Hausbaker 2005

THE AMERICAN CUT GLASS INDUSTRY

T. G. Hawkes and his
Competitors

THE AMERICAN CUT GLASS INDUSTRY

T. G. Hawkes and his Competitors

Jane Shadel Spillman

ANTIQUE COLLECTORS' CLUB
IN ASSOCIATION WITH
THE CORNING MUSEUM OF GLASS

British Library Cataloguing-in-Publication Data
A catalogue record for this book is available from the British Library

Printed in England by the Antique Collectors' Club Ltd.
5 Church Street, Woodbridge, Suffolk
on Consort Royal Satin paper
supplied by the Donside Paper Company, Aberdeen, Scotland

Frontispiece. Claret jug, cased cranberry over amber and cut in Venetian pattern with silver mounts, about 1890. H. 34.2cm.   Private collection.

Title page. Three goblets with cut decoration in the color Carder called Wisteria. This dichroic glass is bluish in daylight and pinkish in incandescent light and is usually called alexandrite (after the mineral) by European factories. The left and center ones are shape 7382 and the right one 7383. Steuben Division, Corning Glass Works, about 1920-1930. H.(left) 19.9cm. Gift of Corning Glass Works (CMG 69.4.239B, 75.4.802, 69.4.239C).

The Antique Collectors' Club

The Antique Collectors' Club was formed in 1966 and quickly grew to a five figure membership spread throughout the world. It publishes the only independently run monthly antiques magazine, *Antique Collecting*, which caters for those collectors who are interested in widening their knowledge of antiques, both by greater awareness of quality and by discussion of the factors which influence the price that is likely to be asked. The Antique Collectors' Club pioneered the provision of information on prices for collectors and the magazine still leads in the provision of detailed articles on a variety of subjects.

It was in response to the enormous demand for information on 'what to pay' that the price guide series was introduced in 1968 with the first edition of *The Price Guide to Antique Furniture* (completely revised 1978 and 1989), a book which broke new ground by illustrating the more common types of antique furniture, the sort that collectors could buy in shops and at auctions rather than the rare museum pieces which had previously been used (and still to a large extent are used) to make up the limited amount of illustrations in books published by commercial publishers. Many other price guides have followed, all copiously illustrated, and greatly appreciated by collectors for the valuable information they contain, quite apart from prices. The Price Guide Series heralded the publication of many standard works of reference on art and antiques. *The Dictionary of British Art* (now in six volumes), *The Pictorial Dictionary of British 19th Century Furniture Design, Oak Furniture* and *Early English Clocks* were followed by many deeply researched reference works such as *The Directory of Gold and Silversmiths*, providing new information. Many of these books are now accepted as the standard work of reference on their subject.

The Antique Collectors' Club has widened its list to include books on gardens and architecture. All the Club's publications are available through bookshops world wide and a full catalogue of all these titles is available free of charge from the addresses below.

Club membership, open to all collectors, costs little. Members receive free of charge *Antique Collecting*, the Club's magazine (published ten times a year), which contains well-illustrated articles dealing with the practical aspects of collecting not normally dealt with by magazines. Prices, features of value, investment potential, fakes and forgeries are all given prominence in the magazine.

Among other facilities available to members are private buying and selling facilities, the longest list of 'For Sales' of any antiques magazine, an annual ceramics conference and the opportunity to meet other collectors at their local antique collectors' clubs. There are over eighty in Britain and more than a dozen overseas. Members may also buy the Club's publications at special pre-publication prices.

As its motto implies, the Club is an organisation designed to help collectors get the most out of their hobby: it is informal and friendly and gives enormous enjoyment to all concerned.

For Collectors — By Collectors — About Collecting

ANTIQUE COLLECTORS' CLUB
5 Church Street, Woodbridge Suffolk IP12 1DS, UK
Tel: 01394 385501 Fax: 01394 384434
and
Market Street Industrial Park, Wappingers' Falls, NY 12590, USA
Tel: 914 297 0003 Fax: 914 297 0068

Contents

Acknowledgments

I am grateful to the staff of The Corning Museum of Glass for assistance with the research and writing of this book. Members of the staff of the Rakow Library, especially Norma P. H. Jenkins, Virginia Wright, and Gail Bardhan helped me to find my way through the intricacies of the Hawkes and Carder archives and related papers and trade catalogs in their care. Jill Thomas-Clark and Nicholas Williams managed the photography and Priscilla Price kept meticulous records of the objects borrowed for photography. Many collectors offered access to their collections for study or offered photographs for use and I am most grateful for their assistance.

Photographs

Unless otherwise noted in the captions, all objects, both glass and paper, are in the collection of The Corning Museum of Glass; and the photography is the work of Nicholas Williams. Some objects were graciously loaned to the Museum for photography by Mr. Williams, including those belonging to Paul Efron, Frank Swanson and to three other private collectors, as well as the objects from the Jones Museum of Glass and Ceramics. The John Hay Library of Brown University, custodian of the Gorham Archives, arranged for special photography of Gorham scrapbooks for this project. We are indebted to the Chrysler Museum, Hillwood Museum, the Lightner Museum, the National Museum of American History, Smithsonian Institution, and the Sandwich Museum for photographs of objects in their collections. Mr. Maurice Crofford kindly photographed objects in the collections of Tom and Marsha de Graffenreid, George and Billie Harrington and Lowell and Zoe Switzer for us, Martin Folb provided photographs of the objects in his collection, and the Forsyth Gallery of Texas A. & M. University provided color photography of objects in the collections of Dowlton and Ruth Anne Berry, Cinthia Hampton, George and Billie Harrington, Tom Jacks, Don and Suzy Kosterman, Lowell and Zoe Switzer and Del and Elone Tipps. We appreciate the courtesy of all of these collectors and museums in allowing us to illustrate and/or photograph their glass.

The Cut Glass Industry
and the Hawkes Archives

The cutting of glass is a luxury craft that did not at first flourish in the United States. Although Benjamin Bakewell of Pittsburgh produced glass tableware cut in the latest London patterns as early as 1818, American cut glass always had to compete with more prestigious imported wares, especially in Eastern cities where they were readily available. The depression of 1873, during which a number of banks and businesses failed all over the country, was especially hard on the sellers of luxury goods. In the 1870s, America's principal manufacturers of blanks for cutting were the New England Glass Company, the Boston & Sandwich Glass Company, and the Mt. Washington Glass Company, all in Massachusetts; Christian Dorflinger in Pennsylvania; and the Corning Glass Works in Corning, New York. Cut glass was produced by all of these firms except the Corning Glass Works. John Hoare cut blanks supplied by the Corning factory, and there were a few independent cutting shops in New York City and Brooklyn. However, aside from some decorative engraving of inexpensive tableware, the fine glass industry of the 1870s was limited to the above-mentioned companies.

Philadelphia's Centennial Exhibition in 1876 marked a turning point in this situation. Although many Midwestern firms filled their booths with pressed glass, the New England companies and Dorflinger showed exceptional cut and engraved pieces, which attracted a great deal of attention. Another highlight of this exposition was the complete glass factory that Gillinder & Sons of Philadelphia operated on the grounds.

The interest generated by these exhibits and America's growing prosperity led to a new era in the cut glass industry. Although the number of factories supplying blanks did not grow substantially, production increased and independent cutters and cutting shops proliferated. The demand for cut glass increased every year thereafter until World War I. By 1895, the principal manufacturers were located in White Mills, Pennsylvania; Toledo, Ohio; New Bedford, Massachusetts and Corning, New York. The C. Dorflinger & Sons glasshouse in White Mills employed about 500 workers at its peak. It supplied blanks to cutting shops all over the East, and it produced finished cut goods in its own shop. The Libbey Glass Company in Toledo was a new firm, an offshoot of the New England Glass Company in Massachusetts, which had closed. It also supplied blanks to cutting shops in many locations and cut its own glass. The Mt. Washington Glass Company, in New Bedford both manufactured and cut glass, although it sold few blanks to outsiders. The Corning Glass Works sold most of its blanks to T. G. Hawkes & Company and J. Hoare & Company, two large cutting shops in Corning. These six firms dominated the cut glass industry, which reached the height of its prosperity around 1905.

Small cutting shops, each of which had ten to 50 employees turning out less expensive goods, mushroomed between 1900 and 1910. Eventually, their cheaper wares drove the better-quality cut glass off the market. Cut glass became less fashionable, and the entire industry went into a decline after 1910, which resulted in the closing of most of the small shops and many of the larger ones as well. The firms that stayed in business, such as Libbey in Toledo, and the Corning Glass Works, managed to do so by altering their product line to meet changing demands.

Because the industry was basically small, the proprietors of the glass factories and cutting shops were well acquainted with one another. They worked together in an effort to weaken the fledgling labor movement, and they often exchanged blanks and occasionally collaborated on orders. The recent discovery of thousands of letters sent to the Hawkes firm by suppliers and customers in the 1880s and early 1890s provides a much clearer picture of the inner workings of the industry as a whole. Thomas Gibbons Hawkes can be seen as a leader who pioneered the use of advertising and trademarks and produced innovative design patterns. His animosity toward organized labor was typical of his fellow proprietors, but it earned him the particular dislike of the Knights of Labor. On the other hand, he was not entirely an "oppressor of humanity", as the unions represented him; he paid a fair wage for the time and adopted an attitude of benign paternalism toward his employees.

The wares of the biggest cutting firms were sold mainly through jewelers or through china and glass retailers. The Hawkes letters show that prices were often negotiable, not just between the factory and the store, but also between the retailer and the customer. This was a way of doing business that is unknown today. Competition for the patronage of customers was intense, and it seems to have been a buyer's market to a surprising extent in the 1880s. Although records similar to the Hawkes letters have not survived to document in detail the business of other firms, the Hawkes company can be viewed as indicative of practices in the American fine glass industry at the turn of the century.

In 1865, Corning, New York, was a village in an agricultural area. Steuben County was lightly settled, although the advent of the railroads had helped to boost the population. Three railroad lines converged in Corning, thereby increasing its importance. Lumber and coal from northern Pennsylvania were shipped to market through the village, and some local investors were eager to attract a manufacturing plant. The Corning glass industry began in 1868, when the Houghton family, principal owners of the Brooklyn Flint Glass Works, decided to relocate their company. In doing so, they hoped to avoid the labor agitation in New York City, and they thought that the upstate site, with both river and rail transportation, would be advantageous. Their new factory opened in October to general rejoicing in the village, and it initially afforded employment to about 50 men and boys, some of whom had come from Brooklyn. The company's principal products were blanks for cutting, pressed tableware, lantern globes, and some pharmaceutical and scientific glassware. The Corning Glass Works, which today is known as Corning Incorporated, is still located in Corning. It is the area's major employer, a position it has held since the turn of the century.

During the first half-century of glassmaking in Corning, however, ornamental glass cutting was equally important, and as many people were employed in the area's glass cutting shops as at the Corning Glass Works. The two biggest cutting chops were operated by John Hoare, who, like the Houghtons, had brought his business to Corning in 1868; and Thomas G. Hawkes, who had been Hoare's superintendent before he left to start his own cutting shop in March 1880. In the 1890s, Oliver Egginton and his son Walter, and Thomas Hunt and his son Harry, left T. G. Hawkes & Company to start their own small firms. In 1904, H. P. Sinclaire Jr., second in command at the Hawkes firm, opened his own company, which in the 1920s both made and cut glass. There were several other cutting shops in Corning, but they were all much smaller, and most of them were in business for only a few years.

By 1890, Corning was promoting itself as the "Crystal City". In 1902, the village was so well known as a producer of cut glass that a New York City newspaper ran a lengthy story entitled "Cut Glass City of New York State". It reported that:

"The house was the ordinary frame dwelling of a workingman, and similar homes sprawled over the side of one of the twin hills that shut the Chemung River in a beautiful valley. It was the home of a man who might earn $2.00 a day – enough in an upstate city like Corning to provide a large family with necessities.

The door of the dining room was open and the table was set for the noonday meal. Nothing strange about that. Yet there was something strange about that table. Scattered about in careless profusion, looking a little out of place on the cheap red cloth, were pieces of cut glass – real cut glass.

There was no doubting their genuineness. They gleamed with white light and prismatic color, and their facets glittered as only cut glass facets can. It was the cut glass from the sideboards and tables of the rich. A closer inspection might have discovered flaws in each piece, perhaps a crack in the neck of the vinegar bottle or a chip out of the base of a tall glittering vase. The slightest flaw is enough to prevent a cut glass piece from going to market. Yet seen through the door of the humble home, it was beautiful.

And the stranger wondered how it came there – that is, until he remembered that he was in Corning, the cut glass city of New York State, in which, it is asserted, more high grade glass is cut each year than in any other city in the country."[1]

The number of glass cutters in Corning grew steadily until it peaked in 1905 at 490, according to the city directory. At least double that number were employed by the cutting shops, where there were sometimes more inspectors, packers, and office employees than cutters. By 1903, a dozen cutting firms were listed in the directory.

The English glassmaker Frederick Carder came to Corning in March 1903 to observe the village's glass business and also to sign the contract with T. G. Hawkes that led to the opening of the Steuben Glass Works. He was struck by the high quality of American cut glass and by the fact that American cut glass manufacturers were "forging ahead" of English ones. "Where we used to sell them thousands of pounds worth of Cut Glass per annum it has dwindled down to a few pounds & in fact they are sending their Cut Goods over to Great Britain

1. "Cut Glass City of New York State," *New York Sunday Tribune*, November 23, 1902.

instead of vice versa," Carder said. He also noted that "they do not produce so many designs, either in form or cutting, as we do," and he explained that "this enables them to get larger orders for one design and consequently the men turn out more work." He described Corning as a "city of 13,000 where in one factory they have 400 men, another in the same city 200 men, another 80 & one or two more with from 60 to 30 men so that it will be seen that in one factory they employ nearly as many cutters as there are employed in the whole Stourbridge district."[2] At this time, according to Amory Houghton Jr.'s testimony in a legal suit, the Corning Glass Works had ten furnaces and employed more than 1,000 people, doing a business that grossed in excess of $700,000.[3] Thomas Hawkes, with more than 400 employees, did about half a million dollars' worth of business a year.[4]

The demand for cut glass and the business of the firms that supplied it peaked between 1905 and 1910. Many of the smaller companies then went out of business before or during World War I. The Hoare firm closed in 1920, shortly before James Hoare's death. After H. P. Sinclaire Jr. died suddenly in 1928, his family decided to close his company. Over the years, the Hawkes company changed its products to suit changing tastes, but eventually, in 1962, it also succumbed after a long post-war decline.

Because the Hawkes firm was in the same location in Corning for most of its existence, few of its records were thrown away. It thus accumulated a large quantity of archival material, including catalogs, scrapbooks, and designs from both Hoare and Sinclaire that were acquired when the two companies went out of business in the 1920s. The Corning Museum of Glass bought some of this material in 1962 and 1970, and it was given more in 1977, when the Hawkes family sold the building that had housed their company. Many more records were thrown away or dispersed piecemeal through sales in the 1960s. In 1967, an agent appointed by the family sold many of the leftover glass blanks, unfinished pieces, plaster casts of glass, pattern files, and thousands of letters – the detritus of eight decades – to a glass collector who placed them in storage in a basement and forgot about them for 20 years. After her death, this dirt-covered miscellany was purchased at auction in 1990 by The Corning Museum of Glass.

This purchase was something of a gamble because the contents of the boxes were in no particular order and it was hard to see what much of the material was. However, this treasure trove included the nearly complete incoming business correspondence of the Hawkes Rich Cut Glass firm from 1880 to 1890, the first ten years of its existence. There are also two bound notebooks containing carbon copies of typed outgoing letters for some of 1888, 1889, and 1892. It is thus possible to trace both inquiries and responses in some of this correspondence. The incoming letters amount to some 15,000-20,000 pieces of paper that document the way the Hawkes company, and others like it, did business in the 1880s. There are letters from Hawkes's customers and from his suppliers, letters from other glass manufacturers, applications for employment, and personal bills

2. These comments are taken from a manuscript in Carder's hand that is in the Carder Archives in the Rakow Library of The Corning Museum of Glass. It formed the basis for an article about Carder that was published in the Brierley Hill newspaper in 1903, just before he moved to Corning.
3. *Corning Glass Works vs. Corning Glass Company et al.*, 126 A.D. 919, 75 A.D. 629 (Fourth Dept., 1902), p. 85, testimony of March 4, 1904.
4. Hawkes Cash Book, 1900–1904, Hawkes Archives, Rakow Library, The Corning Museum of Glass.

Water lamp base engraved with swimming fish, probably 1920-1940. H. 36.3cm, trade-marked on foot.   Courtesy Susie Herpel.

for clothing and groceries (Hawkes did not keep his personal expenses separate from his business ones).

The correspondence was filed alphabetically by year in rubber-banded bundles. As might be expected, there are fewer letters in the early 1880s and many more in

1888 and 1889 as the business grew. It is too much to expect that every single incoming message would be present for those years, but certainly most of them are. The only exception is in the correspondence of 1886, which is so small in comparison to that for 1885 and 1887 that half of it is probably missing. Perhaps it was discarded by mistake in the 1960s. That letters received after 1891 were bound into ledgers is suggested by a cache of letters from 1892 and 1893 that was recently presented to the Museum by Walter Poeth. Ledgers, daybooks, employment files, records of blanks received, master lists of shapes, catalogs, advertisements, and loose catalog pages are all among the papers acquired in 1970, 1977, and 1990, and among those more recently given to the Museum by Sarah Hawkes Thornton (granddaughter of T. G. Hawkes) and Mrs. Penrose Hawkes.

The material from the Hoare firm includes two large scrapbooks divided into sections by shape names. The company ordered these books in 1909, and it cut up its own catalogs as well as those of competitors in order to keep track of what all of these firms were selling. Samuel Hawkes gave one volume of this scrapbook to Dorothy Daniels, the first researcher of American cut glass, in the late 1940s and Mrs. Daniels left it to the Rakow Library of The Corning Museum of Glass, in 1968. Twenty years later, the second volume of this pair was located by a dealer, and it was subsequently presented to the Museum library by Mr. and Mrs. James Parks, along with other Hoare material located with it. More Hoare catalogs came in separately as they were found. The 1990 Hawkes purchase included a two volume set labeled "Templates & Drawings" by Hoare; it is uniform in binding with the scrapbooks, and it holds profile drawings of Hoare shapes, as well as a loose-leaf book of clippings from Gorham catalogs.

The Sinclaire Design Archives, consisting of several hundred folders of design drawings, and a number of plaster casts of engraved Sinclaire pieces were included with the 1990 purchase of the Hawkes material. In addition, Estelle Sinclaire has presented to the Rakow Library much of the archival material relating to her grandfather's firm. The Museum continues to seek material relating to Corning's cut glass industry.

The Hawkes correspondence has now been sorted and microfilmed, and it is available to researchers on microfiche. The Museum staff is grateful to members of the American Cut Glass Association's Eastern Lakes Chapter who donated many hours of time to helping sort and clean the letters and other materials, and to the Association's board of trustees and chapters that provided the funds to have these items microfilmed. We also want to thank the many donors who have enriched our library with documents relating to Corning's cut glass and added treasured pieces to our collection.

Unless otherwise noted, all letters cited are in the Hawkes Archives of the Rakow Library, The Corning Museum of Glass. The letters to T. G. Hawkes are mostly handwritten originals, the ones from Hawkes are copies, most unsigned, of typed letters.

John Hoare and the Beginning of Cut Glass in Corning

John Hoare was born in Cork, Ireland, in 1822. He was the son of a glass cutter named James Hoare, who worked at Cork and later in Belfast, where John learned the trade of glass cutting. In 1842, John went to England where he worked first for Rice Harris and Sons in Birmingham, for Thomas Webb at Wordsley, and finally as foreman for Lloyd and Summerfield. In 1845, he married Catherine Dailey, the daughter of a family in the glass cutting trade, and in 1848, he started his own shop. This was not particularly successful and after five years he decided to bring his wife and growing family to the United States. According to tradition,[1] they landed in Philadelphia in 1853 with exactly half a sovereign in capital, but since he was a trained and experienced cutter he had no difficulty in finding a job with Haughwout & Dailey. Haughwout's partner may have been a relative of Catherine Dailey, but no proof of that has been found.

This firm was one of the largest china and glass retailers in New York; it employed both china painters and glass cutters to decorate wares to order. The porcelain was ordered primarily from France, but American glass from the Brooklyn Flint Glass Company was listed in their advertisements and on their billhead. John S. O'Connor, who later worked as foreman of the Dorflinger cutting shop in White Mills, worked for Haughwout at this time. The late nineteenth century accounts of Hoare's various partnerships are contradictory, but it is clear that John Hoare found one or more partners and started his own cutting shop first on 2nd Avenue and then on 18th St. in Manhattan soon after his arrival

1. Harlo Hawkes, ed., *Landmarks of Steuben County*, Syracuse, 1896, p.52.

1-1. *Fruit or Salad bowl in a variation of Wheat pattern, about 1885–1895. D. 29cm. (CMG 79.4.99).*
N.B. All illustrations in Chapter 1 are of objects produced by J. Hoare & Company.

1-2. *Fruit or Salad bowl and underplate, Wheat pattern, about 1885–1895. Dia. of plate, 35.2cm.*
Courtesy of George and Billie Harrington. T. A. & M photo.

in New York. By 1857, he had new partners, and the firm of Hoare, Burns & Dailey bought the 'cutting department' of the Brooklyn Flint Glass Company and moved into their premises at 44 State Street in Brooklyn where Hoare continued to cut glass for Haughwout as well as for other customers. A reporter visited the Brooklyn factory in 1863 and reported that the partnership of Gould and Hoare was running both the blowing and cutting operations at the plant.[2] Joseph Dailey (Catherine's brother) and John Hoare were still partners when the Houghtons and other investors bought the Brooklyn Flint Glass Company in 1864. They also had a cutting shop at Greenpoint, in the Dorflinger glass works, after it was built in 1861.

2. *Scientific American*, January 31, 1863.

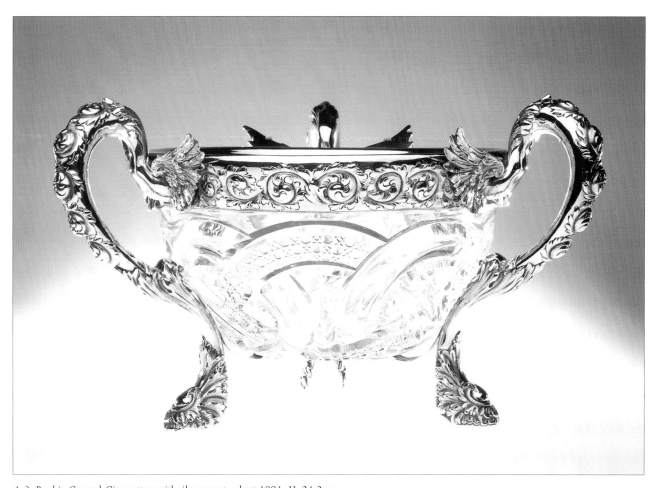

1-3. *Bowl in Crystal City pattern with silver mounts, about 1891. H. 21.2cm.*

Courtesy of Tom Jacks. T. A. & M photo.

The close relationships in Brooklyn of all of these cutters (most of them born and trained and perhaps already acquainted in England) is emphasized by the association of all of them with the service of glassware made for Mary Todd Lincoln in 1861. The Englishman Enoch Egginton worked in Brooklyn at this time, with Dorflinger and/or Hoare. When Egginton went to Portland, Maine to superintend the building of the Portland Glass Company in 1863, a local newspaper story mentioned that he had previously made a service of glassware for Mrs. Lincoln. His brother, Oliver, joined him in Portland, and in 1867 went with him to Montreal, to run a glass factory there. Enoch died in Montreal and in the 1870s Oliver brought his family to Corning to work for Hoare. *The Corning Journal's* 1895 review of glassmaking in Corning reported that "before coming here" the glass works had made a set of glassware for the Lincolns.[3] The Lincolns only ordered one set of glassware from Brooklyn, which was made, tradition says, at the Dorflinger glasshouse in Greenpoint. Unfortunately, no solid documentary evidence exists to tie this set to any specific factory, but it looks as if the blowing and the cutting were done by some combination of Dorflinger's Greenpoint works, the Brooklyn Flint Glass Company, and John Hoare's firm.

Amory and Francis Houghton had sold their interest in the Union Glass Company of Somerville, Massachusetts around 1864, and bought the property of the Brooklyn Flint Glass Company. The factory suffered from a bad fire December

3. *Corning Journal*, Special Trade Edition, September 4, 1895.

3, 1866 and both Hoare & Dailey and the Houghtons sustained extensive damage. An 1867 broadside of the Brooklyn Flint Glass Works refers to the fact that the factory had been rebuilt and enlarged and offers "Rich Cut, Plain Blown and Pressed Glassware,/ in plain flint and colors" as well as apothecary and scientific glassware.[4] However, in 1868, due primarily to labor unrest in Brooklyn, the Houghtons decided to move their plant and by October of that year they were blowing glass in Corning and making blanks for Hoare & Dailey's Corning branch, located on the second floor of the glass factory.

The Glass Works had a number of financial problems in the early years and for a short time in 1870 was in receivership, but Hoare stayed in business in Corning in spite of that. A newspaper story of 1870 reported that Hoare employed about 50 men in Corning and he presumably had about the same number in Brooklyn. By 1873, the Hoare family had moved to Corning, along with the rest of their employees, and the Brooklyn cutting shop was closed. The number of employees in Corning nearly doubled and was almost as many as were employed at the Glass Works, which was running only an eight pot and a ten pot furnace and sometimes only one of those. After its reorganization in 1875, Corning Glass Works dropped its pressed tablewares and concentrated on blanks for cutting and glass for apothecary and industrial use especially for the railroads which were constantly growing. Around this time, Dailey's name was dropped from the company and its name was 'John Hoare, Rich Cut Glassware' Their advertisement in a trade paper in 1875 read:

JOHN HOARE,
(Successor to HOARE & DAILEY)
Manufacturers of all Descriptions of
FINE CUT, ENGRAVED AND PLAIN
TABLE GLASS WARE
FACTORIES AT CORNING, N.Y.
ATTENTION GIVEN TO MATCHING UP ODD ARTICLES IN GLASS

Rich Cut and Engraved Gas and Car Lamp Globes, Richly Cut Flat Glass; also
Pickle Jars, Castor Bottles, Etc. and all Glass pertaining to the Silver and
Plated-Ware Trade, Constantly on Hand and Made to Order
James Hoare, 34 Church Street, near Barclay, N.Y.[5]

James Hoare was John's oldest son, born in England and trained by his father in the Brooklyn business. John Hoare quickly became a leading citizen of Corning and was elected mayor of the village in 1875. In October 1876, a fire at Corning Glass Works destroyed a lot of Hoare's equipment and stock, but within a few days Hoare had set up cutting and engraving equipment in a storeroom and was at work again. By December, the paper carried a story describing the new quarters of the cutting shop:

"The re-building of the burned portion of the Glass Works has been an

4. Printed single-sheet flier headed "Office of Brooklyn Flint Glass Works" and ending, "A. Houghton, Treasurer," dated December 1867.
5. Crockery & Glass Journal, November 11, 1875.

1-4. Bowl in Crystal City pattern, about 1891, D. 19.7cm. Gift of Mr. and Mrs. J. T. Sisk (CMG 83.4.149).

improvement, the mansard roof being dispensed with, as the walls were carried up three stories. Thus there is so much room gained in the third story, that the glass cutting and engraving are now carried on there, instead of occupying the second and third stories. Capt. Hoare has made also much improvement in arranging the machinery, and because of the late dreadful accident in the temporary shop he has the line shafting so placed that if by accident an employee is caught when adjusting a belt no fatal injury will result, as there is ample space between the shaft and the roof or walls. Capt. Hoare has imported grindstones of superior grain, and the fixtures are costly and of the latest improvement, so that now every arrangement is made for convenience and dispatching work. An elevator suspended by wire ropes leads from the basement to the third story. The stairway on the west is of iron and also a stairway, which has been put up on the south to reach the commodious office of Messrs. Houghton & Co. The Glass Works is by far the most important manufacturing interest in Corning. Its establishment here in 1868 gave a remarkable impetus to the prosperity of the village, and its successful management during the three past years of financial stringency and prostration of business reflect much credit upon the enterprise and sagacity of the proprietors of both 'departments'."[6]

The new arrangement of the belt was because of an accident which had occurred while the men were using the temporary quarters, when one of the employees was caught in the belt and fatally injured. However, the belt was still cut occasionally, probably to give the men and boys a day off, since it usually took that long to get it fixed. "Some one cut the main belt connecting with the machinery at John Hoare's cutting shop, Saturday, and work had to be stopped for half a day. This is the second occurrence of this kind within a month. Mr. Hoare offers $50 reward for the detection of the rascal", said one story.[7]

In 1889, the glass works built itself new offices and the Hoare company

6. *Corning Journal*, December 28, 1876.
7. *Corning Journal*, June 29, 1882.

1-5. Claret decanter with Gorham
silver mount dated 1893. H.
33cm.
    Courtesy Martin Folb. Folb photo.
The Gorham records indicate that
the glass is from Hoare.

1-6. Decanter in Croesus pattern,
1890s. H. 32.5cm.
Courtesy Tom Jacks. T. A. & M
photo.

1-7. Ice tub in Monarch pattern.1890s. W. 25.4cm.   Courtesy Tom and Marsha de Graffenreid. Crofford photo.

occupied their old ones. The newspaper story described the new Corning Glass Works offices for H. P. Sinclaire and the Houghtons with their costly desks, coal grates, massive oak mantels and polished cherry floors as "among the most magnificent and luxurious of any between New York and Buffalo."[8]

"The late quarters of the Glass Company will be occupied by J. Hoare & Co., as an office and for the much ampler display of cut glass. The elegant samples of their work are not seen to advantage in the small room now used. In their new offices, there will be five times the space for the display of the goods manufactured in their cutting shop. The engraved or cut glass makes a brilliant exhibition and has no superior in elegance or finish anywhere."[9]

There is comparatively little correspondence between the Hoare and Hawkes firms in the archives since they were so close and except for blank borrowing and occasional order sharing didn't have a lot of business with each other. The tone of the letters was usually friendly, as when James Hoare inquired "Would it inconvenience you to Engrave 2 dozen Globe Wine Bottles *Ivy leaf* at once or are Your Engravers too Busy. The Bottles are ready and cut. Please Answer at once and Oblige."[10] In 1888, Richard Briggs ordered an oval sugar and creamer "cut to sample" along with other objects and Hawkes wrote back that Hoare would make the sugar and creamer, as it was his blank.[11] There were occasional disputes over workmen or pattern copying, but basically the relationship was one of respect and cooperation.

Over the years John Hoare took out several design patents, as well as one for a mold, and assigned them to his company. The first of these, when he was still in New York, was a design for a glass castor bottle (#4,752, April 4, 1871). His

8. *Corning Journal*, July 18, 1889.
9. Ibid.
10. James Hoare for J. Hoare & Company to T. G. Hawkes, October 10, 1887.
11. T. G. Hawkes to Richard Briggs, Boston, December 12, 1888.

second patent covered a design for a "Bouquet Holder or Vase" which was in the form of a shell, frosted by grinding and then the edges cut into scallops. The object ended in a peg which could be inserted in a silver holder. This was design patent #8,187, granted March 2, 1875. In 1879 and 1882, he registered two more designs for ornamented castor bottles (#11,217, June 3, 1879; #12,651, Jan. 3, 1882). On April 8, 1884, John Hoare was granted patent #296,691 for a mold for manufacturing glass baskets with attached handles. His catalogs show a number of cut glass baskets of various shapes with these handles, so presumably it was a successful design which was probably made for him by Corning Glass Works.

On February 15, 1887, George L. Abbott, a Hoare associate, was granted design patent #17,110 which he assigned to John Hoare. The patent was for a simple geometric pattern which is shown in the earliest company catalog as the *Mikado* pattern. The last Hoare design patent was granted to John Hoare for a pattern of interlocking circles (#20,504, granted Feb. 3, 1891) which appears in the second

1-8. Demijohn in a variation of Monarch pattern, 1890s. H. 46cm.

> Courtesy George and Billie Harrington. Crofford photo.

1-9. Demijohn, cut on the same blank as Fig. 1–8. 1890s. H. 39cm.

> Courtesy Lightner Museum.

1-10. Decanter in Croesus
pattern with a silver stopper, about
1887–1897. OH. 26.1cm.
(95.4.269).
This shape was also supplied by
Hawkes to Gorham for silver
mounting; the blank is from
Corning Glass Works.

1-11. Bowl in Eleanor pattern,
1890s. D. 23.4cm.
    Courtesy Cinthia Hampton. T. A.
                    & M photo.

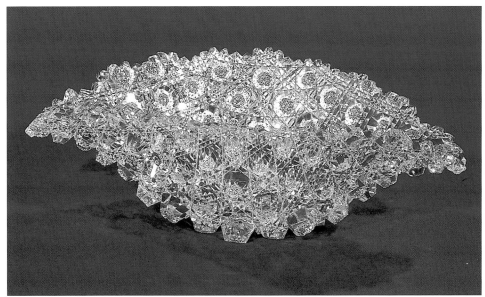

1-12. Bowl 8882 in Kohinoor
pattern, around 1910. L 34.2cm.
Courtesy Martin Folb. Folb photo.
This bowl, cut on an "extra heavy
blank" is shown in the 1911
catalog where it cost $40.

Figs. 1–13 to 1-15 and 1-19
through 1–24 are pages from a
Hoare catalog printed in 1896.
Much of this glass probably did
not have a trademark. Some of
these patterns were in production
until after the acid-stamped
trademark came into use in the
early 20th century however.

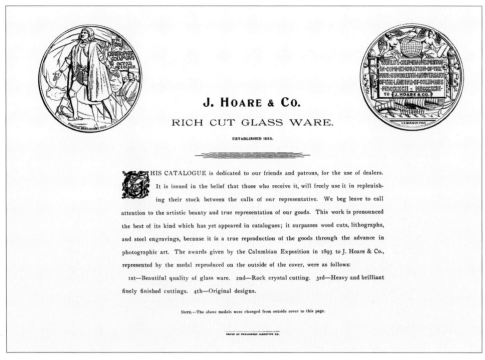

1-13. First page of catalog.

company catalog as the *Crystal City* pattern. The bouquet holder and castor bottles probably were not made after 1885 and both of the patented rich-cut designs are rare. The interlocking rings on the *Crystal City* patterns were difficult to cut and it was quite expensive. Pieces in these patterns are not likely to bear trademarks due to the early date of their manufacture, but the *Crystal City* pattern is so distinctive that it is easy to recognize and no other company cut it, as far as is known. In 1897, George L. Abbott took out a patent for a locking stopper for a bottle. This may have been a closure for a Tantalus set. (#588,211)

John Hoare sold the business to his son James and George L. Abbott as equal partners in 1887, and they changed the name of the firm to J. Hoare & Company. One of his other sons, John Jr., worked in the family business as well, running the New York office until 1887 and then as foreman of the cutting shop until his death in 1894. Abbott (who was a son-in-law of Amory Houghton) was the chief salesman, and at the time of the name change 'Captain Hoare' as he was called locally, retired from active participation. He died in June, 1896.

Like all manufacturers specializing in luxury goods, the cut glass firms of Corning sought prestigious special orders of cut glassware from prominent customers. The local newspapers frequently exaggerated the quantity and price of these special orders, but not their prestige. For example, on December 22, 1870, the *Corning Journal* reported, "The Corning Glass Works have received an order from President Grant for one thousand dollars worth of glassware." It is difficult to identify that particular order in White House files because the only one placed around that time was a November order to J. W. Boteler & Brothers, crockery and glass merchants in Washington, for three dozen each of goblets, champagnes and wine glasses for $145.[12] This must be what was made in Corning, and it could be an addition to the state service, assuming that the glasses ranged in price from $4 to $5 apiece. It may also have been an order for Grant family use rather than for

12. *Corning Journal,* December 22, 1870.

28

Plate 6.

CHAPTER ONE

No. 8608 SHAPE, CUT "SOUVENIR."

1-14. *Plate 6 shows stemware in Souvenir pattern.*

No. 8234 SHAPE, CUT "ROCK CRYSTAL."

1-15. *Plate 7 shows stemware in the Rock Crystal pattern. See Fig.1–25 for glass in this pattern.*

1-16. *Claret Decanter in Newport pattern*, about 1910. H. 50.7cm.
  Courtesy Martin Folb. Folb photo

1-17. *Vase* in Newport pattern, cut on shape 1906 in 1910. H. 55.8cm.
  Courtesy Martin Folb. Folb photo

state dinners, cut in the current style but without engraving of the White House crest. Whatever the pattern was, it was cut by John Hoare whose cutting firm occupied space on the second floor of Corning Glass Works, and used Corning blanks.

Hoare received one of the earliest Corning orders for the state service in 1873. The procedure for ordering White House furnishings was usually to order from a retailer, who then placed the order with a supplier of his choice, although sometimes bids were sought from several manufacturers. In 1873, the order went from the White House to J. W. Boteler & Brothers, a firm which had supplied the White House several times before. Boteler placed the order with John Hoare's company and it was announced in the Corning paper on August 1, 1873: "Mr. John Hoare, of the glass cutting department of the Corning Glass Works, has received an order for several thousand dollars worth of glass ware for the State dinner service, at the White House."[13] In October, the paper reported: "The elegant glass ware (to supply the President's State Dinner Service) made at the Corning Glass Works, and cut and engraved in the Cutting Department, by Mr.

13. *Corning Journal*, August 1, 1873.

1-18. *Vase, cut around 1910 by George Barnes at Hoare. H. 30.3cm. Gift of Mrs. Theodore Barnes (CMG 81.4.49).*

Plate 9.

HEAVY EDGE F. BOWL AND PLATE, CUT "SOUVENIR."

HEAVY EDGE F. BOWL AND PLATE, CUT "REGAL."

No. 8234. F. BOWL AND PLATE, CUT "ROCK CRYSTAL."

No. 8775. F. BOWL AND PLATE, CUT "ZENDA."

1-19. *Plate 9 shows fingerbowls and plates in Souvenir, Regal, Rock Crystal and Zenda patterns.*

Hoare, will be on exhibition at the Glass Works, during each day and evening, next Wednesday, Thursday, Friday."[14] The extent of national curiosity about the furnishings of the presidential mansion is shown by an article in an Oakland, California newspaper about the glassware. It was titled "Republican Simplicity" and the paper reported that: "At the Corning Glass Works, a set of glass destined for the Presidential mansion has just been completed. It consists of two dozen goblets, which are cut about half way up the bowl, the remainder of the bowl being richly engraved, and prominent among it is the United States coat-of-arms; four dozen champagne glasses and saucer bowl, two dozen regular champagne glasses, six dozen canary colored hock glasses, seven dozen ruby-bowl, flint stem sauterne glasses. These colored glasses are very superior, three dozen punch glasses with handles, four dozen ice cream plates, cut and engraved as the glasses. The value of the glass is about $2000."[15]

Although the newspaper had the quantities of glassware wrong, its descriptions of the cutting and engraving and of the handled punch glasses permit the identification of the glass, which matched the service originally ordered by Mary Todd Lincoln in 1861. The fact that the quantities of each shape varied from less than a dozen to more than six dozen makes it clear that these were replacements rather than a new service.

The same year, Hoare received an order from George W. Childs, publisher of the *Philadelphia Public Ledger*, for twelve large burner globes for its editorial rooms, specially engraved with portraits.[16] The cost of the globes was $80 apiece, a handsome sum which equaled several weeks' wages for a master cutter or engraver and several months' pay for a beginner. At this time, the Hoare firm employed about eighty to one hundred men, including Thomas G. Hawkes, the foreman, and John S. Earl, each of whom was soon to leave to start his own

14. *Corning Journal*, October 31, 1873.
15. Oakland (Calif.) *Daily Herald*, January 5, 1874.
16. *Corning Journal*, May 23, 1873

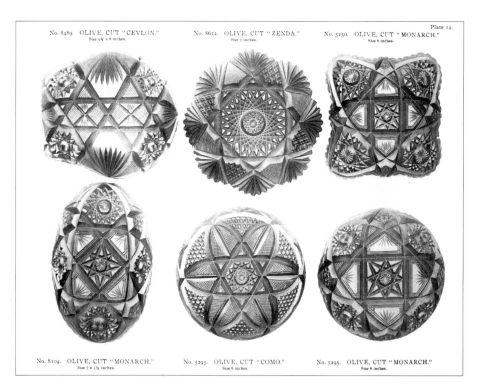

Plate 12.

No. 8489. OLIVE, CUT "CEYLON."
Size 5¼ x 6 inches.

No. 8652. OLIVE, CUT "ZENDA."
Size 7 inches.

No. 5250. OLIVE, CUT "MONARCH."
Size 6 inches.

No. 8104. OLIVE, CUT "MONARCH."
Size 7 x 4½ inches.

No. 5295. OLIVE, CUT "COMO."
Size 6 inches.

No. 5295. OLIVE, CUT "MONARCH."
Size 6 inches.

1-20. Plate 12 shows glass in Ceylon, Zenda, Monarch and Como patterns.

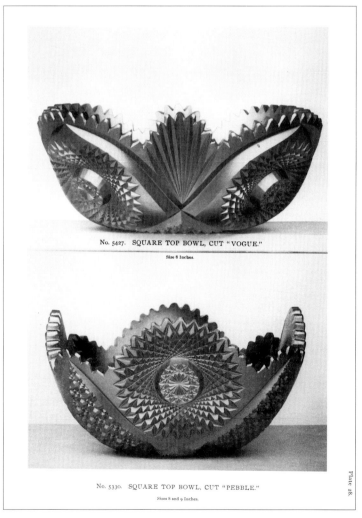

No. 5427. SQUARE TOP BOWL, CUT "VOGUE."
Size 8 Inches.

No. 5330. SQUARE TOP BOWL, CUT "PEBBLE."
Sizes 8 and 9 Inches.

Plate 28.

1-21. Plate 28 shows bowls in Vogue and Pebble patterns.

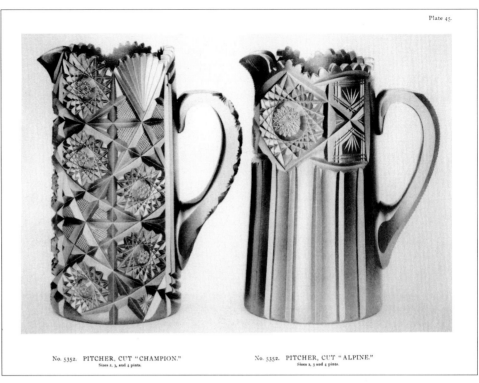

Plate 45.

No. 5352. PITCHER, CUT "CHAMPION."
Sizes 2, 3, and 4 pints.

No. 5352. PITCHER, CUT "ALPINE."
Sizes 2, 3 and 4 pints.

1-22. Plate 45 shows jugs in Champion and Alpine patterns

business. In the next decade, both George W. Childs and the White House were Hawkes' customers, not Hoare's.

There is not much more information about special orders for the Hoare firm, but fortunately some of them were described in the local newspaper. In 1879, John Hoare's shop cut a pair of pitchers for Mrs. William B. Astor of New York, imitations of rare porcelain ones which had been broken. The Hoare pair was said to "excel the originals" although it's hard to imagine how cut glass pitchers could imitate porcelain ones.[17] A few years later, a story in the paper described: "Two large decanters made of ruby glass, were shipped to New York last week from Captain Hoare's Glass Cutting Shops. They were ordered by William H. Vanderbilt, some time before his death and were of the most finished workmanship. Their value has been placed at $100 each."[18] The following week, the reporter went to see "three elegant cut glass articles, two candelabra and a flower stand… the three being worth several hundred dollars."[19] The flower stand was a shape which was very popular in England, but wasn't made by many companies in the United States. Unfortunately, there is no illustration in the story.

An 1885 article in the *Pottery & Glassware Reporter* describes a display in New York which must have been cut by Hoare:

"Corning Glass Works, at their branch warerooms here, display a noteworthy collection of cut glass goods which in some important respects cannot be excelled by any other articles of the same description in the market. The colognes and toilet bottles exhibited are beautiful specimens of workmanship, and similar commendation is due to the table glassware on exhibition."[20]

There is an illustration of the massive punch bowl which the company sent to the Chicago World's Fair in 1893,[21] from the local newspaper, but the bowl was not cut in a pattern which shows up in any Hoare catalogs yet found, although it

17. *Corning Journal*, January 30, 1879.
18. *Corning Journal*, January 7, 1886.
19. *Corning Journal*, January 14, 1886.
20. *Pottery & Glassware Reporter*, December 3, 1885, p.5.
21. *Corning Journal*, Special Trade Edition, September 4, 1895.

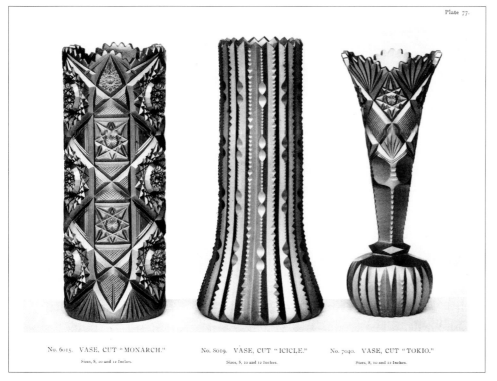

Plate 77.

No. 6015. VASE, CUT "MONARCH."
Sizes, 8, 10 and 12 Inches.

No. 8019. VASE, CUT "ICICLE."
Sizes, 8, 10 and 12 Inches.

No. 7040. VASE, CUT "TOKIO."
Sizes, 8, 10 and 12 Inches.

1-23. *Plate 77 shows vases in* Monarch, Icicle *and* Tokio *patterns.*

Plate 98.

No. 8774. SMALL SYRUP,
CUT "SIGNORA."
White Metal Plated Top.

No. 8772. SYRUP, CUT "8772."
White Metal Plated Top.

No. 8773. SYRUP, CUT "NEW YORK."
Sterling Silver Top.

1-24. *Plate 98 shows syrup jugs in* Signora, 8772 *and* New York *patterns.*

1-25. Stemware in Hoare's Rock Crystal pattern which is part of a set ordered through J. E. Caldwell and Company of Philadelphia about 1912. Some of the pieces in this set were marked "SINCLAIRE", some were marked "HOARE" and some were unmarked. H. (tallest):14.7cm. Gift of Thurman Pierce (CMG 93.4.71A–E). Sinclaire called this pattern R.C.105. Stevens & Williams in England also engraved this pattern, as early as 1879. They may have supplied some of the blanks for this set.

is somewhat related to the *Signora* pattern. There are no contemporary descriptions of the Hoare exhibit in Chicago, even though it won a prize. Possibly this was because the Fair opened May 1, and at that time the cutters were still finishing up the final pieces in Corning. The last pieces were not shipped until June and when the first example of the big punch bowl broke, the Hoare cutters had to make a second one. The bowl was 24 inches in diameter, 18 inches high and weighed about 70 pounds before it was cut, and the blank may have been made at the Union Glass Company in Somerville, Massachusetts, or at White Mills, since Corning Glass Works did not usually make large size blanks.

The Hoares purchased most of their blanks from Corning Glass Works until after 1905 when the Glass Works began to phase out this part of their business. Amory Houghton testified in a suit in 1904 that Hoare had purchased about 75% of his blanks from Corning up until that time.[22] Most of the rest seem to have come from Dorflinger (stemware and bowl blanks in a great variety of shapes and sizes) and from Union.

By 1909, when the Glass Works was no longer making blanks, the Hoare template books show that they were buying them from Union, Pairpoint, Steuben and Sinclaire. A number of the blanks seem to have been shared with the Elmira Cut Glass Company, which was a subsidiary of Hoare in 1913. The exact relationship between the two companies is undetermined as yet, but after the Elmira Company closed in 1913 because of labor difficulties, its address and its president were listed for one year in the Corning directory and were the same as

22. *Corning Glass Works vs. Corning Glass Company et al.,* 126 A.D. 919, 75 A.D. 629 (Fourth Dept., 1902) p. 383, testimony of March 4, 1904. Hereafter cited as CGW suit.

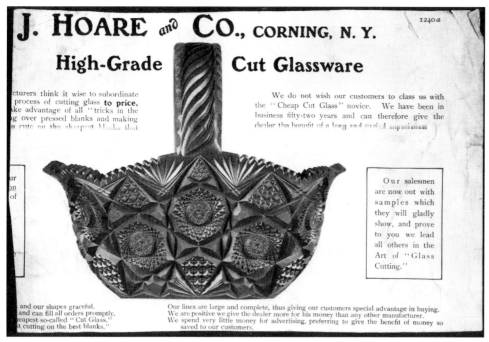

J. HOARE *and* **CO.**, CORNING, N. Y.

1240a

High-Grade   Cut Glassware

...cturers think it wise to subordinate
...process of cutting glass **to price,**
...ke advantage of all "tricks in the
...g over pressed blanks and making
...

We do not wish our customers to class us with
the "Cheap Cut Glass" novice. We have been in
business fifty-two years and can therefore give the
dealer the benefit of a long and...

Our salesmen
are now out with
samples which
they will gladly
show, and prove
to you we lead
all others in the
Art of "Glass
Cutting."

...and our shapes graceful,
...and can fill all orders promptly.
...eapest so-called "Cut Glass."
...t cutting on the best blanks."

Our lines are large and complete, thus giving our customers special advantage in buying.
We are positive we give the dealer more for his money than any other manufacturer.
We spend very little money for advertising, preferring to give the benefit of money so
saved to our customers.

1-26. *Advertisement for a cut glass basket, cut from a trade journal, 1905.*

those of J. Hoare & Company.

The template books also show that Hoare was still supplying glass for silver mounting to both Gorham and Tiffany and did so until the Corning firm closed in 1920. (See Chapter 11 for further information on Hoare's relationships with these companies.) One special vase which was produced in 1910 is documented in the template book with a large cutout of its shape and the following two notes: "Vase 1906 Designed after a suggestion by Maria 11/9/1910 22"; 12/13/10 – Two Vases Rec'd one bad & one good. Good Vase cut 231/8" when finished, …weighed 41 1/2#… Union charged flat price at rate of about 50 cents a pound. H. W. B. Cut Newport, 6 around, like on vase 1902." The partially finished vase was recorded in a photograph for Hoare's files, which was mounted in the company scrapbook.[23] There's no record of who Maria was, but H. W. B. was Hasell W. Baldwin, the firm's treasurer; his initials on most of the templates in the book indicated that he took an inventory of molds and patterns around this time. The "good vase" is illustrated in Fig.1–16.

Apparently J. Hoare & Company was in financial difficulties shortly after 1900. A. B. Houghton audited the company books at the request of the Glass Works president, early in 1907 and reported that no profit had been made from 1903 to 1906 and that orders were dropping during this period in spite of the fact that every other cutting shop in Corning was growing. In spite of this, both Abbott and Hoare had been withdrawing large sums of money from the company in addition to their salaries of $10,400 a year apiece. The company was doing a business of about $190,000 annually, and its chief problem seems to have been careless business practices, and a certain amount of rivalry between the partners.[24] It was apparently these conditions which led to a formal incorporation in 1908. When George Abbott died in 1911, James Hoare was in poor health and his only son, John S. Hoare, was running the Hoare branch factory in Wellsboro which

23. *J. Hoare and Company Cut Glass,* Corning, N.Y., A.C.G.A., 1992, p.94.
24. A. B. Houghton to A. Houghton Jr., Corning, 1907. Courtesy Archives, Corning Incorporated

1-27. Kohinoor pattern punch bowl and ladle around 1910. D. 24.8cm. OH. 20.6cm. Gift of the Davis family in memory of Helen Moore Davis (CMG 83.4.54).

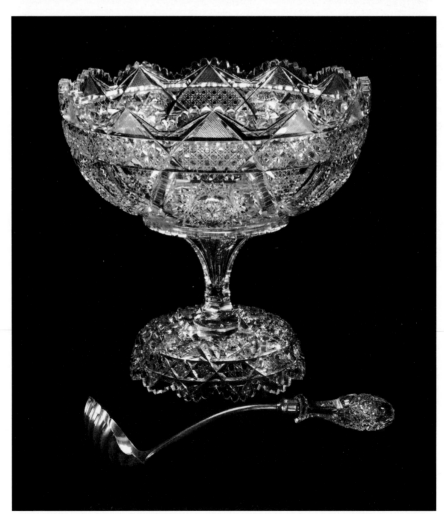

1-28. Compote-footed punch bowl with Gorham ladle, 1909. D. 36.4cm, OH. 32.3cm. trademarked. Gift of the Davis family in memory of Helen Moore Davis (83.4.53). This was a gift from Mrs. Davis's father, Michael Moore, a Hoare cutter, to her mother to celebrate their daughter's birth.

1-29. *Vase cut in a variation of Russian pattern, about 1905–1915. H. 25.8cm. Gift of the Oliver family (CMG 83.4.50).*

was in operation from 1906 until 1914. Baldwin became a partner in 1908 and was running the company by 1913, although his title was still Vice-President and treasurer. In a letter to A. A. Houghton dated Dec. 4, 1913, he negotiated the Hoare firm's continuing status as a tenant of Corning Glass Works and agreed to vacate the new large shop with seventy-five frames and go back to the old one with only fifty frames available. Eventually, in 1915, the Hoare company did move out and in 1917, Baldwin sold control back to the Hoares. In 1920, when the company closed, A.A. Houghton put James Hoare on the Corning payroll with a friendly note welcoming him to the firm, underscoring the long and friendly relationship between the Hoare and Houghton families.[25] Hoare died shortly after, and his son, John S. Hoare, left the glass business and Corning.

The two extant catalogs from this period, a complete one of 1911,[26] and an

25. A. A. Houghton to James Hoare, Corning, August 7, 1920. Courtesy Archives, Corning Incorporated
26. This catalog is owned by the Toledo Museum of Art; a microfiche copy is in the Rakow Library of The Corning Museum of Glass.

1-30. *Queens pattern decanter cut by Frank Clark in 1917 at Hawkes. H. 31.1cm. Gift of Robert Smith in memory of Bernice Clark Smith (CMG 83.4.42).Pitcher in a pattern similar to Queens. H. 20.1cm, stamped with Hoare trade-mark. Gift of the Davis family in memory of Helen Moore Davis (CMG 83.4.55).*

assembled one with several different kinds of pages which dates from between 1906 and 1914, both list "Factories at Wellsboro and Corning" which seems to indicate that the same wares were produced in both places. Given the financial difficulties which seemed to have plagued the company from 1903 until 1920, it is remarkable that it turned out so much fine quality glass in this period.

The Hoare company did very little advertising and although their trademark registration papers, filed in 1914, say that they had been using the company trademark since 1895, it does not show up until a very few local advertisements in 1910.[27] It is also in the two twentieth century catalogs, but not in the complete 1896 one. It seems likely that, whether or not the trademark was adopted before 1900, it was not acid-stamped on the glass until 1901 or 1902, although it might have been on a paper label. Various trade papers have Hawkes advertisements in nearly every issue after 1890 and scattered advertisements for other Corning companies including J. F. Haselbauer & Sons, the Corning Cut Glass Company, the O. F. Egginton Company (which says "Trademark on every piece" in 1905), Giometti Brothers, J. N. Illig, and H. P. Sinclaire & Company, between 1905 and 1915, but the only Hoare advertisements are from the teens and only a few of those illustrate the trademark.

The earliest Hoare 'pattern book' in the Rakow Library is a leather bound book

27. *Corning Daily Journal*, December 19, 1910.

1-31. Bowl cut on pattern 1958 on shape 5134 about 1910. D. 20.5cm. Gift of the Davis family in memory of Helen Moore Davis (CMG 83.4.56). This piece is in the 1910 catalog.

of small photographs which is stamped "John Hoare Cut Glass Manufacturer" on the cover. This has no pattern names, only a few early patterns (mostly *Hobnail*, *Sharp Diamond*, *Strawberry Diamond*, and *Russian*) and shows a number of unusual shapes. It probably dates from the early 1880s and a few illustrations from it were reprinted by the American Cut Glass Association in their Hoare catalog reprint of 1992.

The next catalog is a small format book which J. Hoare & Company called a "Price List" and which they must have put out between 1887 and 1890, judging from the fact that it contains the *Mikado* pattern, patented in 1887, but not the *Crystal City* pattern, patented in 1891. Under the heading, "Some of our different cuttings", it lists *Block Diamond*, *Chair Bot. Hobnail*, *Moscow*, *Persian*, *Quarter Diamond*, *Russian*, *Sharp Diamond*, *Strawberry Diamond* and *Wheat* as old patterns and *Amazon*, *Arabesque*, *Basket Pat'n*, *Corning*, *Corona*, *Croesus*, *Eclipse*, *Harlequin*, *Meteor*, *Mikado*, *Oriental*, *Paragon*, *Pearl Edge*, *Prism*, *Richelieu*, *Spider Web*, *Twin City*, and *Universal* as new patterns. All but *Chair Bot. Hobnail*, *Corona*, *Spider Web* and *Universal* are illustrated in a grid of tiny squares on the first page, but the actual catalog illustrations show only a few patterns and the price list shows prices for a full range of shapes in only a few patterns.

Between 1891 and 1893, Hoare put out a printed catalog, rather than a photographic one. There is no entire copy of this, but cut-out pages survive in the two volumes of the Hoare scrapbook and permit us to put together a list of the patterns shown. Many of them have pattern numbers rather than names, mostly four digit numbers beginning with 5, but the following pattern names appear: *Arabesque*, *Corning*, *Croesus*, *Crystal City*, *Cleveland*, *Grecian*, *Hobnail*, *Hobnail & Fan*, *Mikado*, *Keystone*, *Prisms*, *Persian*, *Pillars*, *Pillars & Fans*, *Richelieu*, *Russian*, *Russian & Fan*, *Russian & Pillars*, *Strawberry Diamond*, *Strawberry Diamond & Fan*, *Strawberry Diamond & Pillars*, *Twin City*, and *Wheat*. There may well have been other patterns, since the catalog is cut up and disassembled. This is the second appearance of *Croesus* which was made until about 1900 and the first of *Crystal City* which was probably made for only a few

1-32. *Vase, mold-blown and engraved, probably 1910–1920. H. 29.1cm. Gift of the Davis family in memory of Helen Moore Davis (CMG 83.4.52).*

years. It marks the last appearance of *Hobnail, Mikado, Pillars, Russian, Strawberry Diamond* and *Wheat* and most of their many variations. As far as J. Hoare & Company was concerned, these old-fashioned patterns were no longer in the line by 1896 although they were undoubtedly available in matchings.

The next catalog in the series is one acquired just recently by the Museum. It is undated, but since it features a picture of Captain Hoare along with the information that he died during its preparation, we can be fairly certain it came out for the Christmas season of 1896. Because some pages of it are in the Hoare scrapbooks, some of these designs were published in 1979 with a tentative date of 1905–1910.[28] However, we know that the following patterns were in production in 1896: *Alpine, American, Argand, Atalanta, Aztec, Ceylon, Champion, Como, Coyote, Croesus, Crystal, Delft, Eleanor, Elfin, Golf, Icicle, Lenox, Monarch, Manitou, New York, Pebble, Rock Crystal, Oxford, Regan, Signora, Souvenir, Strawberry Diamond & Fan, Tokio, Wheat, Vogue, X-Ray, Yquem, Yucatan, Zenda.* The price list pages in the back indicate that stemware was available in only about half of the patterns, and quite a few of the patterns listed above seem to be available in only one form. One decanter in *Croesus* is shown and one bowl in a very simplified version of *Wheat. Alpine, Delft, Strawberry Diamond & Fan, Tokio* and *Zenda* are the cheapest patterns at $14 for a 9 in. bowl; *Eleanor* is the most expensive at $30 for the same bowl. The *Rock Crystal* stemware, like *Champion* and *Regal*, is one notch less than *Eleanor* in expense, the *Croesus* and *Crystal* decanters are in the same price range and the *Wheat* variant bowl and plate are $50, while a larger bowl and plate cut in *Eleanor* on the same page are $80. This catalog does not mention any trademark although it does list 1853 as the year the company was established.

The next catalog has several different kinds of pages, both photographic and printed, and must have been assembled sometime after 1906, when the Wellsboro factory opened. It can probably be dated to about 1906–1909 since the scrapbook shows that printed catalogs were issued in August, 1910, in 1911, 1912 and in 1913. The 1906–1909 catalog shows almost no continuation of older patterns (only *Champion* and *Monarch* from 1896) and the introduction of many new ones, most of which stayed in the line through 1913 and probably later. The new patterns are *Acme, Beryl, Bolo, Carolyn, Florence, Haydn, Harvard, Heron, Hindoo, Iola, Limoge, Marcus, Marquise, Messina, Newport, Niagara, Pond Lily* (an engraved pattern), *Pluto, Rock Crystal* (simpler than the one of the 1890s), *Quincy, Sparkler, Steuben, St. James, St. Louis, Victoria* and *Venice*. The later catalogs which are very similar, continue most of these (only seven were dropped) and add *Aqua, Carlisle, Cleary, Colonial, Comet, Crosby, Erie, Fleuron, Jersey, Kohinoor, Leo, Lily, Lotus, Mecca, Naples, Narcissus* (an engraved pattern), *Nassau, Oxford* (different from 1896), *Peerless, Prism, Rookwood, Saturn, Tokio, Trellis, Wild Rose* (an engraved pattern) and *Versailles* as well as many numbered patterns. There were no dated additions made to the scrapbook after 1913 and no other complete catalogs are in the Museum library, but it is likely that few patterns were introduced after 1913 and no new catalogs were printed. A line of satin-finished floral and fruit engravings on both lightweight and heavy blanks, similar to Hawkes Gravic designs was introduced around 1911 and shows up in the 1912 and 1913 catalogs, but does not seem to have been very successful since few examples have turned up. The patterns were *Apples, Cherries, Chrysanthemum, Cornflower, Flower and Ferns, Gooseberries, Grapes, Poppy, Roses, Strawberries, Thistle,* and *Wild Rose*.

John S. Hoare took over the Wellsboro plant for his own business from 1914 to 1916 while Hasell Baldwin was running the parent company. The few advertisements of John Hoare's Wellsboro cutting shop which can be found in 1914 show a trumpet vase in a nondescript pattern. His company was in existence for only a couple of years and its products were probably not marked. After he went back to Corning and took over the family firm, he began to engrave Pyrex for Corning Glass Works, but the Hoare business was very small by that time, and it closed completely in 1920. For many Corningites, the closing of Corning's first cutting firm marked the end of an era as less expensive glassware dominated the business from then on.

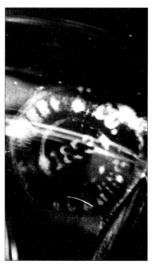

1-33. *Hoare and Hawkes trademarks acid-stamped on the base of a decanter. Probably 1910–1920. OH.29.2cm.*

Photo courtesy Marshall Ketchum. It is likely that this piece was left over when the Hoare factory closed and that it was sold to Hawkes along with other leftover glass and equipment. A few other pieces have turned up with similar double marks.

28. Estelle S. Farrar and Jane Shadel Spillman, *The Complete Cut and Engraved Glass of Corning,* New York, Crown Publishers, 1979, pp.47–59, figs. 95–109.

Thomas Gibbons Hawkes, Entrepreneur

NB. All of the glass illustrated in Chapter 2 was produced by T. G. Hawkes & Company, or its predecessor, T. G. Hawkes Rich-Cut Glass.

Thomas Gibbons Hawkes was born at Surmount, in County Cork, Ireland, in 1846, a scion of the landed gentry, but a younger son in a very large family. He was sent to Queen's College, in Cork, where he studied Civil Engineering for two years, but in 1863, at the age of seventeen, he decided to try his fortunes in the New World. Landing in New York, he was at first unable to find a job, but by chance he encountered John Hoare, another Irishman, who hired him as a draftsman. Thomas apparently was a diligent worker as well as an enterprising one, and he learned the cut glass business quickly, rising rapidly to foreman. He gained experience as a salesman as well, and for a short time ran a branch shop in Rochester, New York engraving lamp chimneys. John Hoare closed the Rochester shop after opening his shop in Corning and by 1870, Tom Hawkes was supervisor of the Corning branch of Hoare's operation, a position he held for ten years. He married a local girl in 1876, started a family, and by 1880 he felt sufficiently confident to open his own cutting shop on West Market Street, literally a stone's throw from Corning Glass Works and John Hoare, at the foot of Walnut Street.

Hawkes and John S. Earl, Hoare's foreman, had both owned small shares of Hoare's business, according to a newspaper story of 1877.[1] Oliver Egginton, who left Hoare's employ along with Hawkes, had not owned a share of the Hoare firm,

1. *Corning Journal,* January 4, 1877, p.3.

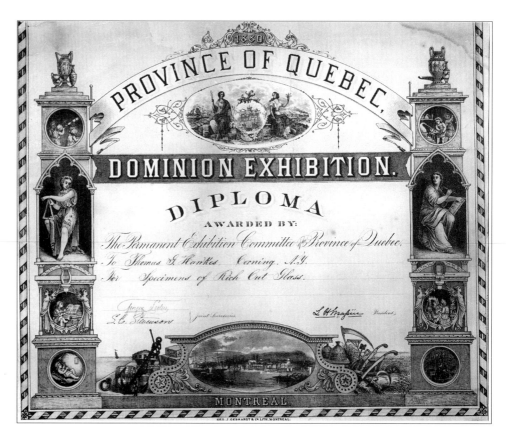

2-1. *Diploma awarded to Thomas G. Hawkes for specimens of rich cut glass at the Dominion Exhibition of Quebec in Montreal, in 1880. Unfortunately, none of the correspondence refers to this exhibition and the diploma may have been awarded simply for participation.*

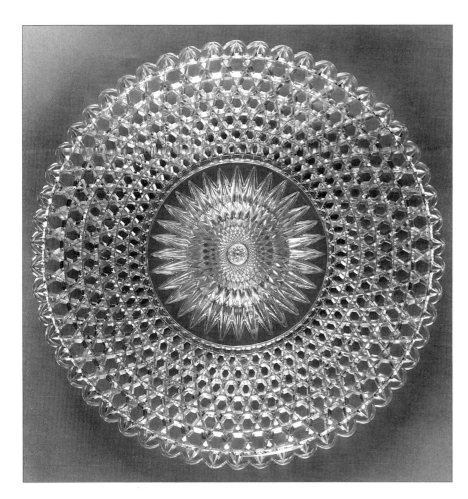

2-2. Plate cut in Hobnail pattern, 1880–1900. D. 33.4cm. Gift of Mr. and Mrs. Frederick V. Martin in memory of T. G. and Samuel Hawkes, The Chrysler Museum. This piece descended in the Hawkes family.

2-3. Ringstand cut in Venetian pattern, about 1890. D. 12.4cm.

The Lightner Museum.

2-4.*Cheese dish, cut in a variation of Venetian pattern, 1890s. D. 26.6cm. Gift of Mrs. Richard O'Brien in memory of Mr. and Mrs. John Ryan. (CMG 86.4.6).*

although eventually he did own a small share in the Hawkes business when Hawkes incorporated in 1890. Although no record has been found, it is possible that Corning Glass Works, or the Houghton family, backed Hawkes financially in the beginning. Certainly, the correspondence between Charles F. Houghton and Thomas G. Hawkes indicates that the Houghtons referred many orders to Hawkes in spite of the fact that Hoare's business was occupying space in their building. The patent for the *Russian* pattern was signed by Quincy Wellington, a Corning banker, and George T. Spencer, both of whom were original investors in the Corning Flint Glass Works, and this may indicate some financial involvement on their part. The later patents were all signed by Hawkes' employees rather than investors. If John Hoare was unwilling or unable to expand his business, the Houghtons may have been trying to develop another customer for their output of blanks.

Around 1881, Thomas Hunt, an English glass cutter, moved from White Mills to Corning to work for Hawkes, and in 1883 H. P. Sinclaire, Jr., the son of Corning Glass Works' corporate secretary, joined Hawkes as book-keeper, manager and, eventually, chief salesman. In 1895, 1896, and 1904, Egginton, Hunt and Sinclaire left to form their own cutting firms in Corning, as Hawkes had left Hoare in 1880. Sinclaire, like Hawkes an experienced manager, was markedly more successful than Hunt and Egginton, the skillful craftsmen.

The Hawkes firm grew rapidly, expanding from seven or eight employees at its founding in March 1880, to thirty or forty men in 1882, and double that by 1890. Some time in the 1890s, the Hawkes company passed Hoare's in size, and by 1902 it was easily the largest cutting shop in Corning with about 400 employees, three shops (two adjacent to each other on Market Street and one a few blocks away on Erie Avenue; the two on Market Street are still standing) and

2-5.*Wineglass, cut in Russian pattern with Russian cut foot, 1882–1895. H.11cm.(CMG 85.4.24).*

2-6. *Wineglass engraved in the Horse pattern, 1880–1900. H. 10.7cm. Gift of F. S. Blake (CMG 69.4.29).*

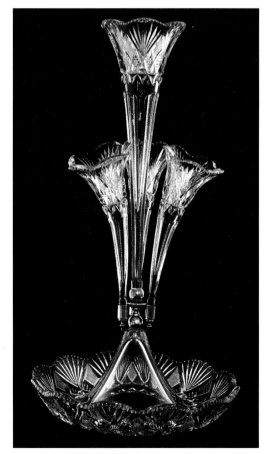

2-7. *Epergne, cut in St. Regis pattern, on Steuben blank 1470, about 1903–1905. H. 46cm.*
Courtesy George and Billie Harrington. Crofford photo.

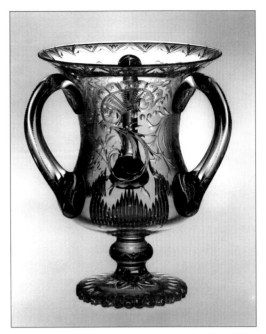 

2-8. *Loving cup, engraved with scrolls, about 1900. H. 23cm, trade-marked. Gift of Charles A. and Isabel S. Hungerford (CMG 84.4.117).*
This piece is shown in the second edition of the Hawkes booklet produced after 1900. The blank is Steuben #955; it was a wedding gift from the Houghton family to Mr. Hungerford's parents in 1900.

2-9. *Punch bowl with silver-gilt stand by Gorham, dated 1904. D. 35cm, trade-marked. Gift of Walter P. Chrysler, The Chrysler Museum.*

several small subcontractors. The cash flow was considerable and Thomas Hawkes was building his fortune through outside investments as well. In the early 1890s, he purchased Iniscarra House, an estate near his father's home in Ireland, and began spending summers there.

In 1901, Hawkes had acquired the Payne foundry building on Erie Avenue to house another cutting shop; in 1903, he announced triumphantly that he had hired Frederick Carder, manager of design at Stevens & Williams in Stourbridge, England, to run a new glass factory, Steuben Glass Works, in the Payne building. Carder's diaries show that, when he visited Corning in March, 1903, the agreement with Hawkes had already been made; his visit was primarily so that Hawkes could make a public announcement. Carder was only in Corning a few days then, but went on to Pittsburgh and Philadelphia at Hawkes' expense to see about constructing furnaces and ordering raw materials.[2] Although Carder was trained as a designer, his work in the English glass industry, and his inquiring mind, had made him equally familiar with the operation of furnaces and blowing rooms, knowledge that Hawkes didn't have. Undoubtedly, this was the period of greatest prosperity for T. G. Hawkes & Company, a prosperity that soon was shattered by changes in the economy and in public taste.

In 1904, H. P. Sinclaire left Hawkes to found his own cutting firm, perhaps for some of the same reasons that brought Carder to Corning. Both had worked as 'second-in-command' at large companies where the boss had a son ready to take over his position. When John Northwood died and his son John II became chief designer at Stevens & Williams, Carder came to Corning. When it became clear

2. Carder's notebooks, Carder Archives, Rakow Library, The Corning Museum of Glass.

2-10. Gravic compote, about 1903–1910. D. 34.6cm. Gravic trademark.
Courtesy of the Jones Museum of Glass and Ceramics.

2-11. Shallow bowl cut on an extremely heavy blank, about 1901–1910. D. 25cm, trademarked. Gift of Mr. and Mrs Marvin Ashburn (CMG 88.4.13).

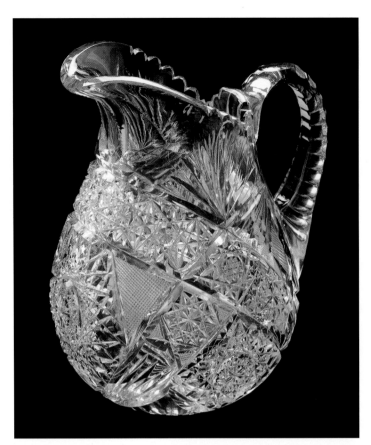

2-12. *Pitcher, about 1890, cut by Frank Clark, about 1890–1900. H. 22.9cm. Gift of Rhea Stasch (CMG 88.4.34).*

2-13. *Goblet cut in Russian pattern, 1882–1895. H. 14.3cm. (CMG 90.4.13). Originally this goblet was taller, but it was cut down, probably to remove chips.*

that Samuel Hawkes would step into his father's shoes and his ideas were different from Sinclaire's, Sinclaire left the Hawkes firm. The same situation had existed when Tom Hawkes left Hoare's shop. James Hoare, somewhat younger than Hawkes, was clearly going to become the boss; the letters between the two indicate that there was no love lost, although Hawkes got along well with John Hoare.

One of Hawkes' last business decisions was to hire a silversmith in 1912 and begin to provide his own silver mounts for glass instead of relying on purchases from the Gorham Manufacturing Company and other firms. Although the department was a one- or two-man operation for the forty-five years it existed, the Hawkes company could now sell more silver mounted glassware, a line that seems to have been especially popular in the 1920s and 1930s.

Thomas Gibbons Hawkes died in 1913, leaving a personal estate of about half a million dollars. His business was in the hands of his only son, Samuel Hawkes, who had started in the firm in about 1895 when he left St. Paul's school. Other Hawkes family members in the firm were Townsend de Moleyns Hawkes, a first cousin of T. G., and Penrose Hawkes, a nephew, both of whom were considerably younger than the firm's founder. In 1915, the directors of the firm decided to hire Pierce and Bickford, architects, of Elmira, to modernize their plant. The four

2-14. *Salad bowl on stand with serving pieces, cut in Russian and Pillars, about* 1890. *OH* 20.1cm. *Gift of Mr. and Mrs. John C. Huntington, Jr. (CMG 84.4.58).*

existing small frame buildings were combined into a single brick building with a unifying facade and decorative window frames; packing, shipping, and storage were on the first floor, offices, stockrooms, and assembly rooms were on the second floor and cutting rooms on the third. The showrooms were across the alley in a frame building erected in 1902 and reached by a bridge over the alley; gilding, enameling, and other decorative work was done in 'Factory No. 2' slightly west on Market Street and separated from the headquarters by a small building whose owner refused to sell. The company moved into these new

2-15. *Ice cream tray cut and engraved in a Gravic fruit pattern, 1911–1915. L. 35.1cm. Gift of Blake's Antiques in memory of Carl C. Jansson (CMG 84.4.119).*
This piece is shown in a Hawkes photograph labelled "Gravic, 4/1911".

quarters early in 1916, after the Christmas rush, and finally vacated for good the building just west of the Hayt Mill at the Walnut Street/Market Street intersection which they had rented from Stephen Hayt since 1882. In January 1924, a fire damaged the plant, but by March the press could announce that elaborate new display rooms had been installed in the former shipping area on the second floor. A designer from the Tiffany firm in New York City created the decor which included light fixtures with Steuben aurene shades, although the Hawkes family no longer owned Steuben Glass Works. They had been forced by wartime economic conditions to sell the plant to Corning Glass Works in 1918. They continued to purchase blanks from Steuben (and others) until 1933, except for the years 1918 and 1919 when Steuben turned out mostly tubing, light bulb blanks and other mundane but necessary products.

Even before Thomas Hawkes' sudden death, the Hawkes firm had seen the need to diversify. Hawkes had always supplied fine engraving on glass as well as the popular rich cuttings; in 1903 he had introduced "Gravic" engravings and even registered a separate trademark for them. Originally these were elaborately engraved wares with both polished and matte surfaces, but later they were simplified. Both Tom and Sam Hawkes understood the need to innovate and to change their product line as the customers' tastes changed. This was probably the reason why Thomas Hawkes encouraged Frederick Carder to produce decorative designs and colors in addition to the blanks for cutting, which were his original reason for founding Steuben.

Before 1917, when Samuel Hawkes presented a gift of glassware to the U.S. National Museum, he was producing gilded and enameled wares as well as

2-16. *Gravic Strawberry bowl,*
about 1905–1915. D. 20.6cm,
Gravic trademark.
Gift of Irene Worth (CMG
84.4.106).

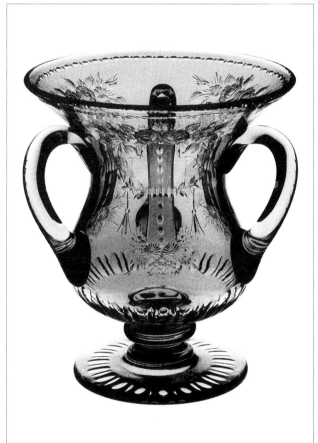

2-17. *Engraved loving cup, about 1910–1920. H. 26.7cm, trade-marked.*
Courtesy of the Lightner Museum, gift of Samuel Hawkes.

2-18. *Engraved vase, about 1910–1920. H. 24.1cm, trade-marked.*
Courtesy of the Lightner Museum, gift of Samuel Hawkes.

53

2-19. Claret jug, cased cranberry over colorless glass and cut in Venetian pattern with silver mounts, about 1890. H. 30cm.
Private collection.

2-20. *Claret jug, cased cranberry over amber and cut in Venetian pattern with silver mounts,* about 1890. H. 34.2cm.

Private collection.

2-21. *Two wineglasses with engraved decoration: Left, probably after 1920, right, signed "H. Fritchie", about 1904–1916. H. (left) 14.8cm.* Hawkes collection.
The difference in quality of the two glasses, the larger one a factory sample done by one of the journeymen engravers and the smaller one done by master engraver, Hieronimus Fritchie, can clearly be seen in the illustration.

reproductions of eighteenth century Anglo-Irish cut glass. Complete descriptions of the Hawkes product lines can be found in Chapters 6 and 8; information acquired from the Hawkes archive has enabled us to redate some of the catalogs published in 1978.[3] The earliest photographic catalog in the museum library dates from the early rather than the late 1890s,[4] although since it was a loose-leaf book, it was updated constantly and the library copy cannot be dated to any one year. The next catalog, chronologically, in the library was probably produced before 1905.[5] The stemware brochure, "Hawkes Glass Services", was probably printed between 1915 and 1920 rather than in the mid-twenties.[6] The catalogs showing "Old English" patterns and colored wares are from about 1915–1925 rather than later,[7] since examples of several pieces shown were given to the U.S. National Museum in 1917 and 1918. The Waterford line, named in the 1920s, was produced until Hawkes closed in 1962; the enameled and gold-decorated wares were phased out in the late 1930s. One thing that was not made clear in these catalogs is the difference, if any, between the "Gravic" and "Satin Engraved" lines, both of which

3. Estelle S. Farrar and Jane Shadel Spillman, *The Complete Cut And Engraved Glass Of Corning*, New York, Crown Publishers, 1979, pp.61-116.
4. Ibid., p.61, figs.174-206.
5. Ibid., p.61, figs.207-239.
6. Ibid., p.60, figs.120-121.
7. Ibid., pp.100–109, figs.333-382.

2-22. Plate cut with Willow
pattern center and blazed edge,
probably T. G. Hawkes & Company
about 1905—1910. D. 25.4cm.
*Courtesy Tom and Marsha de
Graffenreid. Crofford photo.*

2-23. Bowl cut in Willow
pattern with engraved center,
probably T. G. Hawkes & Company
about 1905—1910. D. 15.8cm.
*Courtesy Lowell and Zoe Switzer.
Crofford photo.*

2-24 Lamp, cut in Odd pattern
1890s. H. 62.8cm. Gift of Helen
Chambers in memory of Marvin
Chambers (CMG 82.4.9).
This piece, with this chimney, is
shown in the second edition of the
Hawkes booklet produced after
1900.

2-25. Nappy, cut in Venetian pattern, 1890s. W. 14.9cm. Gift of Mrs. Margaret Buchholz. (CMG 87.4.36).

feature matte surface engraving. Satin Engraved may be simply a new name for Gravic, as "Singing Waterford" is the new name for Old English.

The Hawkes firm continued to use Steuben blanks along with those from Pairpoint and Sinclaire, especially for colored wares in the 1920s. After 1933, however, they were forced to rely on blanks from the plant in Tiffin, Ohio as well as cheaper blanks purchased from a variety of sources. After 1956, the company failed to turn a profit for its owners and the Hawkes family reluctantly decided to liquidate in 1962. The name, trademark, and patterns were sold to the Tiffin Art Glass Company of Tiffin, Ohio, who had been their major supplier of blanks for some time, and for a period in the late 1960s and early 1970s, the Tiffin company produced Hawkes stemware patterns and marked them with the Hawkes name.[8] The increasing demand for Hawkes cut glass from collectors has led to a number of pieces of modern glass cut in old patterns and bearing one of the Hawkes trademarks, appearing on the market. Unfortunately it is very easy to have a trademark stamp made and acid-stamp both old unmarked and new pieces. Collectors need to be sure that the piece in question has other earmarks of authenticity (shape, pattern, cutting, color) without relying just on a trademark.

8. Fred Bickenheuser, *Tiffin Glassmasters*, Grove City, Ohio, 1985, pp.64-71.

2-26. Design drawing by W. Le Brantz, probably 1920s. See Fig. 2–28 for glass in this pattern.

2-27. Engraved perfume, probably 1930s. H. 15.6cm. (CMG 90.4.274ab). This was a leftover from T. G. Hawkes & Company

2-28. Goblet, wine and cordial, probably 1920s. H. of goblet 19.5cm, trade-marked "HAWKES".
  Courtesy Lightner Museum, gift of Samuel Hawkes.

2-29. Vase engraved by Karl Sarter at Hawkes about 1915–1935. H. 40cm. Gift of Mrs. Francis Konstanzer (CMG 86.4.178).

2-30. Goblet and champagne, 1924. H. (goblet) 15.8cm. Gift of Mrs. Edwin S. Underhill (CMG 85.4.6AB).

2-31. *Vase cut in a pattern of hobstars similar to Festoon, about 1900–1910. H. 53.5cm, trademarked.*

Courtesy Martin Folb. Folb photo.

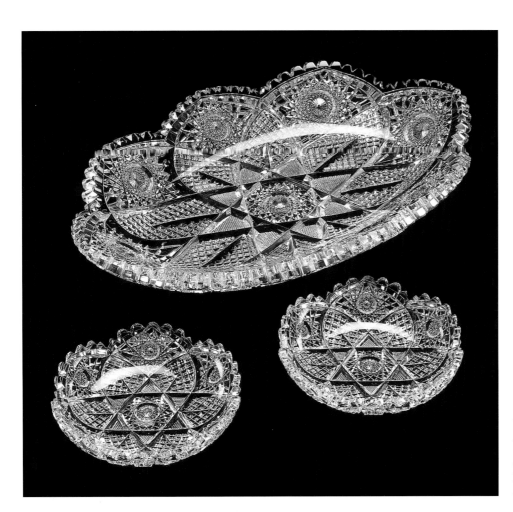

2-32. Ice cream set cut in Aberdeen pattern, about 1900–1910. L. of tray: 39.9cm, trade-marked. Gift of Mr. and Mrs. Milan J. Krasnican (CMG 85.4.84, 86.4.87A,B).

2-33. Punch set in Chrysanthemum pattern with Gorham silver rim with date stamp for 1900. Said to have been produced for exhibition by Gorham at the 1900 Paris Exposition. D. (bowl) 61cm, cups trade-marked. Courtesy Martin Folb. Folb photo.

2-34. Plate engraved with flowers, 1920–1940. D. 30cm, trade-marked.

Courtesy Lightner Museum, gift of Samuel Hawkes.

2-35. Punch bowl, engraved with a ship, probably in the 1930s or 1940s. W. 29cm, trade-marked. Gift of Betty Gruene Spier in memory of Helen McKearin (90.4.120).
The blank for this piece seems to have been made from the bottom of a carboy. It was acquired by Helen McKearin in the 1950s and must have been intended to look 'antique'.

2-36. Candelabra cut in Gladys pattern, about 1900–1910. H. 53.4cm, trade-marked.
Courtesy of Don and Suzy Kosterman. T. A. & M photo.

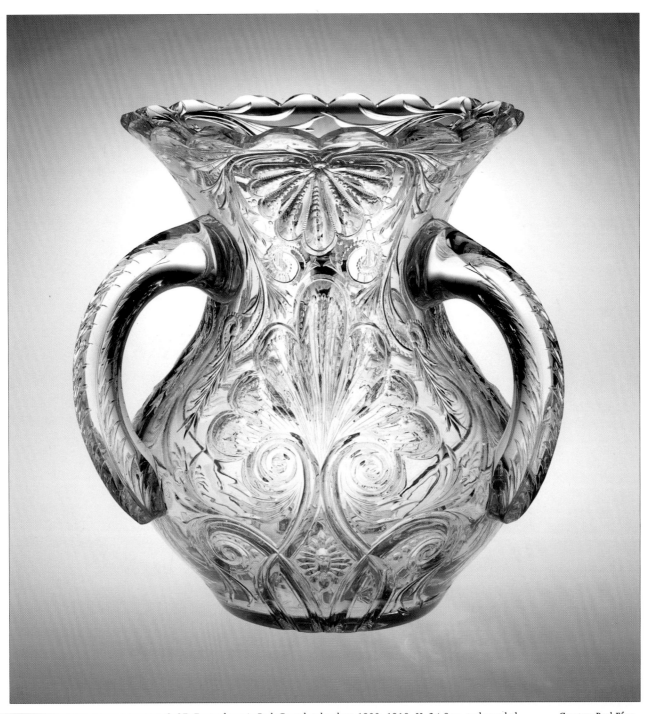

2-37. *Engraved vase in Rock Crystal style, about 1900–1910. H. 24.8cm, trade-marked.* Courtesy Paul Efron.

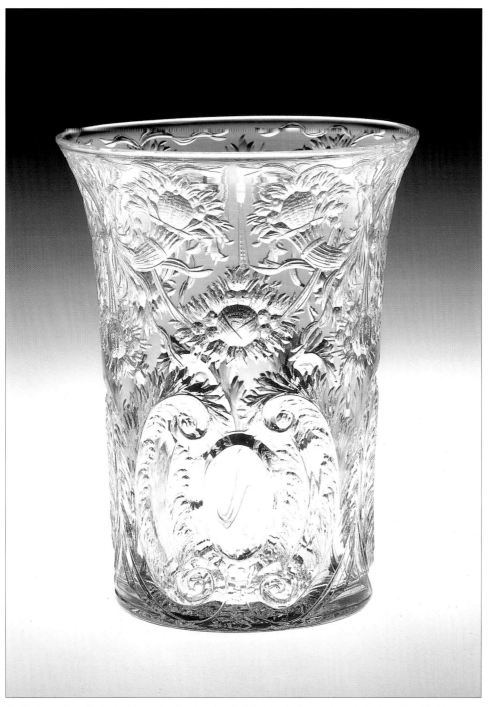

2-38. *Engraved tumbler in Rock Crystal style, about 1900–1910. H. 9.7cm, trade-marked. (CMG 95.4.268).*

2-39. Gravic ice cream plate, about 1903–1910, L. 39.9cm, Gravic trademark.   Courtesy Dorothy-Lee Jones

2-40. Waterford pattern bowl with engraved paradise birds, designed by Samuel Hawkes, 1930s. L. 30.7cm, trade-marked. This was made for an exhibit circulated by the firm in the late 1930s to 1940.

Courtesy of Howard J. Bacon.

2-41. Jack-in-the-Pulpit vase,
about 1900–1910. H. 31.6cm,
trade-marked.
Courtesy Del and Elone Tipps.
T. A. & M photo.

2-42. Plate engraved in an underwater pattern, about 1900–1910. D. 18cm, trade-marked.

Courtesy of the Jones Museum of Glass and Ceramics.

2-43. Ginger jar in cased amber over colorless glass and engraved with birds, probably T. G. Hawkes & Company, about
1910–1920. H. 24.2cm.   Courtesy Lowell and Zoe Switzer. T. A. & M photo

2-44. Lifebuoy decanter, cut in pattern 1401 about 1903–1918. H.28cm. trade-marked. This blank is shape #1307, made by Steuben for Hawkes.   Courtesy Martin Folb. Folb photo.

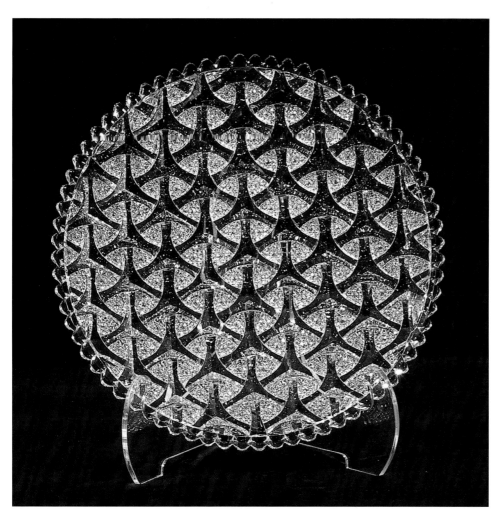

2-45. Tray cut in Pueblo pattern,
about 1905–1910. D. 38.5cm,
trade-marked.
    Courtesy Martin Folb. Folb photo.

2-46. Bowl cut in Panel pattern,
about 1905–1910. D. 25.4cm,
trade-marked.   Private collection.
The cutting on this piece is
exceptionally deep.

2-47. Epergne cut in Queens
pattern, about 1905–1910. H.
61cm, trade-marked.
   Courtesy Dowlton and Ruth Anne
   Berry. T. A. & M photo.

2-48. Goblet with silver foot, engraved in a heraldic pattern, about 1920–1935. H. 15.2cm, marked "HAWKES STERLING" on foot.

Hawkes collection.

2-49. Four goblets engraved with heraldic patterns, about 1920–1935. H. (tallest) 18.2cm, all marked "HAWKES" on foot.
Courtesy Lightner Museum, gift of Samuel Hawkes.

2-50. Vase with silver foot designed by Samuel Hawkes for the exhibition circulated by Hawkes to jewelry stores in 1940. H. 23.3cm, marked "HAWKES STERLING" on silver foot and "SAMUEL HAWKES" on glass, acid-stamped trademark on base.
Courtesy Howard J. Bacon.

2-51. Cocktail glass with enamel decoration by Joseph Lalonde, 1930s. H. 11.6cm, trade-marked.
Hawkes collection.

2-52. Goblet with rock crystal style engraving in the Empire pattern, 1925-40. H. 21.6cm, marked on base, "*HAWKES*". Gift of James Strauss (CMG 79.4.570).

2-53. Tumbler, enameled by Joseph Lalonde and signed "*Lalonde*" at the lower edge. 1930s. H. 15.3cm, acid-stamped "*HAWKES*" on base. Gift of Otto Hilbert (CMG 79.4.231).

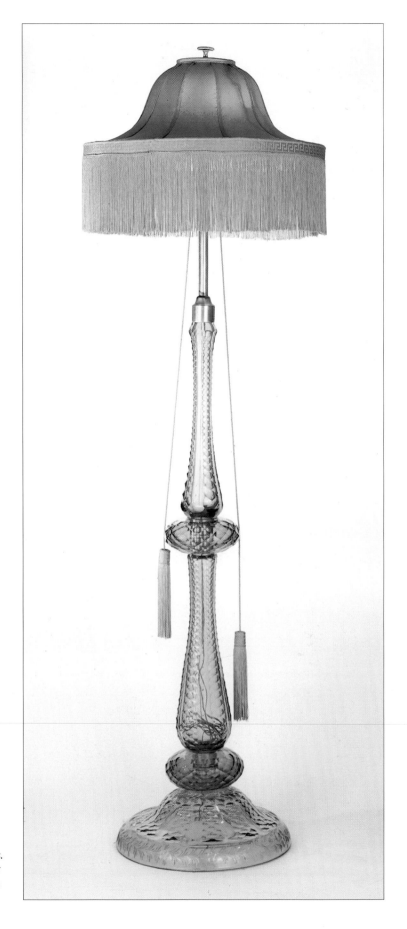

2-54. Floor lamp in amber glass with cut stem and silk shade, probably made in the 1930s. H. 240cm, engraved "HAWKES" on stem.

    Courtesy Lightner Museum, gift of Samuel Hawkes. This is undoubtedly a unique item although the parts for another were in the Hawkes building in the late 1950s and are now in a private collection.

2-55. *Vase cased green over colorless glass and cut probably in the 1940s. H. 30.2cm, trade-marked.   Private collection.*

2-56. *Water lamp base engraved with swimming fish, probably 1920-1940. H. 36.3cm, trade-marked on foot.*

Courtesy Susie Herpel.

Two or three of these have turned up, but the design was probably never produced commercially and does not appear in any catalogs.

2-57. Two wineglasses cut in a streamlined style, probably in the
1940s. H. (taller) 16.4cm, trade-marked.   Courtesy Frank Swanson.
These may be prototypes for new designs which were never
commercially produced.

2-58. Pair of vases cased blue over colorless glass and cut in
Thousand Eyes pattern, probably 1920–1940. H. 33.2cm,
trade-marked.   Courtesy Lightner Museum, gift of Samuel Hawkes.
The blank was made by the Pairpoint Corporation of New Bedford,
Massachusetts.

2-59. Plate engraved with fruit and flowers, 1920–1940. D.33.6 cm., marked "HAWKES".
    Courtesy Lightner Museum, gift of Samuel Hawkes.

2-60. Vase engraved with flowers and scrolls, 1920–1940. H. 25.9cm, trade-marked.
    Courtesy Lightner Museum, gift of Samuel Hawkes.

CHAPTER THREE

Labor Relations In The
Glass Industry

When Thomas G. Hawkes opened his glass cutting shop on Market Street, he had only a few employees, but it is likely that at least one engraver, Joseph Haselbauer, was among them. All of Hawkes's first employees were probably recruited from the ranks of John Hoare's workmen, but within a year or two Hawkes was receiving applications for employment from outside of Corning. In August 1883, John Tomey wrote: "Dear Sir hearing from Mr. Singleton that you were in want of a good glass Engraver. I beg to offer myselfe to your notice. I am a good general workman. I have just come over from England and shall be glad of a Favourable reply from you."[1]

In October of the same year, Arsene Ratel wrote: "I take the liberty to offer you my services as glass cutter of great experience. This morning I showed specimen of my work at Mr. Hoare's New York office & was advised to apply to you for employment in your factory. Please reply & oblige."[2] Hawkes' reply to the second letter brought further information: "I last worked at the White Mill, in Pennsylvania, in the department of 'rich cutting' for the period of eight months without stoppage. I was originally brought up as a diamond Cutter at Bacara France, where I worked continuously for 17 years. I can however do the cutting of many faced stoppers. In preference to forwarding you specimen of my handy work I will take them to you in person as I will travel farther on if I am not accepted in your place."[3]

There are half-a-dozen similar letters in the archives, all of which mention the writer's past experience and most of which do not mention wages. It seems to have been a buyer's market in the 1880s. Another engraver who applied for work was J. Johne, who wrote: "I have been informed that you are doing a good Business in Cut & Engraved Glassware. I would be glad to do your Engraving to your own Price and promptly and it will be done well, as if you Should require a Man to do your Engraving at your Shop I would be glad to come."[4] Hawkes replied, inquiring about his experience and Johne wrote again: "Yours received as regards the Pollished Engraving. I can Produce the same as Thomas Webb of England. I have Made a sample for Davis Collamore, they tried to get it done by other Engravers but could not. I am able to do all you have in the Pollished Engraving if you wish you can see the Sample at Davis Collamore."[5] The following week, he wrote again: "I send you to Day the 2 Flasks Engraved, if you should require work done Cheaper, I can do it but it will not be done so well. These 2 Flaskes has taken me 2½ Days hard Work. I can make you work According to your own Price."[6]

The cutters were paid from $12 to $20 a week, depending on their experience and skill, and this seems to have been standard across the industry, although it was much higher than European rates of pay. This inequity ensured that a steady stream of experienced cutters and engravers would come to the United States from England and the Continent, and many of them found their way to Corning.

One of the most interesting developments that can be tracked in the Hawkes correspondence is the determination of Hawkes to shut out the fledgling labor

1. John Tomey, Boston, to Mr. Hawkes, Corning, August 23, 1883.
2. Arsene Ratel, New York to T. G. Hawkes, Corning, October 15, 1883.
3. Ratel to Hawkes, October 22, 1883.
4. J. Johne, New York to Thomas Hawk, Corning, December 6, 1883.
5. Johne to Hawkes, January 18, 1884.
6. Johne to Hawkes, January 23, 1884.

movement and to control the workmen on his own terms. To begin with, there were agreements among Thomas Hawkes, his chief Corning competitor John Hoare, and Christian Dorflinger in nearby White Mills, Pennsylvania, that they would not hire each other's men. On August 23, 1882, John S. O'Connor, the Dorflinger foreman, wrote to Oliver F. Egginton, Hawkes' foreman, to confirm that: "I have had two applications for work from Corning which I do not intend to answer for as you say it would be to our mutual intrest for each to have those we have taught. Mr. Hoare and I have an understanding to the same efect, and I believe it to be a benefit to both parties, for instance two of his young men applyed to us for work some time ago but I would have nothing to do with them (although we wanted hands very mutch at the time) then again we had a young man to work a couple of weeks, he told me he worked for John Taney in Brooklyn (and he suted us very well) but when I found out he was one of Mr. Hoare's hands we let him go, so you may depend on us acting honorable towards you."[7]

John Hoare himself wrote to Hawkes on November 21 of that year somewhat more bluntly: "Man or boy leaving and working in another Place for a month or so is no Excuse for me I do not employ them."[8] At least twice, the Dorflingers sent back workmen whom they had hired without realizing that they had broken Hawkes contracts.

More distant glass cutting firms sought the same protection, although not with formal agreements. George Hatch of the Meriden Flint Glass Company wrote Hawkes on May 11, 1881 about the union: "I enclose a list of 15 Glass Cutters, all of whom are Society [Knights of Labor] men, and have given us constant trouble. We changed our system of work, and contracted with the old foreman to do our cutting and these Society men refused to work for him. They were, of course, discharged by this Company, but have been exceedingly malicious and done what they could to prevent our getting men. We shall consider it as a mark of courtesy if you see fit to refuse to employ them."[9]

On July 13, 1887, a representative of T. B. Clark & Company in Honesdale, Pennsylvania, near White Mills, wrote to Hawkes, "We wired you this morning that our men had struck. We trust you will protect us in this matter and not hire any of them until the strike is over."[10]

Thomas Hawkes endured a strike by his own cutters from September 26, 1886 until March 24, 1887. Neither the newspaper accounts nor the existing correspondence gives a complete account of the trouble, but it seems to have come to a head over the issue of apprentices. The union thought Hawkes was training too many glass cutters, which would drive down wages, and that he was letting the apprentices do work which should have gone to the more highly paid workmen.[11] The real issue seems to have been whether or not Hawkes would permit union activists from the Knights of Labor to run his shop. Local newspaper accounts give an ugly picture of fistfights between the strikers and the twenty-five or so 'scabs' Hawkes hired to replace them,[12] but the letters show how he managed to stay in business by subcontracting work to Dorflinger, John Maris &

7. John S. O'Connor for The Dorflinger Glass Company, White Mills to O.F. Egginton, Corning, August 23, 1882.
8. John Hoare, Corning to Thomas G. Hawkes, November 21, 1882.
9. George Hatch, Meriden, Connecticut to T. G. Hawkes, May 11, 1881.
10. T. B. Clark & Company, Honesdale to T. G. Hawkes, July 13, 1887.
11. Estelle S. Farrer and Jane Shadel Spillman, The Complete Cut and Engraved Glass of Corning, Crown Publishers, 1979, p. 55.
12. Ibid.

3-1. *Thomas G. Hawkes, engraving from Landmarks of Steuben County, ed. Harlo Hawkes, 1896.*

Company of Philadelphia, and the firms of William H. Lum (the New York agent for the Mt. Washington Glass Company) and John McCue in New York City. This sometimes had to be done secretly since workers at the other shops were often in sympathy with the strikers.

A letter from McCue's partner, John Earl (the former Hoare foreman), to "Friend Tom" explains: "After writing to you Saturday, we had a Committee of the Shop to say they understood that we was cutting work for you we neither admitted or denied it but told them we would not have any trouble about that this morning they said they thought there was more goods in the shop for you if that was the case they could not do it they spoke of 4 decanters hobnail & star P. told them we was to send them to D. C. & Co. that satisfied them now you know this puts us in bad shape and you must try to help us out. Cannot you let us ship the good direct to your Customers or send the goods you must have in Corning to

3-2. *John Hoare, engraving from* Landmarks of Steuben County, *ed. Harlo Hawkes, 1896.*

D.C. or any other Place you may name & have them ship there to you. We intend to do all the work you may send us and to have some say in running the shop but we do not want a strike just at present. Some time later on will be better."[13]

At the same time, Hawkes was receiving complaints from his major customers that he was taking too long to fill orders. Hawkes also wrote letters asking that his competitors not hire any of his strikers, and he saw to it that two hired under assumed names by Dorflinger and then by Clark were discharged.[14]

Dorflinger also supplied goods to Hawkes at cost during this period in a deliberate attempt to help break the "Society."[15] A letter from John J. McCue in New York to Hawkes, demonstrates the helpful attitudes of the other cutting shop owners: "Within the past few days, it has come to my knowledge that one of the men in my employment (who had formerly worked for you) on a recent visit to Corning he is reported to have said that if I had the room I was willing and would

13. John Earl for John J. McCue, New York to T. G. Hawkes, February 21, 1887.
14. Louis Dorflinger, White Mills to T. G. Hawkes, January 12, 1887.
15. Dorflinger to Hawkes, January 5, 1887.

3-3. Building occupied by T.G. Hawkes & Company from the 1890s until its closing in 1962, Market Street, Corning, N.Y. Hawkes' Factory No. 2 was to the left, separated from this one by a small building. Both buildings still stand; this one is presently occupied by Vitrix, a small glass business.

be glad to put all the men at work who left you on account of the strike at your place. I wish to contradict that story, it is false in every particular and if you will say that you heard it on what you consider good authority the man will be no longer in my employment."[16]

An exchange of letters between the Phoenix Glass Company and Hawkes further underlines the owners' attitude.[17] "Mr. Howard has requested me to answer your letter in regard to see if there is any of your men working for us. In reply state that I have two men working for me from White Mills & Honesdale this I know from their Transfer Cards from the A.F.G.W.U., ...I knew there was a strike at your place but as for the amount of cutting done out West it is so little that it wouldn't justify any men to come here." Hawkes responded by asking for the names of the two men as he wanted "...to find out if they were our men who had contracts with us which we knew had got situations somewhere but we could not tell where, but since writing you we have ascertained where the men have been working. Their employers have discharged them as no responsible manufacturer will employ another mfr's men who are under contract."

A letter on February 12 from Louis C. Dorflinger explains: "Please let us know what the result of the arrest of the strikers will be. Hope you can get them punished ...was in Meriden on Thursday and Bergen promised to discharge the two strikers of yours that he has there at work. Please keep this quiet."[18]

An exchange of letters between Thomas Hawkes and E. D. Libbey, then still in New England, explains the owners' views. Libbey wrote: "Will you please inform us what you pay for first class journeymen Glass Cutters, lowest & highest price.

16. John J. McCue, New York to T. G. Hawkes, January 12, 1887.
17. J. C. Riordan, Phoenix Glass Company, Monaca, Pennsylvania to T. G. Hawkes, January 25, 1887 and penciled draft of reply written on reverse of above letter.
18. Dorflinger to Hawkes, February 12, 1887.

Our men have joined something & seem to feel quite strong support judging by their demands, actions &c &c." and Hawkes replied: "When our men struck, 70 of them went out. Our wages were from $12 to $17 per week. There were three or four who we paid $18.00 to but they had been with us since we started in business, & we did not recognize them as a standard for what wage we paid. We are led to believe that the Knights of L. have withdrawn their support from our men. The contributions that have been coming here for the last few weeks have been from the different cutting shops in the country. The largest contributions seem to come from E. Cambridge. Between $80 – $100 at a time. We found that the rate of wage men paid made it very difficult to compete with the English manufacturers as you can see we have been paying 100% more than the English glasscutters receive."[19]

At the conclusion of the strike, most of the manufacturers wrote to Corning to find out what points Hawkes had conceded to the union. Henry Spurr, General Manager of the Boston & Sandwich Glass Company, wrote several times in dismay because his men were celebrating the end of the strike as if the union had won.[20] Unfortunately, Tom Hawkes' replies do not survive, but he claimed victory in the struggle.

The trouble continued at other firms in the summer of 1887. Louis Dorflinger wrote to Hawkes in August that: "Bergen of Meriden writes us his men are asking more wages and doing ⅓ less work—All this since July 1. Everyone seems inclined to fight the cutters — if they don't do it now the longer its put off the worst it will be."[21] Eventually, in November of that year, the New England proprietors, Frederick Shirley and Edward Drummond Libbey, took the lead in arranging for the owners of glass-cutting businesses to meet at the Astor House in New York City to agree on a united front.[22] Hawkes was not able to attend, but John Hoare represented Corning at the meeting. He reported to Hawkes in person so the exact outcome of the meeting is not recorded here. However, it apparently concerned the formation of an association of the manufacturers.[23] "I think it is important for all concerned in the rich cut glass trade to work together in harmony. I know it pays well in the Glass Mfg part & such an association of Mfg. cutters as we now have in the Factory dept. will be money in our pockets every year", said Louis Dorflinger.

Trouble in White Mills followed shortly after the strike in Corning and on January 23, 1888, Louis Dorflinger wrote Hawkes:[24] "We have discharged nine of our cutters… They are the leading Society men here and are all good cutters. A couple of them are well acquainted with Mr. John Hoare & may go up there looking for work. Will you please ask Mr. Houghton to speak to Mr. Abbot & see that none of these men are hired by Mr. Hoare. There is no other place for them to look for work but in Corning."

George L. Abbott was Hoare's partner and a son-in-law of Amory Houghton. The following day, Dorflinger reported: "About sixty of our cutters walked out of the shop this morning, this because we discharged the leaders of the Union. We

19. E. D. Libbey, for W. L. Libbey & Son, New England Glass Works, Boston to T. G. Hawkes, January, 1887 and draft reply on reverse, January 24, 1887.
20. Henry Spurr, Boston & Sandwich Glass Company, Sandwich, Massachusetts, to Thomas G. Hawkes, March 27, 1887.
21. Dorflinger to Hawkes, August 29, 1887.
22. Edward D. Libbey, East Cambridge to Thomas G. Hawkes, November 14, 1887.
23. Dorflinger to Hawkes, November 22, 1887.
24. Dorflinger to Hawkes, January 23, 1888.

will not experience much trouble, we think we will be able to run abt. 40 frames regularly, will keep you posted. Our men gave us no notice whatever. Asked for the reinstatement of discharged men, this we positively refused and they simply walked out.[25]

The strike at Dorflinger's apparently spread to the blowers and continued for six months. Dorflinger met it by refusing to give in to the union and importing new men from Europe. At times, his communications to Hawkes took on a cloak and dagger aspect as when he said on February 16: "We wrote under name of John Dawson to Dithridge & Company asking for work, Please note the reply enclosed herewith. How would you like your shop run on these principles."[26] The logical assumption is that Dithridge was willing to employ 'John Dawson' even though he was a striker. In July, Dorflinger sent to Amory Houghton, via T. G. Hawkes, proof that several of his men were union members although he asked Hawkes to show "the book" to no one else.[27]

In August, Dorflinger wrote: "We started today another first class castor place shop [a team of men who made mold-blown glass] and in the course of ten days we will be prepared to make anything you may require in best goods. We have two more first class shops coming over, (one shop supposed to be the best in Europe for large work) and in the course of next 30 days you will see some work done in this 'scab' workshop that will do your heart good. The Union is working hard against us, but we are now on top & propose to stay there."[28]

An entire exchange of letters between Dorflinger and Hawkes had to do with a cutter named Elwell who tried to move from Hawkes to White Mills. He arrived in White Mills on August 14, 1888, and applied for work; Louis Dorflinger immediately instructed John O'Connor, his foreman, to telegraph Oliver Egginton, Hawkes's foreman, and find out why he had left.[29] Elwell had apparently been under contract to Hawkes and by August 17, Louis Dorflinger had persuaded him to return to Corning and had even bought him a railway ticket so that he could do so.[30] In September, two former workmen of both Hawkes and Hoare's, named Delahunty and Mulford, left Corning to work for T. B. Clark and Company, but the workmen at Clark's refused to work with the two Corningites and they came to Dorflinger's.[31] The indefatigable Louis Dorflinger investigated the matter and found that the Corning cutters had not paid their union dues in Corning and thus their "mates" at Hoare's had written ahead to try to stop Clark from hiring them.[32] A letter from Delahunty himself to Thomas Hawkes tells the story slightly differently and makes it clear that the attempt to find employment in Pennsylvania was really a feint to enable them to seek re-employment with Hawkes without upsetting John Hoare.[33] Eventually, on September 28, Dorflinger wrote: "Mr. Delahunty the glass cutter, Artist & Designer leaves us today. He returns to Corning and expects to go to work for you. He tells me he leaves here much to his regret, but his wife does not wish to leave Corning just now. He tells others he leaves for Corning because there are not churches enough here (he pretends to be unusually religious) to others he says he leaves because the

25. Dorflinger to Hawkes, January 24, 1888.
26. Dorflinger to Hawkes, February 16, 1888.
27. Dorflinger to Hawkes, July 18, 1888.
28. Dorflinger to Hawkes, August 22, 1888.
29. Dorflinger to Hawkes, August 14, 1888.
30. Dorflinger to Hawkes, August 17, 1888.
31. Dorflinger to Hawkes, September 4, 1889.
32. Dorflinger to Hawkes, September 7, 1889.
33. J. Delahunty, White Mills to T. G. Hawkes, Corning, September 7, 1889.

3-4. *Interior view of a cutting shop in Corning, about 1890-1900. This is the way all of the shops looked, with belts running from an overhead shaft. Judging from its size, this is either the Hawkes or the Hoare shop.*

standard of wages is not high enough in the shop. We paid him 16.00 a week and that was all he was worth. He is an awful talker and honestly I am glad he has left us. If you need him put him to work, but I think he will bear watching for I don't think he is blessed with any more common sense than falls to the lot of most men. I don't put much confidence in these great talkers, particularly when they try to impress me with their deep desire to never miss attending church at least three times on Sunday.[34]

According to another letter from Louis Dorflinger, the trouble at T. B. Clark's had more to do with the union's dislike of Tom Hawkes than with Delahunty's unpaid dues. "The fact of their being non union did not amount to anything, but particular stress was put on the necessity of preventing you from getting men… It will be well for you to remember these things, some day it may be your turn to do the dictating."

This correspondence makes it clear that the workers found it difficult to make any sort of move without the owners' knowledge. The Corning-White Mills connection was close geographically as well as personally and although the New York City and New England shops were farther away, the owners were in frequent communication. Even in the larger shops which employed 150 to 250 men (Hoare, Hawkes, Dorflinger and later, Libbey in Toledo), the foremen and the owners knew the names and histories of most of the workmen, and they were vigilant in guarding against the encroachment of the Knights of Labor and paternalistic in their attitudes toward the men and their families.

34. Dorflinger to Hawkes, September 28, 1889.

T.G. Hawkes and
C. Dorflinger & Sons

From 1887 until 1903, Thomas G. Hawkes and C. Dorflinger & Sons in White Mills had a very close relationship, which involved sales in both directions. The 1887-1892 correspondence shows almost daily letters between Louis J. Dorflinger and Tom Hawkes or Harry Sinclaire, and some visiting between the two to consult on matters of importance. Correspondence after 1892 is not available, but that the relationship continued is demonstrated in both the Hawkes cash books and the Dorflinger blanks records. The Hawkes cash books and day books are available for many years from December 1900, and the Dorflinger Factory office record of blanks[1] covers the period from the early 1890s until the mid-teens.

Hawkes ordered 427 different blank shapes in the period covered, mostly in the 1890s but some in 1909 and 1910. J. Hoare and Company, Dorflinger's next largest customer for blanks, bought 259 different shapes. Hawkes spent about $35,000 annually in the peak years from 1900 to 1903 buying blanks from Dorflinger, more than from any other source and more than half of the firm's total expenditure on blanks. Although the financial records from the 1890s are missing, it seems likely that the replacement of Corning Glass Works by Dorflinger as the chief blank supplier to the Hawkes firm was a gradual one. For both Hawkes and Hoare, blank purchases from Dorflinger started in 1885, when a strike at Corning closed the glass works for a short period. During the Hawkes strike of 1886–1887, the Dorflingers supported him extensively, supplying blanks at favorable prices and probably doing some cutting for Hawkes as well. In the Dorflinger strike which followed, in early 1888, Tom Hawkes returned the favor.

In January, most of the glass cutters in the Dorflinger factory struck in support of the leaders of the fledgling union, who had been discharged. The strike of cutters soon spread to the blowing room. It continued for six months and Dorflinger met it by refusing to give in to the union and importing new men from Europe. However, by August, Louis Dorflinger could report to Tom Hawkes: "We are doing first rate in the cutting shop and before long we trust to be running as of old. When we get well stocked up with cut goods, we propose going for the new customers in the west & if you will lend us a hand as you are now doing we can by working together make things lively for the other fellows and have a good trade for ourselves."[2]

The two strikes began this relationship, and apparently it proved profitable to both companies. In December 1887, just before the Dorflinger strike, Louis Dorflinger wrote, "If you have any cut goods in hand now that you cannot use, for your regular trade we may be able to run some of it off for you; if you will send us samples and prices we will try to dispose of it for you."[3] Just before the strike, he wrote, "We expect to largely increase our work with you, as we intend to push sales of cut glass this year to the fullest extent and be prepared with a large stock to fill orders promptly."[4] During the strike, Dorflinger wrote: "Please accept thanks for goods sent. We don't expect you to cut our goods at cost. Please charge us a fair profit on our orders & we will be perfectly satisfied."[5] A couple of months

1. The original book, in Louis Dorflinger's distinctive hand, along with other Dorflinger material, was purchased by the Museum from John Dorflinger's heirs shortly after his death. Unfortunately it was stolen by a Dorflinger researcher in 1987 but a photocopy remains in the Rakow Library of The Corning Museum of Glass. Only notes are left on the contents of some of the other original Dorflinger records which were part of the group. If any of these records are ever found, the Museum is most anxious to recover them.
2. C. Dorflinger & Sons, White Mills to T. G. Hawkes, August 22, 1888.
3. C. Dorflinger & Sons, White Mills to T. G. Hawkes, December 2, 1887.
4. C. Dorflinger & Sons, White Mills, to T. G. Hawkes, January 3, 1889.
5. C. Dorflinger & Sons, White Mills to T. G. Hawkes, February 23, 1888.

later, he ordered more glass and asked, "Would you like more work from us, We can send you more work if you want it and have a chance to do it, We are running now but are short on good workmen,"[6] and Hawkes drafted a reply on the back indicating that he was not busy and would be glad to cut anything for Dorflinger. Throughout the remainder of 1888, then through 1892, nearly daily letters indicate that Hawkes was not only buying blanks but was also cutting substantial quantities of glass ordered by the Pennsylvania firm.

By the fall of 1888, Hawkes was also supplying glass directly to Dorflinger's New York City sales shop on Murray Street on consignment as well as to White Mills on order. Louis Dorflinger wrote: "Our alterations and repairs being now complete at our N Y store, we would be glad to have you send us on consignment and with lowest prices the fancy pieces you spoke to writer about in Corning. We can without doubt get rid of these for you."[7] The only matter left unclear in the letters is whether the glass sold from the shop was sold as Hawkes or as Dorflinger glass. There are several existing lists of the glass in the shop on consignment, but they do not clarify this.

A letter from the Murray Street store (which seems to have been a retail store, as well as a display space) says: "In reply to yours…to White Mills. Please find enclosed herewith report of goods sold to date. On the last lot of goods sent us on consignment, one of the Amber hocks, 'Hob & Star' was broken. Will you please cut us one to make this dozen complete…"[8] Attached to this letter is a list of the goods sent on consignment which had been sold in the previous two months, for a total of $934. In reply, Hawkes says that he will send the bill for the goods sold to White Mills and supply the broken amber hock.[9] The monthly statements in 1889 show that Dorflinger was paying Hawkes several hundred dollars a month for these goods. A letter from White Mills to Hawkes says: "If you have any odd rich Decanters handled or unhandled, please send them by Express at once. We have a chance to sell a few odd pieces of this description, and if you have any that you would like to dispose of please send them, and we can put them in with our goods."[10] Whether or not these were being marketed through the store is not stated, but it seems less likely that Dorflinger was selling them to a wholesale customer. On the other hand, when Dorflinger sent photographs of Hawkes's glass to a customer, as happened occasionally, they must have been identified as Hawkes products.[11]

The objects ordered from and sent to White Mills were probably being sold as Dorflinger's glass, perhaps with the Dorflinger paper label which had apparently been adopted in the fall of 1888.[12] In August, Dorflinger wrote: "We send today some 8in & 9in Round nappies. Please cut 12 9in in Cobweb, 6 9in in Russian, 6 9in in Hobnail, 10 8in in Cobweb, 4 8in in Russian, 4 8in in Hobnail. Will send you some for S/ & Fan cutting next week." This is obviously an order for stock, rather than a special order since these are standard patterns and shapes being ordered in quantity.

Between 1887 and 1892, Hawkes provided hundreds of articles in the

6. C. Dorflinger & Sons, White Mills to T. G. Hawkes, April 27, 1888.
7. Louis Dorflinger, White Mills to T. G. Hawkes, October 6, 1888.
8. W. F. for C. Dorflinger & Sons, New York to T. G. Hawkes, December 31, 1888.
9. T. G. Hawkes to C. Dorflinger & Sons, New York , January 1, 1889.
10. C. Dorflinger & Sons, White Mills, to T. G. Hawkes, May 31, 1889.
11. C. Dorflinger & Sons, New York, to T. G. Hawkes, December 22, 1891.
12. G. P. Riker for Gilman Collamore & Company New York to "Friend Hawkes" October 5, 1888, refers to label.

following patterns to Dorflinger: Block Diamond, Brazilian, Cobweb, Fan & Diamond, Grecian, Grecian & Hobnail, Hob Diamond, Hob & Russian, Hobnail, Japanese, Large Hob Diamond, Large Hobnail, Large Russian, Mirror Block, Parisian, Persian, Peacock, Pillars, Pillar & Concave, Princess, Prisms, Russian, Russian & Pillars, Silver Diamond, Star & Hobnail, Strawberry Diamond & Fan, Table Diamond, and Venetian. Some of these are patented Hawkes patterns; others were in the public domain. In 1888 and 1889, Cobweb and Parisian were ordered most frequently, but by 1892, the cheaper Strawberry Diamond & Fan was the most common pattern in the orders. For most of these, Dorflinger supplied the blanks. However, in some cases, Hawkes got the blanks in Corning or from somewhere else.

In January, 1888, Louis Dorflinger wrote: "Since my return home we have been talking over the matter of getting blanks from England & we have almost decided to send our Mr. Martin over to England to look into the matter & place the orders & make the necessary arrangements for regular supplies…if we decide to send him over he can do your business for you as well as ours, or, as I suggested to you, we can import these goods together & in this way reduce the cost to both."[13]

Tom Hawkes was glad to give the Dorflingers advice on where to go in England, but he said that he did not need any of the blanks at that time as he had reduced his workforce and planned to keep the business small for several months. A letter of May 1887, shows that the Dorflingers were using substantial quantities of imported lapidary stoppers at that time. "We find we can import them cheaper & better than we can make & cut them here," said Louis Dorflinger.[14]

When the Parisian pattern was first introduced in the late 1880s, it was being made in quantity by Hawkes for Dorflinger. One letter from White Mills says: "We could not afford to pay over $14 to $15 a doz. for the Parisian tumblers. We think you can cut them for this; our boys can cut Parisian in such work as tumblers, nappies &c."[15] The phrasing of that particular letter leads one to think that it was because Hawkes had better cutters rather than because Dorflinger had too many orders that Dorflinger turned to them for assistance, but that might have been because of the strike in White Mills. The emphasis on 'boys' in that letter may also imply that Parisian tumblers were easy to cut and the work could be done by boys, that is, at a lesser price. On the other hand, some of the work supplied by Hawkes may have been sold as Hawkes glass, particularly the Cobweb, Venetian, and Brazilian pieces, all of which were Hawkes's patented patterns. After an urgent order for a pair of water bottles cut in the Cobweb pattern, which Hawkes could not supply in the time allowed, Dorflinger wrote: "We are very sorry you cannot get out the pair Water Bottles. We now lose sale of an entire set of this ware. We know this is a bad time to ask for special favors, but as we respect your rights in the Cobweb cutting and have never cut any here, we…relied on you to help us out…"[16]

Another time, Dorflinger wrote: "By freight today we sent you 3 doz. 521 assorted colored Hocks, 1 — 8 doz. 520 assorted colored Hocks, 2 doz. 520 assorted double colored Hocks. Please cut one dozen of each of these Brazilian,

13. Louis J. Dorflinger, White Mills, to T. G. Hawkes, January 9, 1888.
14. C. Dorflinger & Sons, White Mills to T. G. Hawkes, May 28, 1887.
15. C. Dorflinger & Sons, White Mills to T. G. Hawkes, May 3, 1888.
16. C. Dorflinger & Sons, White Mills, to T. G. Hawkes, May 11, 1888.

foot to be cut patent star but not scalloped. The cutting of the balance I will send you later. There are four green 520 Hocks short to make the 2 dozen these we will send very soon, In cutting the dozen of each please distribute the colors equally as we sell them in sets. The stem of the 520 Blue and Ruby Hocks are made heavier than the others, please see that these are cut down to correspond in thickness with the other ones."[17]

However the goods were being sold, Dorflinger frequently tried to negotiate lower prices. "Can't you allow us 10% on D. Water Bottles in Cobweb and Parisian. We are selling that at just what you charge us for them. Please look into this and see if you can't do it."[18] Even the cutters must have had trouble telling Hawkes from Dorflinger some of the time, as the shapes were often the same. In 1888, Hawkes wrote: "Please send us... round nappies, heavy enough for Russian cutting. As your moulds are the same size and shape as ours, it will not be necessary for us to send you moulds for these goods."[19] The next year, Dorflinger wrote: "If Mr. Hawkes cannot come soon, writer will go to Corning as we wish to talk over some matters for coming season. We have quite a number of new goods and we want to arrange to have you cut some during the dull season. The trouble with metal is all over. Our lot of material raised the devil for a time until we got it straightened out."[20]

As the Dorflinger factory increased in size after the strike, they wished to sell more and wrote several times to Hawkes about supplying the Corning firm with more and better blanks. In the fall of 1889, Louis Dorflinger wrote: "When I was at Corning last, you spoke about our making ruby work for you such as linings and that class of work. We are now in good shape to make these things, as we have a shop (French) who make a specialty of this work on the other side...You showed me a hand made nappy that you were getting from England, I wish you would let us try a lot of these for you when in want again. You know our capacity is now large and we want to secure all the work we possibly can.[21]

The most puzzling aspect of the relationship is that both companies seemed to wish to keep it secret. In 1892, Hawkes wrote, "We have given notice to our packer to mark all glass 'blanks' and are sorry the mistake should have occurred...Will hurry the salads Str[awberry] Diam & Fan, some of them are now being cut."[22] The following month, Hawkes complained: "We are in receipt of letters from our agent now in the west complaining that he is handicapped by statements made by your salesman, Mr. Shipman, that C. Dorflinger & Sons, furnish us blanks, etc. You can understand the impression created by such statements and the difficulties in overcoming them with the educated trade. We would ask your kindly interference in the matter."[23]

On the same day, Hawkes wrote to his salesman, W. H. Bryant, that he had written to Dorflinger and that Mr. Shipman would get a lecture. "We do not especially claim that our glass is better than Dorflinger's as far as the color goes, but we do claim it is better in design and finish, and the general care that is taken in its production...Every time that Dorflinger's agent quotes us using their blanks

17. C. Dorflinger & Sons, White Mills, to T. G. Hawkes, May 15, 1889.
18. C. Dorflinger & Sons, White Mills, to T. G. Hawkes, January 26, 1889.
19. T. G. Hawkes to C. Dorflinger & Sons, White Mills, August 29, 1888 .
20. C. Dorflinger & Sons, White Mills to T. G. Hawkes, February 11, 1889.
21. Louis J. Dorflinger, White Mills, to T. G. Hawkes, November 20, 1889.
22. T. G. Hawkes & Company to C. Dorflinger & Sons, White Mills, August 24, 1892.
23. T. G. Hawkes & Company to C. Dorflinger & Sons, White Mills, September 21, 1892.
24. T. G. Hawkes to W. H. Bryant in Indianapolis, Indiana, September 21, 1892.

only disounts their own standing, which of course redounds to our advantage.[24]

Later, Hawkes said to Bryant, "Our water bottles Str. Dia. & Fan is superior in cutting to Dorflinger's also in quality of glass however, if the trade demands it, after this year we will get up a cheaper bottle, that will still be a little superior to his, although the glass will be no better. We think we can get them out for $3.00 each in dozen lots."[25]

In June of that year, Hawkes had written to a long-standing Syracuse customer that he would not sell to "dry goods houses", and that he did not sell "Corning" glass, "Our goods are sold as the 'Hawkes Glass' and that fact is becoming generally known and the frequent inquiries our customers have for the 'Hawkes glass' convinces us that all the efforts we have made by our liberal advertising to bring the fact before the public, that there will be no conflicting our goods with those put upon the market as 'Corning Glass'."[26]

The reference here is to Hoare's glass rather than to that produced by Corning Glass Works, since Hoare advertised his cut glass as "Corning Cut Glass", but Hawkes certainly seems anxious to conceal the principal sources of his blanks which at this time were still coming in quantity from Corning Glass Works as well as Dorflinger. As he remained on good terms with both the Houghtons and the Dorflingers, this business policy of separating himself from his suppliers of blanks must have been one upon which all were in agreement.

The existing documents in the Hawkes Archives do not show when the firm stopped cutting for Dorflinger. The letters after 1893 are missing and the ledger books of 1901 and after do not show Dorflinger as a customer for finished goods, only as a supplier. Therefore, at some point between 1892 and 1901, Dorflinger stopped ordering cut goods from Hawkes. However, there can be no doubt that from 1887 until 1893, and probably for several years after, T. G. Hawkes supplied a significant amount of cut glass to C. Dorflinger & Sons for resale as Dorflinger glass.

25. T. G. Hawkes, to W. H. Bryant in Dayton, Ohio, October 3, 1892.
26. T. G. Hawkes, to Jos. Seymour Sons & Company, Syracuse, June 7, 1892.

CHAPTER FIVE
Technical Matters

When Thomas Hawkes started his business, he began with assurance from Corning Glass Works and Amory or C. F. Houghton that blanks would be available. No copy of any agreement exists, and it was probably an unwritten one, but he began using Corning blanks immediately. The first bill is dated March 31, 1880, and is for about $50 worth of blanks, but it included "4 10½ in Ribbed flanged epergnes" and four plain ones. Evidently, Hawkes intended to make some expensive pieces. The bill of April 30 was for $105.41 and the bill of May 28 for $532.44. For the rest of that year and the next, the bills for blanks averaged several hundred dollars per month and there is nothing to indicate that Hawkes was buying blanks from anyone else. A typical monthly statement, dated May 1882, shows that the blanks were charged either per piece or by weight. The bill, which remains in the archives, is part of a running tally sent by Corning Glass Works to Hawkes, rather than an official statement. It includes the following:

96	7in Plates K.M.	111 lbs.
26	2oz 3 ring extracts samples	
12 doz	1oz straight extracts diamond	
2	Qt. Whisky Flasks & stoppers	1 50 ea.
2	3 Pt. Tankards K.M.	1 75 ea.
2	1 " " "	1 00 ea

5-1. Group of samples and unfinished objects acquired with the Hawkes archival material about 1900–1920.

4	small sugars & covers to pat.	1 00
4	medium " " "	1 00
2 7/12 Doz.	Punch Plates iron mo. K.M.	
3 9/ "	5in Nappies " " "	
8 3/ "	51/4in ' " " "	72 lbs.
3 8/ "	61/2in ' " " "	43 "
3 10/ "	Individual Olive dishes K.M. small	
7/12 "	Faw Ice Cream Plates K.M.	
2 5/ "	T. E. Punch Cups "	
10	Ice Cream Tray Iron Mo. K.M.	58 lbs
53	Dishes " "	153 1/2
14 2/ Doz	6in Nappies Iron Mo. K.M.	
6 3/ "	T.E. Solid stem Clarets K.M. No. 350	
6 10/ "	" " " Goblets " "	
6 5/ "	" " " Wines " "	
6 7/ "	" " " Saucer Champagnes K.M. No 350	
6 2/ "	" " " Table Tumblers " "	
6 5/ "	" " " Champs " "	
2 8/ "	Colognes Iron Mo. Ba	
6 5/ "	T.E. Champagne Tumblers K.M.	
8	#2500 Goblets to pat lot	3 00
3	" Champs "	1 50
3	" Wines " "	1 25
3	" Finger Bowls "	3 00

The abbreviations K.M. and T.E. stand for "Kiln Metal," which was of better quality, and for "Thin Edge," a distinction applied to some drinking glass blanks. A note from the president of Corning Glass Works refers to returned blanks and distinguishes between the two grades: "We will allow you one cent per pound for batch cullet; two cents per pound for K cullet. Please keep batch separate from K, and also keep our K cullet separate from K cullet made abroad. Any ware returned to us as flown or on account of cords or stones or bad color or bad workmanship, must be returned to us whole; if broken up, we can only allow cullet prices for it."[1] (A blank which had "flown" was one which cracked during the cutting because of poor annealing.) A receipt from Corning Glass Works on April 7, 1888, is for $300 for interest to April 1, presumably interest on the unpaid balance of the account, a situation which suggests both a close relationship between the two firms and large monthly orders.

Hawkes had started buying blanks in great numbers from C. Dorflinger & Sons in 1887 and continued to do so until 1903. Information on blank suppliers between 1893 when the available correspondence stops, and 1900 when the available ledgers begin, is not available, but the picture is likely to have stayed the same. Amory Houghton, Jr. testified in 1904 that his firm supplied about 40% of Hawkes blanks at that time.[2] The turn-of-the-century cash books show payments

1. Amory Houghton, Jr. Corning Glass Works, to Thomas Hawkes, April 10, 1889.
2. CGW suit, p.382.

5-2 and 5-3. Group of profile drawings used for ordering blanks; they have shape numbers and dates.

of several thousand dollars a month to Corning and Dorflinger for blanks and smaller sums to Union, Fry, Libbey, Pairpoint, and other suppliers including some in Europe. After 1903, payments to Steuben begin, and replace first Dorflinger and then Corning Glass Works and substantial payments to Val St. Lambert are also recorded. The record of blanks suppliers is extensive enough to show that Corning was never Hawkes' only source of blanks after 1883, but it is incomplete and so we cannot be certain that all of the blanks suppliers have been identified.

The Hawkes Number Book contains pen and ink drawings of all of the Hawkes shapes starting with shape #100 and continuing until the company closed. Although the numbers are consecutive, there are many gaps, so this may be a new book, started in the late 1880s after some shapes had been discontinued. The existing looseleaf book has typed captions and the first dated entry, #730, is March 10, 1891 on the tenth page, which supports that supposition. The earliest Corning Glass bills do not list the shapes by number, so the whole numbering system may not have started until the mid-1880s. Beginning with number #411 on the first page, the numbers are nearly all continuous so that probably marks

Figs.5-4 through 5-20 are drawings from a notebook of engraved designs; some are signed by William LeBrantz and all may be his work. None are dated, but some of the patterns are from about 1900–1910 and some seem to be from the 1920s and 1930s. There is no indication which were put into production.

5-4. This goblet's complex design is probably from the early 1900s.

5-5. This goblet incorporates a mask into the design.

5-6. This design has a cut stem.

5-7. This design is on a domed foot, which is unusual.

5-8. The foot in this goblet design is thicker than usual.

5-9. This design is signed "WLB" for LeBrantz.

5-10. This design seems to have a cased and cut stem.

5-11. This is a cased and cut pattern which looks European.

5-12. The pattern on this wineglass is Sinclaire's Adam #2.

5-13. This pattern has a flower cluster.

5-14. This pattern features peacocks.

5051 ROSE OF SHARON

5-15. This is shape #5051 engraved with the Rose of Sharon pattern, probably from the 1930s.

5-16. This simple pattern is probably from the 1930s.

5-17. This design has the pattern name, Adam, scribbled in the lower left corner.

5-18. This design is shown on the same blank as 5-16.

5-19. This is a shape from the 1940s and 1950s.

5-20. This is shape #6015 which was used from the 1940s until the firm closed.

the time when the book was started. The blanks shown on the first forty pages came from Corning Glass Works, from Dorflinger and from several other sources, but they aren't identified by supplier although some customers are listed. After 1903, Steuben made some of the same shapes for Hawkes, and added more. It is impossible to tell at what point in the number book the blanks began to be mostly Steuben, but it was probably somewhere in the 1400s.

After Corning, Dorflinger was Hawkes's largest supplier of blanks from the late 1880s until Steuben went into operation. Much of the correspondence between the two firms discusses the shapes, prices, quality, and weight of the blanks. Both sides were anxious to maintain the relationship, which must have been profitable for both, but quality and price were always important. A few sample letters give the flavor of this correspondence: "In ordering, please specify weights wanted as we make these bowls different weights according to cutting to go on."[3] "We send you today one... plate, Please make us one move to match it as near as possible in weight, The last ones you sent us were very uneven, some of them weighing more than twice as much as the sample we sent you."[4] "Please send us two dozen 8in 485 rose globes to our wooden model which you have. Please make them medium weight suitable for Hobnail cutting,..."[5] "We are making your matchings, some we are sending today, and balance will go to-morrow or Monday."[6]

Although the quantities specified in the Dorflinger orders are often dozens, blanks were just as frequently ordered by the "move" which was a glass-working term for one shift of about half a day. "We send ... samples ... One 703 Finger bowl; please make us two moves to match it exactly, one 385 wine, one move to match exactly; one whiskey Tumbler, one move to match exactly; one Soda Tumbler, six dozen..."[7] One move probably meant one shop or team of blowers making one move, not the entire complement of blowers, and it was probably several hundred pieces. Like Corning Glass Works, Dorflinger supplied several grades of glass blanks and charged accordingly. "Just as soon as we get ready to make best metal we will write you. We hope very soon to be running another furnace and when we do, we will be in shape to supply best metal."[8] The following year, Dorflinger wrote: "Will you please send by express a plain blown blank, jug, Decanter or anything like this in make, of your best Corning metal. I want it to compare with some metal we are now making & which we think is very good. My object is to try and turn out metal superior to any now in the market. Don't you think metal in stem ware lately very good, it should finish up very bright."[9]

Early in 1889, T. G. Hawkes complained about Dorflinger's prices and spoke freely of his other blank sources: "You charge us fifty cents a pound for handled decanters, this is ten cents more than we can afford to pay, as the handled decanters that we get in Corning only costs us ten cents a pound more than dishes, bowls, etc. Of course you are aware that we import large quantities of glass of every description; for instance – tumbler that you charge us $3.00 a

3. C. Dorflinger & Sons, White Mills, to T. G. Hawkes, October 26, 1887.
4. T. G. Hawkes to C. Dorflinger & Sons, White Mills, February 28, 1889.
5. T. G. Hawkes to C. Dorflinger & Sons, White Mills, March 8, 1889.
6. C. Dorflinger & Sons, White Mills, to T. G. Hawkes, April 26, 1889.
7. T. G. Hawkes, to C. Dorflinger & Sons, White Mills, November 16, 1888.
8. C. Dorflinger & Sons, White Mills to T. G. Hawkes, May 16, 1889.
9. C. Dorflinger & Sons, White Mills, to T. G. Hawkes, May 8, 1889.

Figs. 5-21 through 5-74 are the first 54 pages of the Hawkes Number Book.

5-21. First page of the Hawkes Number Book. These shapes are from the 1880s.

dozen for we can import ones equally as good as you and the Corning Glass Works or any other American factory can make, in fact, our experience has been they run better, at $2.16 a dozen, and all other goods in proportion. When Mr. Louis Dorflinger was here we showed him bills of best metal that cost us landed down in Corning twenty-three and a fraction of a cent per pound. Of course this importing business is nothing new to us, as we have done more or less of it ever since we have been in business. We mention these facts to show you that when you make prices for us, the Englishmen and other foreigners are the men you have to compete against, and not any domestic factory."[10]

That this was no idle claim is borne out by the orders to English and Continental glasshouses in the Hawkes archives. All those presently in the files date from 1883 and after, and they support the assumption that until then, Hawkes used mostly Corning blanks. In July, 1886, Hawkes ordered a small shipment of stemware, tumblers and "finger cups" from John Walsh Walsh of Birmingham. In 1887, there was correspondence with John Davis & Company of the Dial Glass Works in Stourbridge. Davis wrote in February: "When you send your samples we shall undertake to send you metal as good as it is possible to make. We think we have told you that we have supplied goods to your neighbours... Anything in Cruets & Eperns for Silver [illeg] we shall be able to please you with and at prices that will suit your purpose. We hope by this you have come to amicable arrangements with your Customs, they to not give us much trouble here."[11]

A letter in the fall of 1888 apologizes for a delay in filling orders and mentions that the company "thoroughly understands the requirements of the American trade."[12] Further correspondence in 1888 and 1889 indicates that Hawkes

10. T. G. Hawkes to C. Dorflinger & Sons, White Mills, January 10, 1889.
11. John Davis & Company, Stourbridge, England to T. G. Hawkes, February 26, 1887.
12. William S. Davis for John Davis & Company to T. G. Hawkes, September 7, 1888.

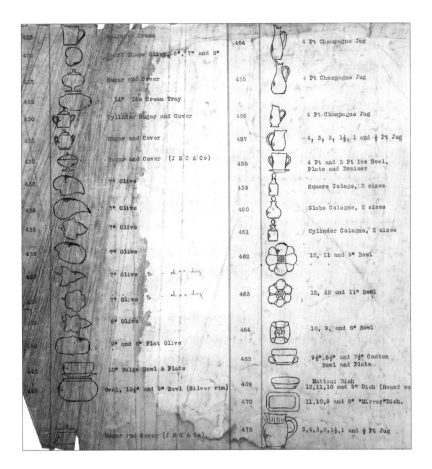

5-22. Note #469, Mattoni dish.

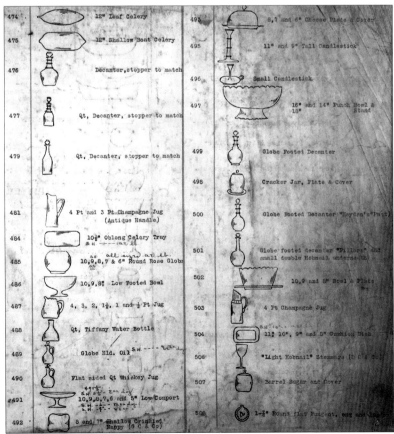

5-23. # 497 at 18in. was the largest punchbowl size.

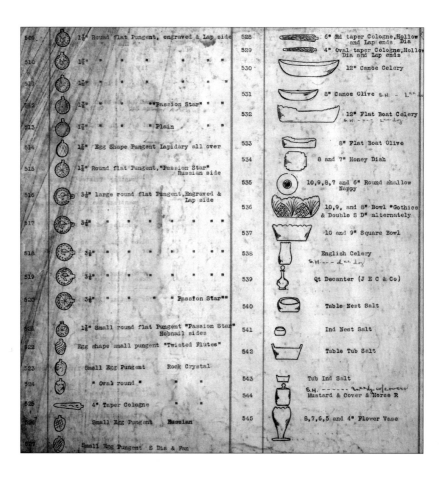

The table in the image (catalog of pungents and glass items):

No.		Description			No.		Description
509		1¾" Round flat Pungent, engraved & Lap side			528		6" Rd taper Cologne,Hollow and Lap ends. Dia
510		1¾" " " " "			529		4" Oval taper Cologne,Hollow Dia and Lap ends
511		1½" " " " "			530		12" Canoe Celery
512		1¾" " "Passion Star" " "			531		8" Canoe Olive S.H. L
513		1¾" " " "Plain " "			532		12" Flat Boat Celery S.H.
514		1¾" Egg Shape Pungent lapidary all over			533		8" Flat Boat Olive
515		1¾" Round flat Pungent,"Passion Star" Russian side			534		8 and 7" Honey Dish
516		3½" large round flat Pungent,Engraved & Lap side			535		10,9,8,7 and 6" Round shallow Nappy
517		3½" " " " " "			536		10,9, and 8" Bowl "Gothics & Double S D" alternately
518		3½" " " " " "			537		10 and 9" Square Bowl
519		3½" " " " " "			538		English Celery S.H.
520		3½" " " " Passion Star" "			539		Qt Decanter (J E C & Co)
521		1¾" Small round flat Pungent "Passion Star" Hobnail sides			540		Table Nest Salt
522		Egg shape small pungent "Twisted Flutes"			541		Ind Nest Salt
523		Small Egg Pungent Rock Crystal			542		Table Tub Salt
524		" Oval round "			543		Tub Ind Salt
525		4" Taper Cologne			544		S.H. Mustard & Cover & Horse R
526		Small Egg Pungent Russian			545		8,7,6,5 and 4" Flower Vase
527		Small Egg Pungent S Dia & Fan					

5-24. The pungents on this page were probably for a silver company.

continued to order stemware and tumblers from John Davis, although not always satisfactorily: "We are very sorry to inform you that we are having very poor luck with the stem glass that you have sent us, more than 25% of which fly in the feet when we come to put the stars on; they are evidently very poorly annealed. Now we cannot possibly think of sending you any more orders for stem glass unless you think you can remedy this difficulty, as when we deduct the breakage, the goods cost us a great deal more than we can get them right here at home for… The tumblers you sent us we had no trouble with, the only fault we found was that the glass was a little low in color, and when cut did not compare very favorably with the general run of our glass. The workmanship on all the glass we considered good."[13]

Evidently, Hawkes was also thinking of ordering goods from Davis at the same time. He wrote: "We send you today two sample cut tumblers, one 350 straw. Dia. & Fan and one 385 Hobnail. Please quote us your very lowest figures for these tumblers in quantities. Please remember the price must be low if we order."[14]

Davis replied: "The two pattern tumblers you sent for quotation have arrived, these two patterns we have done a great many of. Our price for same is 2 8/6 per dozen. These two lines we know are cut very close in the States, we also do wines, fingers etc. of the same patterns… As we cut goods for America very fine, we always get our money as soon as the shippers leave premises. Would you kindly arrange to pay us in the [illeg].'[15]

These were two of Hawkes' cheapest patterns, but it is startling to find that he would consider ordering them already cut. However, there is no evidence in the

13. T. G. Hawkes to John Davis & Company, Stourbridge, January 24, 1889.
14. T. G. Hawkes to John Davis & Company, Stourbridge, February 6, 1889.
15. John Davis & Company, Stourbridge to Mr. Hawkes, February 23, 1889.

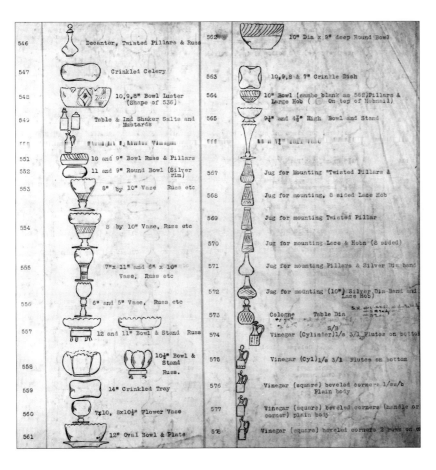

5-25. The jugs in the right column are all for silver mounting by other firms.

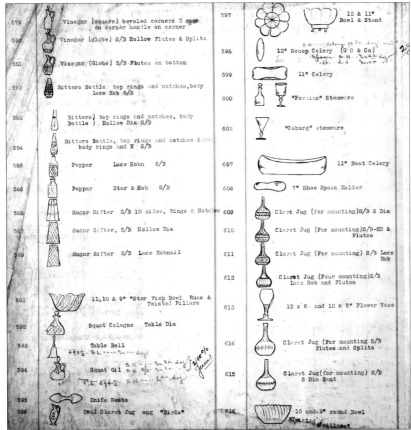

5-26. More claret jugs for silver mounting.

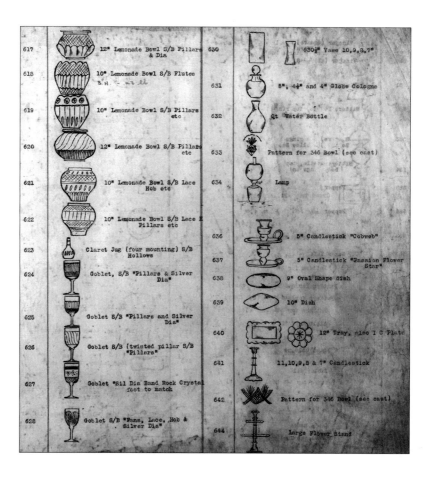

5-27. *This page shows several cut patterns.*

archives that he actually did so.

At the end of 1887, Hawkes was also corresponding with Stevens & Williams about blanks, and about "pattern tumblers" as well.[16] Stevens & Williams wrote to acknowledge an order for 100 dozen tumbler blanks and continued, "We are sorry that the price of our Fingercups is too high."[17] Hawkes complained about the quality of the tumbler blanks and Stevens & Williams offered to replace them, obviously anxious not to lose a customer. "We have now some excellent Tumbler makers, can we make some of these goods for you, we have your pattern here and can now please you in every way."[18] However, Hawkes replied that Stevens & Williams's prices were higher than "we have bought goods elsewhere for" and he did not order more blanks.[19] By the following year, though, Hawkes wrote to inquire about colored blanks, and Stevens & Williams replied: "We make a great variety of colors – single, double and treble casings – extremely charming effects. If you will send us over say a claret glass only of half a dozen of your running cut patterns, we will get you up say sample Dozens of each color, which would then show you the [illeg.] effects. If we sent you plain samples, they would not show you until you had cut them & probably they would be spoilt by your cutters as they would now know the different layers of color."[20]

In 1888 and early 1889, there was a spate of letters between C. Dorflinger & Sons and Hawkes in regard to colored hock glasses which Dorflinger had ordered from England and was sharing with Hawkes. Dorflinger had purchased 100 dozen in six colors and two shapes, with button stems and straight stems, and he found them very satisfactory. The colors were ruby, green, blue, amber, poppy, and Old Gold and it seems likely that they came from Stevens & Williams,

16. Stevens & Williams, Brierley Hill to T. G. Hawkes, December 8, 1887 and draft reply, December 20, 1887.
17. Stevens & Williams, Brierley Hill to T. G. Hawkes, April 11, 1888.
18. Stevens & Williams, Brierley Hill to T. G. Hawkes, June 18 and August 16 1888.
19. T. G. Hawkes to Stevens & Williams, Brierley Hill, August 29, 1888.
20. Stevens & Williams, Brierley Hill to T. G. Hawkes, June 7, 1889.

106

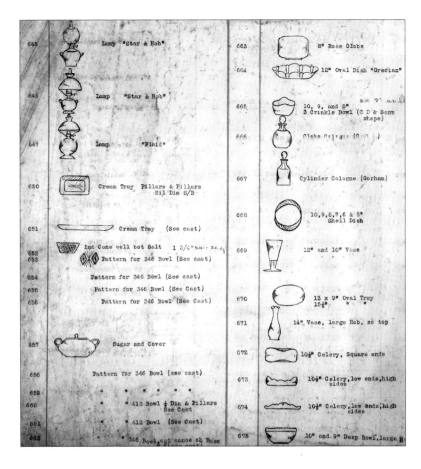

645	Lamp "Star & Hob"
646	Lamp "Star & Hob"
647	Lamp "Plaid"
650	Cream Tray Pillars & Pillars Sil Dia S/B
651	Cream Tray (See cast)
652	Ind Cone well bot Salt 1 3/4"SH-- Ex L
653	Pattern for 346 Bowl (See cast)
654	Pattern for 346 Bowl (See cast)
655	Pattern for 346 Bowl (See Cast)
656	Pattern for 346 Bowl (See Cast)
657	Sugar and Cover
658	Pattern for 346 Bowl (see cast)
659	" " " "
660	" 412 Bowl ½ Dia & Pillars See Cast
661	" 412 Bowl (See Cast)
662	" 346 Bowl cut canoe st Russ

663	8" Rose Globe
664	12" Oval Dish "Grecian"
665	10, 9, and 8" 3 Crinkle Bowl (C D & Sons shape)
666	Globe Cologne (Gorham)
667	Cylinder Cologne (Gorham)
668	10,9,8,7,6 & 5" Shell Dish
669	12" and 10" Vase
670	13 x 9" Oval Tray 15½"
671	14" Vase, large Hob, sc top
672	10½" Celery, Square ends
673	10½" Celery, low ends, high sides
674	10½" Celery, low ends, high sides
675	10" and 9" Deep Bowl, large H

5-28. This page shows the lamps in the line in 1889.

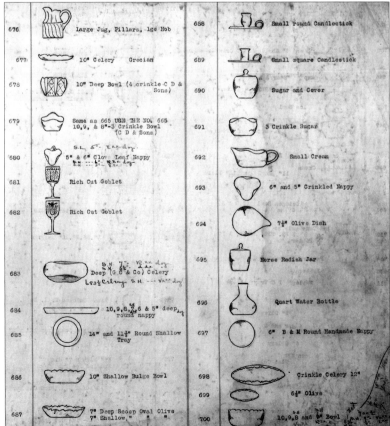

676	Large Jug, Pillars, lge Hob
677	10" Celery Grecian
678	10" Deep Bowl (4 crinkle C D & Sons)
679	Same as 665 USE THE NO. 665 10,9, & 8"-3 Crinkle Bowl (C D & Sons)
680	5" & 6" Clov Leaf Nappy
681	Rich Cut Goblet
682	Rich Cut Goblet
683	Deep (C D & Co) Celery
684	10,9,8,7,6 & 5" deep round nappy
685	14" and 11½" Round Shallow Tray
686	10" Shallow Bulge Bowl
687	7" Deep Scoop Oval Olive 7" Shallow " "

688	Small round Candlestick
689	Small square Candlestick
690	Sugar and Cover
691	3 Crinkle Sugar
692	Small Cream
693	6" and 5" Crinkled Nappy
694	7½" Olive Dish
695	Horse Radish Jar
696	Quart Water Bottle
697	6" B & M Round Handmade Nappy
698	Crinkle Celery 12"
699	6½" Olive
700	10,9,8 and 7" Bowl

5-29. This page shows a blank from Dorflinger, #678.

107

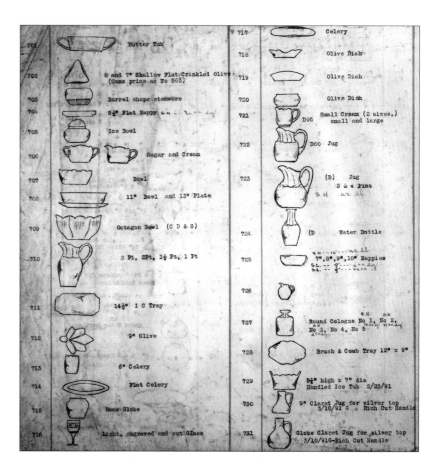

5-30. This page has the first dated designs, made 2/23/91.

although Dorflinger referred to them only as "English."[21] In the last letter of the series, Hawkes described to them as "colored hocks for engraving," and so they may have been cut for rock-crystal engraving before they were sent from England. Several letters indicate that Hawkes's customers occasionally sent English glass to be matched[22] and letters from Davis Collamore refer to the fact that they could get cut glass from England more cheaply.[23]

We find correspondence with several other English glass firms, including Boulton & Mills, from whom Hawkes ordered blanks for ice plates and tumblers, and F. & C. Osler of Birmingham. Hawkes sent identical letters to these two firms on Feb. 6, 1889, along with a wooden model of a bowl with instructions to have a plaster cast taken of the model and an iron mold cast from the plaster, and to send 25 dozen of the bowls, of "your very best glass" at eight pence per pound. "We cut these bowls all over so that if they come out a little rough on the surface, it does not make any difference. The price we name you is what we have been quoted from other English factories, but we prefer to send you this sample order before we make any permanent connection with anybody else, as we rather think that blowing dishes in iron moulds is one of your specialities."

The only difference in the two letters was that Hawkes offered to prepay Osler if the order was accepted and they did not make that offer to Boulton & Mills.[24] Boulton & Mills complained about the price, but completed the order, shipping the bowls on May 10 with a courteous note hoping for further business.[25] Osler however, replied: "On June 22, 1886 we quoted our price for Blowover Bowls in mould 9d per lb. We regret we cannot reduce our price & Therefore cannot accept your order... We shall be glad to prepare the mould you refer to for you, whether

21. C. Dorflinger & Sons, White Mills to T. G. Hawkes, February 13, 1888, November 26, 28, 1888, December 12, 1888. T. G. Hawkes to C. Dorflinger & Sons, December 10, 13, 1888, April 20, 1889.
22. T. G. Hawkes to Richard Briggs, Boston, March 6, 1889; Burley & Company Chicago, to T. G. Hawkes, June 2, 1888.
23. Davis Collamore & Company to T. G. Hawkes, January 29, February 28, 1887, May 28, 1888.
24. T. G. Hawkes & Company to Boulton & Mills, Stourbridge and to F. & C. Osler, Birmingham, February 6, 1888.
25. Boulton & Mills, Stourbridge to T. G. Hawkes, March 7, April 9, May 10, 1889.

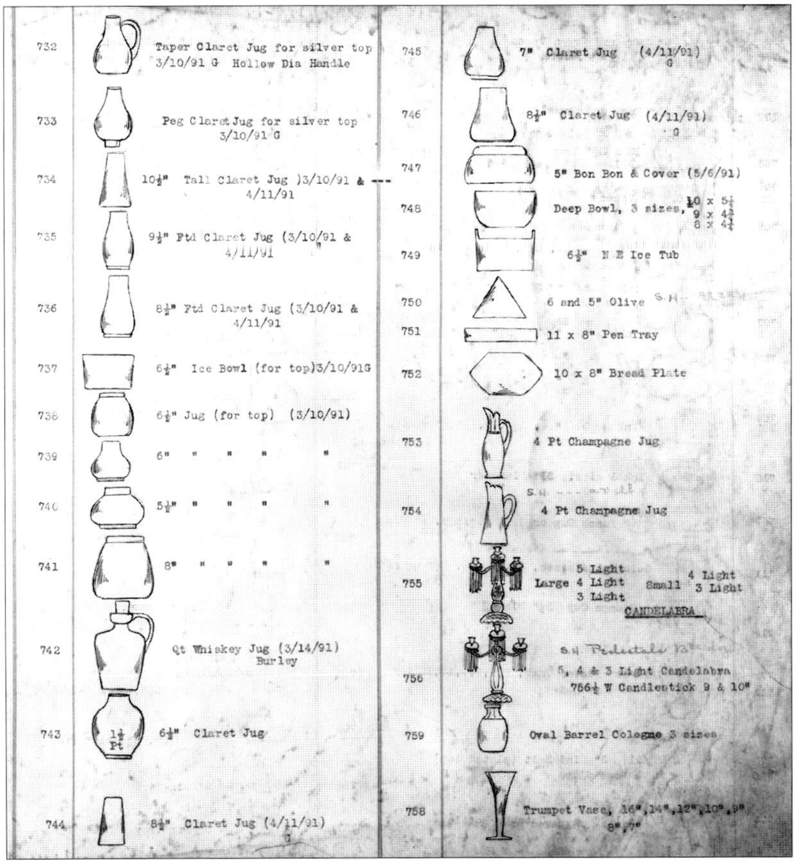

732 Taper Claret Jug for silver top 3/10/91 G Hollow Dia Handle
733 Peg Claret Jug for silver top 3/10/91 G
734 10½" Tall Claret Jug 3/10/91 & 4/11/91
735 9½" Ftd Claret Jug (3/10/91 & 4/11/91
736 8½" Ftd Claret Jug (3/10/91 & 4/11/91
737 6½" Ice Bowl (for top) 3/10/91G
738 6½" Jug (for top) (3/10/91)
739 6" " " " "
740 5½" " " " "
741 8" " " " "
742 Qt Whiskey Jug (3/14/91) Burley
743 1½ Pt 6½" Claret Jug
744 8½" Claret Jug (4/11/91) G
745 7" Claret Jug (4/11/91) G
746 8½" Claret Jug (4/11/91) G
747 5" Bon Bon & Cover (5/6/91)
748 Deep Bowl, 3 sizes, 10 x 5¼, 9 x 4¾, 8 x 4¼
749 6½" N E Ice Tub
750 6 and 5" Olive S.H.
751 11 x 8" Pen Tray
752 10 x 8" Bread Plate
753 4 Pt Champagne Jug
754 S.H. 4 Pt Champagne Jug
755 Large 5 Light 4 Light 3 Light, Small 4 Light 3 Light CANDELABRA
756 S.H. Pedestals 5, 4 & 3 Light Candelabra 756½ W Candlestick 9 & 10"
759 Oval Barrel Cologne 3 sizes
758 Trumpet Vase, 16",14",12",10",9" 8",7"

5-31. *This page shows candelabra.*

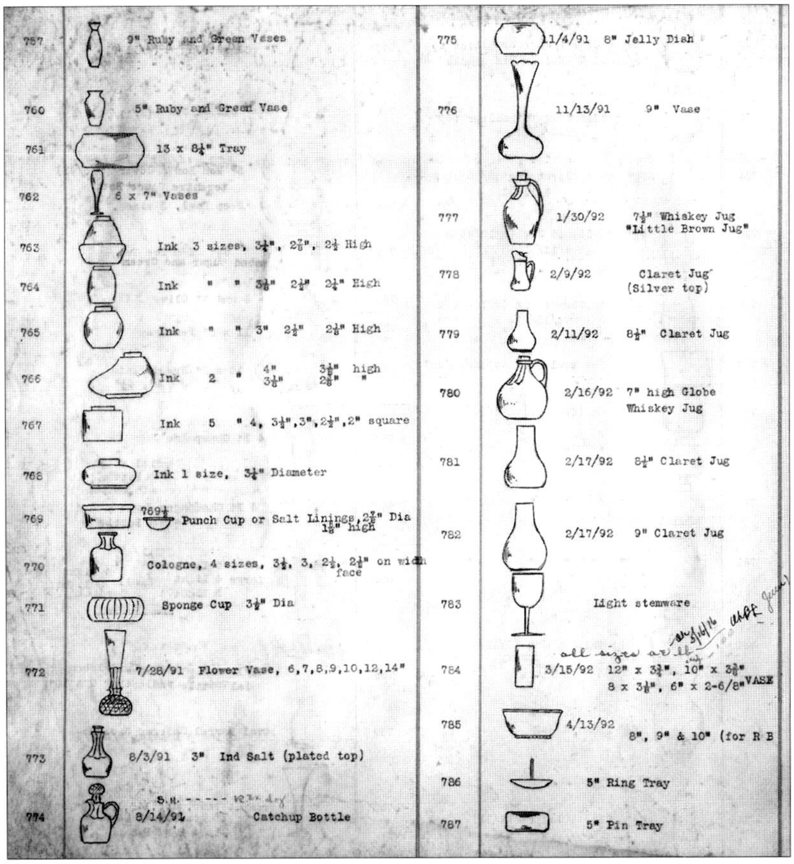

757 9" Ruby and Green Vases
760 5" Ruby and Green Vase
761 13 x 8¼" Tray
762 6 x 7" Vases
763 Ink 3 sizes, 3¼", 2⅞", 2½ High
764 Ink " " 3⅛" 2¼" 2¼" High
765 Ink " " 3" 2½" 2⅛" High
766 Ink 2 " 4" 3½" 3¼" 2⅞" high
767 Ink 5 " 4, 3½",3",2½",2" square
768 Ink 1 size, 3¼" Diameter
769 769½ Punch Cup or Salt Linings, 2⅞" Dia 1⅝" high
770 Cologne, 4 sizes, 3½, 3, 2½, 2¼" on wide face
771 Sponge Cup 3¼" Dia
772 7/28/91 Flower Vase, 6,7,8,9,10,12,14"
773 8/3/91 3" Ind Salt (plated top)
774 S.H. 8/14/91 Catchup Bottle
775 11/4/91 8" Jelly Dish
776 11/13/91 9" Vase
777 1/30/92 7½" Whiskey Jug "Little Brown Jug"
778 2/9/92 Claret Jug (Silver top)
779 2/11/92 8½" Claret Jug
780 2/16/92 7" high Globe Whiskey Jug
781 2/17/92 8½" Claret Jug
782 2/17/92 9" Claret Jug
783 Light stemware
784 all sizes 3/15/92 12" x 3¾", 10" x 3⅜" 8 x 3⅛", 6" x 2-6/8" VASE
785 4/13/92 8", 9" & 10" (for R B
786 5" Ring Tray
787 5" Pin Tray

5-32. *The first two vases on this page were ruby or green.*

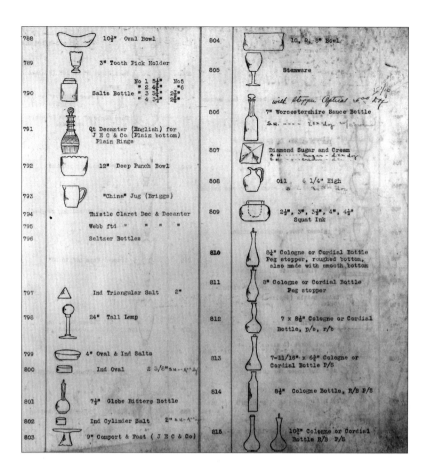

5-33. The English decanter, #791 was cut for J. E. Caldwell & Company

you place the order with us or not. We are quite aware you can get your work at some houses lower than we charge, but do not believe you will be as well satisfied.[26]

Hawkes replied in March, confirming the order at the higher price and the bowls were delivered in May.[27] Correspondence with other English firms and jobbers indicates that the Corning company was continually looking for new (and cheaper) sources of blanks.[28]

R. J. Godwin & Sons was the shipper with whom Hawkes dealt for these English orders and through whom payment was usually dispatched. The suppliers named on some of the invoices are indicated merely by a symbol, and this makes some of the transactions difficult to trace. It is clear, however, that customs duty was charged on most of the shipments as if they contained blanks rather than finished goods. One exception was the "lapidary" knife rests and stoppers which Hawkes purchased from R. Wilkes of the Cross Glass Works in Dudley from 1889 through 1892 and after. These were specifically ordered facet-cut.[29]

Unfortunately, because the correspondence after 1893 is missing, it's impossible to say if the Hawkes firm continued to use many English blanks. However, it seems likely that this was the case at least until 1903, when Thomas G. Hawkes established Steuben Glass Works. According to Samuel Hawkes's daughter, her parents' honeymoon itinerary, in England in 1902, included a preliminary visit to Frederick Carder and doubtless his future association with Steuben and Hawkes was discussed then. However, it was probably Hawkes's continuing search for the best blanks at the best possible price that made him familiar with Carder's work before 1902.

26. F. & C. Osler, Icknield Glass Works, Birmingham to T. G. Hawkes, February 19, 1889.
27. T. G. Hawkes, to F. & C. Osler, March 2, 1889; F. & C. Osler to T. G. Hawkes, May 1, 1889.
28. T. G. Hawkes to W. Woodcock, Dudley, August 30, 1888; T. G. Hawkes to Mills, Walker & Company, Stourbridge, January 28, 1889; T. G. Hawkes to R. J. Godwin & Sons, September 23, 1892 (for blanks from Webb, Shaw & Company Wordsley).
29. T. G. Hawkes to R. Wilkes, Cross Glass Works, Dudley, December 18, 1888, April 9, 1889; R. Wilkes to T. G. Hawkes, January 2, January 14, March 21, April 20, 1889.

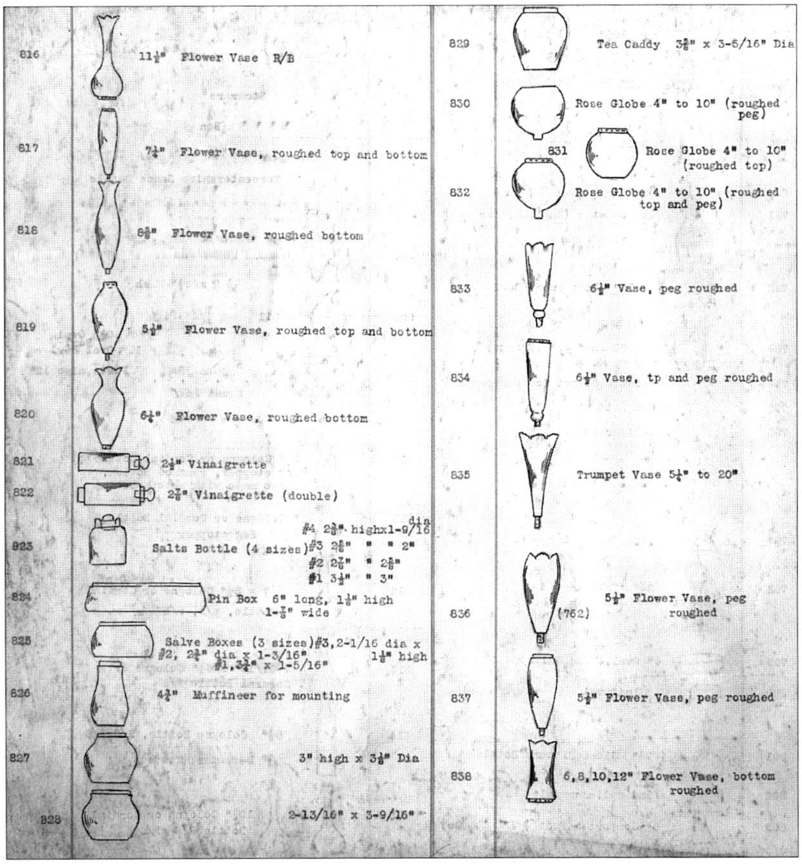
816 11½" Flower Vase R/B
817 7¼" Flower Vase, roughed top and bottom
818 8⅝" Flower Vase, roughed bottom
819 5¼" Flower Vase, roughed top and bottom
820 6¼" Flower Vase, roughed bottom
821 2¼" Vinaigrette
822 2⅞" Vinaigrette (double)
823 Salts Bottle (4 sizes)
#4 2⅝" highx1-9/16 dia
#3 2⅝" " " 2"
#2 2⅞" " 2⅝"
#1 3¼" " 3"
824 Pin Box 6" long, 1½" high 1-⅞" wide
825 Salve Boxes (3 sizes)#3,2-1/16 dia x 1⅛" high #2, 2¼" dia x 1-3/16" #1,3¼" x 1-5/16"
826 4½" Muffineer for mounting
827 3" high x 3¼" Dia
828 2-13/16" x 3-9/16"
829 Tea Caddy 3⅝" x 3-5/16" Dia
830 Rose Globe 4" to 10" (roughed peg)
831 Rose Globe 4" to 10" (roughed top)
832 Rose Globe 4" to 10" (roughed top and peg)
833 6½" Vase, peg roughed
834 6½" Vase, tp and peg roughed
835 Trumpet Vase 5¼" to 20"
836 (762) 5½" Flower Vase, peg roughed
837 5½" Flower Vase, peg roughed
838 6,8,10,12" Flower Vase, bottom roughed

5-34. The flower vases with roughed bottoms were intended to have silver mountings.

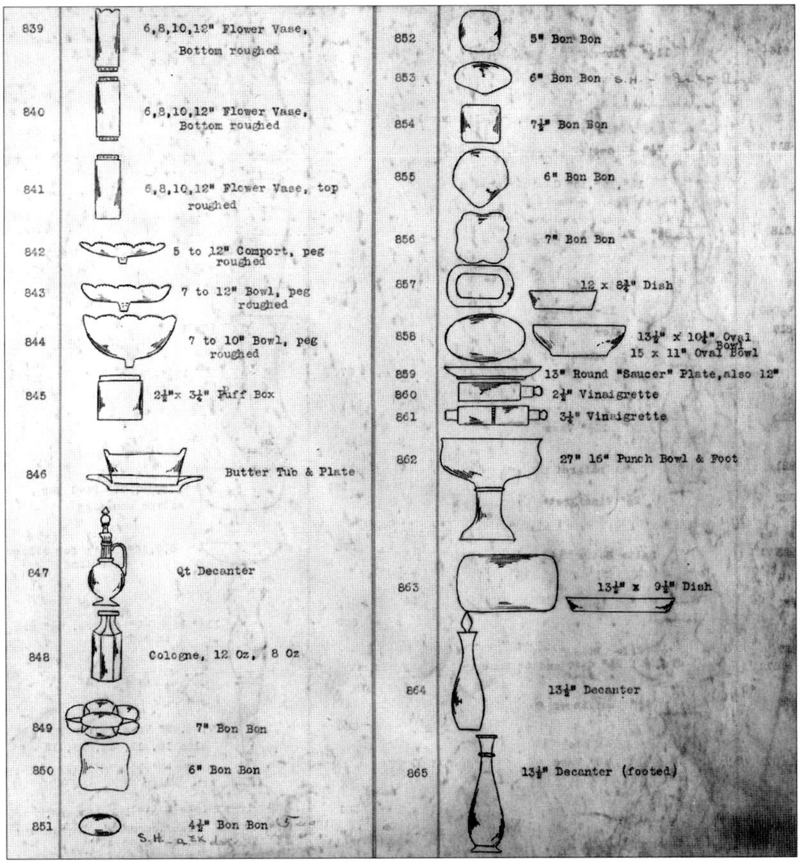
839 6,8,10,12" Flower Vase, Bottom roughed
840 6,8,10,12" Flower Vase, Bottom roughed
841 6,8,10,12" Flower Vase, top roughed
842 5 to 12" Comport, peg roughed
843 7 to 12" Bowl, peg roughed
844 7 to 10" Bowl, peg roughed
845 2½"x 3½" Puff Box
846 Butter Tub & Plate
847 Qt Decanter
848 Cologne, 12 Oz, 8 Oz
849 7" Bon Bon
850 6" Bon Bon
851 4½" Bon Bon
852 5" Bon Bon
853 6" Bon Bon
854 7½" Bon Bon
855 6" Bon Bon
856 7" Bon Bon
857 12 x 8½" Dish
858 13½" x 10¼" Oval Bowl 15 x 11" Oval Bowl
859 13" Round "Saucer" Plate, also 12"
860 2½" Vinaigrette
861 3¼" Vinaigrette
862 27" 16" Punch Bowl & Foot
863 13½" x 9½" Dish
864 13½" Decanter
865 13½" Decanter (footed)

5-35. Punch bowl #862 was 27in. high and 16in. in diameter.

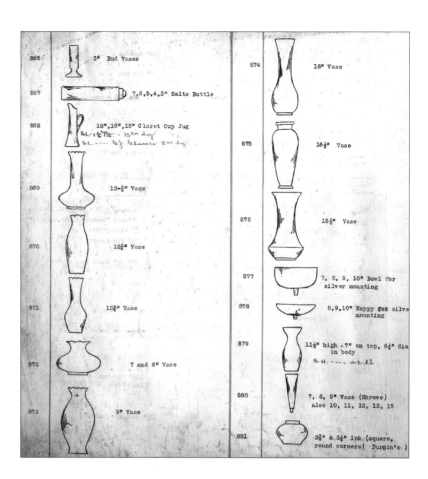

5-36. The 18 in. vase, #874 was one of the largest Hawkes made.

Although Hawkes seems to have used English blanks most often when he ordered from abroad, there is evidence that he also ordered French, Belgian, and Bohemian blanks. The first orders for French blanks are directed to W. H. Glenny & Company, importers, in Rochester, from whom Hawkes ordered "a dozen No. 5 wines" in 1883.[30] In November of that year, Glenny sent a Baccarat catalog and offered Hawkes a special discount. In 1887, he wrote again offering Hawkes colored hocks from both Baccarat and Meyer's Neffe in Bohemia. However, the first small order is the only one found in the correspondence. Baccarat prisms were ordered from C. F. A. Hinrichs in New York in 1886 and 1887,[31] and plain Baccarat tumblers from L. Straus & Sons in 1886,[32] but most of Hawkes's Baccarat blanks seem to have come from Theo. Pabst & Company, a New York importer.

The invoices from Pabst begin in 1883 and continue through 1889 and although Pabst's letterhead indicates he offered "Baccarat, Belgian and Bohemian Glassware," the invoices to Hawkes usually specify Baccarat. At least once, Pabst sent a sample of a Hungarian tumbler which was cheaper than the Baccarat version, but there is no evidence that Hawkes ordered it.[33] Most of the order to Pabst was stemware and tumblers, including colored hocks. Most of the invoices from Pabst have no explanatory letters, but a few do: "We have shipped to you today... 2 1/2 doz. Champagne Tumblers ordered some time ago. The goods sent you last week are the Baccarat ware for Cutting. Our packer is positive that he sent you a fingerbowl with the lot. We will send you tomorrow one fingerbowl and the tumblers which were overlooked in the last shipment. We also enclose the Import price list of the Baccarat ware for Cutting."[34]

The Pabst orders increased in number and size in 1887 and 1888 although

30. Invoice, W. H. Glenny & Company, Rochester to T. G. Hawkes, May 3, 1883.
31. Invoice, C. F. A. Hinrichs, New York to T. G. Hawkes, September 23, 1886, September 23, 1887.
32. Invoice, L. Straus & Sons, New York, to T. G. Hawkes, March 11, April 14, 1886.
33. Theo Pabst & Company, New York to T. G. Hawkes, May 26, 1887.
34. Theo Pabst & Company, New York to T. G. Hawkes, September 15, 1887.

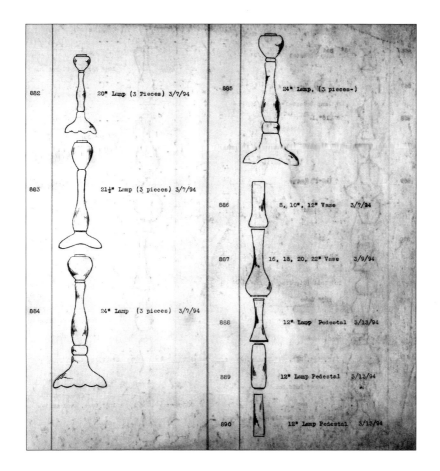

882   20" Lamp (3 Pieces) 3/7/94

883   21¼" Lamp (3 pieces) 3/7/94

884   24" Lamp (3 pieces) 3/7/94

885   24" Lamp, (3 pieces-)

886   8, 10", 12" Vase   3/7/94

887   16, 18, 20, 22" Vase   3/9/94

888   12" Lamp Pedestal 3/13/94

889   12" Lamp Pedestal   3/13/94

890   12" Lamp Pedestal   3/13/94

5-37. The kerosene lamps on this page are very tall and were sold without shades.

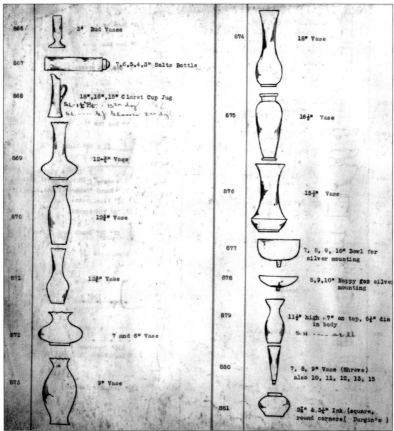

866   3" Bud Vases

867   7,6,5,4,3" Salts Bottle

868   18",16",15" Claret Cup Jug

869   12-¾" Vase

870   12¼" Vase

871   12¼" Vase

872   7 and 6" Vase

873   9" Vase

874   18" Vase

875   16¼" Vase

876   15¼" Vase

877   7, 8, 9, 10" Bowl for silver mounting

878   8,9,10" Nappy for silver mounting

879   11¼" high .7" on top, 6¼" dia in body

880   7, 8, 9" Vase (Shreve) also 10, 11, 12, 13, 15

881   2¼" & 3¼" Ink (square, round corners(Durgin's)

5-38. The first two designs on this page are lamp pedestals which may have been sold to another company for assembly after they were cut.

113

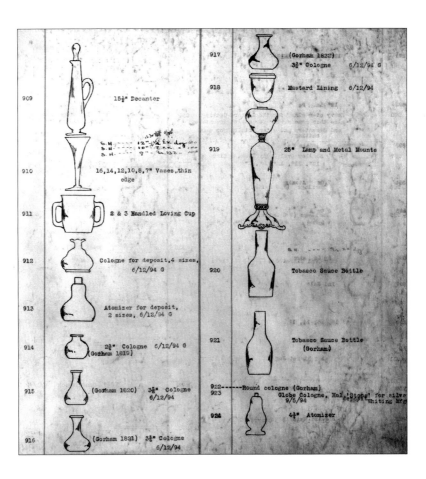

5-39. The #911 loving cup was advertised in the 1890s. See Fig. 6-3.

Hawkes complained about the quality, especially of facet-cut stoppers which he ordered in 1888.[35] Whether Hawkes discovered that he disliked Baccarat's quality or whether he just found he could get cheaper blanks elsewhere is uncertain, but he seems to have stopped ordering their blanks around 1890. A letter to Mermod & Jaccard Jewelry Company in St. Louis in 1892 says, "We would say that the statement made by Mr. Baccarat's salesman to your Mr. Mermod, was a wilful misstatement of the truth. We do not buy any glass of their house, and in fact could not use it at any price, as the heavy metal is entirely inferior in every way with the glass made in this country or in England."[36] That Hawkes had not entirely given up on French blanks, however, is indicated by the fact that he bought blanks from Monot & Stumpf in August of the same year, although the dollar amount was small.[37] By September 1888, when McCue & Earl offered to share an order of Baccarat globe-shaped water bottles "suitable for any cutting", Hawkes wrote back that his "experience with French Glass has not been very satisfactory, and we do not think that we could use any of them."[38]

Most of this unsatisfactory experience probably came from using French blanks for Richard Briggs' Louis XIV pattern. Briggs usually supplied the blanks, but occasionally he expected Hawkes to get them. In 1888, he wanted light tumblers and Hawkes replied: "Your telegram in reference to light Tumblers received, we are sorry we could not ship them to day as requested. Our glass was not suitable to make them. We sent the samples to New York as these are imported Tumblers. We think we can get them for you there at about one half price what it would cost us to make them."[39]

Two weeks later Briggs wanted goblets and got a similar reply: "We do not

35. Theo Pabst & Company, New York to T. G. Hawkes, April 28, 1888.
36. T. G. Hawkes & Company to Mermod & Jaccard Jewelry Company, St. Louis, June 29, 1892.
37. T. G. Hawkes to R. J. Godwin & Sons, New York, August 18, 1892.
38. McCue & Earl, Brooklyn, to T. G.Hawkes, September 11, 1888, reply September 14, 1888.
39. T. G. Hawkes to Richard Briggs, Boston, September 8, 1888.

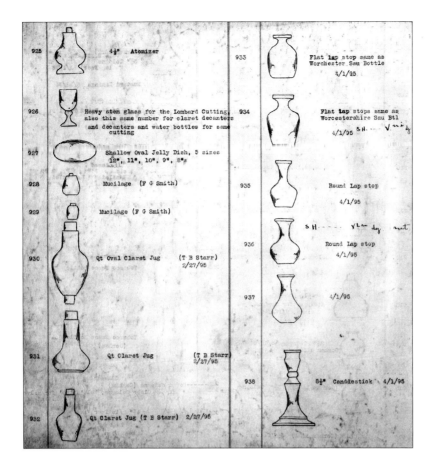

925	4¼" Atomizer
926	Heavy stem glass for the Lombard Cutting, also this same number for claret decanters and decanters and water bottles for same cutting
927	Shallow Oval Jelly Dish, 5 sizes 12", 11", 10", 9", 8"
928	Mucilage (F G Smith)
929	Mucilage (F G Smith)
930	Qt Oval Claret Jug (T B Starr) 2/27/95
931	Qt Claret Jug (T B Starr) 2/27/95
932	Qt Claret Jug (T B Starr) 2/27/95
933	Flat lap stop same as Worcester Sau Bottle 4/1/95
934	Flat lap stops same as Worcestershire Sau Btl 4/1/95
935	Round Lap stop 4/1/95
936	Round Lap stop 4/1/95
937	4/1/95
938	8½" Candlestick 4/1/95

5-40. #926 was used for the Lombard pattern; See Fig. 6-10 for an advertisement for this.

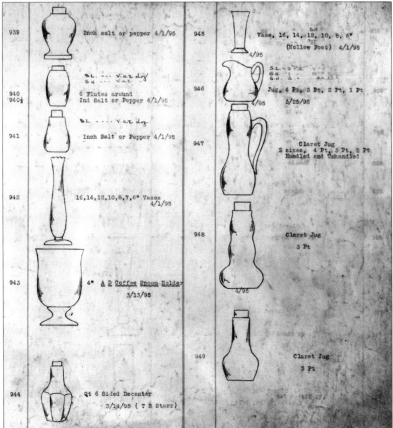

939	Inch salt or pepper 4/1/95
940 940½	6 Flutes around Ind Salt or Pepper 4/1/95
941	Inch salt or pepper 4/1/95
942	16,14,12,10,8,7,6" Vases 4/1/95
943	4" A D Coffee Spoon Holder 3/13/95
944	Qt 6 Sided Decanter 3/14/95 (T B Starr)
945	Vase, 16, 14, 12, 10, 8, 6" (Hollow Foot) 4/1/95
946	Jug, 4 Pt, 3 Pt, 2 Pt, 1 Pt 3/25/95
947	Claret Jug 2 sizes, 4 Pt, 3 Pt, 2 Pt Handled and Unhandled
948	Claret Jug 3 Pt
949	Claret Jug 3 Pt

5-41. #943, the coffee spoon holder, is an unusual item.

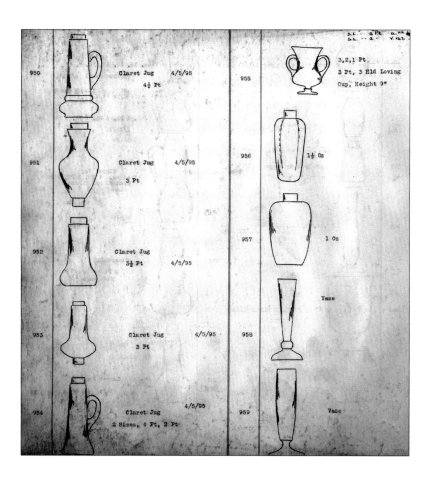

5-42. *The claret jug for silver mounting is dated 4/5/95.*

think that we could make the three doz. Goblets to match the Claret it being so very light and is of foreign manufacture, being blown in paste moulds and cut off afterwards, which is a business of itself, however, if you must have the goods, we will try and make them by hand for you, as light as we can, but we could not make them as light as the Claret you sent."[40] "Paste moulds" are lined on the inside with a chalk-like substance and the glass is turned in the mold to eliminate seams.

The following year, Hawkes provided Briggs with an explanation of why he disliked the French blanks. "Most of the clarets and wines that you sent to have the stems cut, flew in the bowl when working on them. We made them up several times from those we had made over to fill your order, but find now that you are four short. We will have these four made immediately and ship as soon as possible. This Baccate [sic] glass being very hard is very liable to fly in cutting the stems. We have had several hands working on this order since Monday morning so as to be sure to get them off as we promised; sorry we could not send the whole thing complete, but it was not our fault, we tried hard to do so."[41]

Briggs replied by sending "a lot of Baccarat glass" and requested that it be engraved to match some Hawkes samples. Apparently, no matter how much difficulty Hawkes had in the cutting, Briggs preferred French blanks for some of his patterns.

There is also correspondence with Johann Umann & Company near Tiefenwald in Bohemia, a supplier of cut stoppers. However, the samples Umann sent twice must have been unsatisfactory, because no orders followed.[42] The following year, Hawkes wrote to a factory at Schuttenhofen, Bohemia to inquire about blanks but, again, it is not clear if orders followed the initial inquiry. "Please send us at once,

40. T. G. Hawkes to Richard Briggs, Boston, September 28, 1888.
41. T. G. Hawkes to Richard Briggs, Boston, April 3, 1889.
42. Johann Umann, Tiefenbach bei Tannwald, Bohemia, to T. G. Hawkes, February 16, May 2, 1884, September 21, 1885.

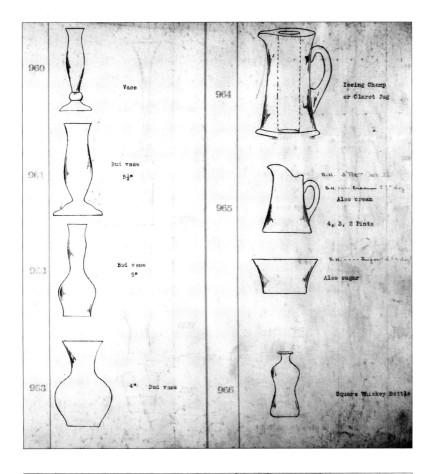

5-43. The icing champagne or claret jug, #964, is unusual.

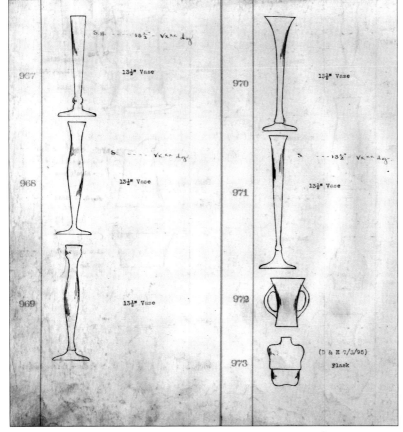

5-44. The pocket flask, #973, is for silver mounting and the initials are those of the customer, probably a silver firm.

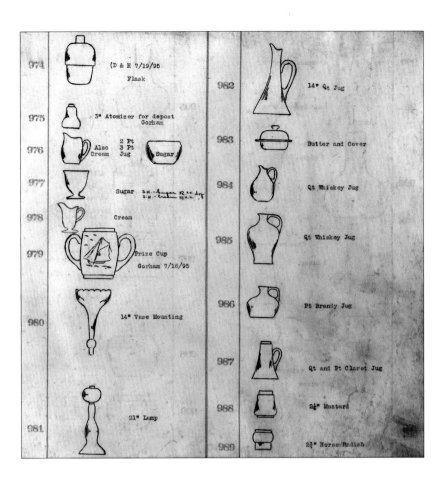

5-45. *The prize cup, probably for a yacht race, was for Gorham to silver mount.*

at our expense, a few samples of plain tumblers, colored hock glasses and crystal stem glass suitable for cutting, and quote prices for quantities. Also send some samples of cut lapidary stoppers if you make them. Can you make glass bowls, dishes, etc. which are blown in iron moulds? If so, how much do you charge by the pound weight? We employ one hundred and thirty glass-cutters, and use large quantities of Glass. We are now buying largely in England, so your prices will have to be low if we do business with you, and the quality must be of the best."[43]

Only a few years later, Hawkes replied to a New York importer, "Our experience with imported glass is that it is not suitable for our class of trade," which may indicate that during the 1890s, he used mostly English and American blanks.[44]

The Hawkes Archives contain cash books and day books which cover the first decade of the 20th century, and several blanks books which show lists of the shapes in use at specific periods. A ledger headed "Glass, Silver" which was started by December 15, 1896, but must have been in use for at least ten years, has a list of blank sources for specific shapes. This indicates that Corning Glass Works supplied stemware blanks in shapes called *Church, Mitchell, Empire, Gibson,* and *Thistle* as well as the numbered blanks, 350, 375, 385, 500, 506, 600, 602, and 3840, and three pages of blanks for other shapes. Dorflinger supplied two pages of stemware blanks only, including 176, 350, 375, 385, 500, 602, 783, 805, 926, 1000, 1020, 1044, 1051, 1060, and 3840 at lower prices than the Glass Works. Libbey supplied a mixture of blanks including stemware and Fry, Pairpoint, and Union were listed on one page each with a mixture of shapes that did not include stemware. Steuben blanks covered two pages, including 350, 1044, 1085, 1110, 1255, 1413, 1459, 1467, *Versailles* and *Star of India*, also at

43. T. G. Hawkes to Jos. Ed. Schmid, Schuttenhofen, Bohemia, January 25, 1889.
44. T. G. Hawkes to Fensterer & Ruhe, New York, August 9, 1892.

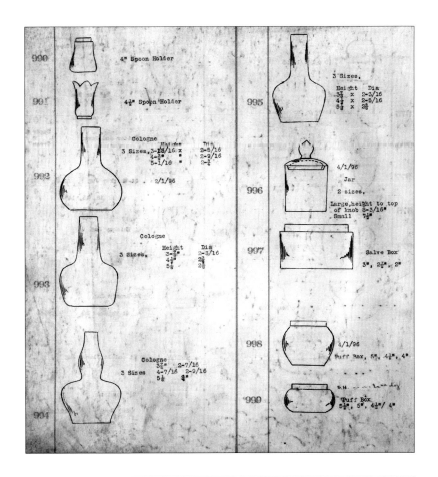

5-46. The first two items are spoon holders which were old-fashioned by this time.

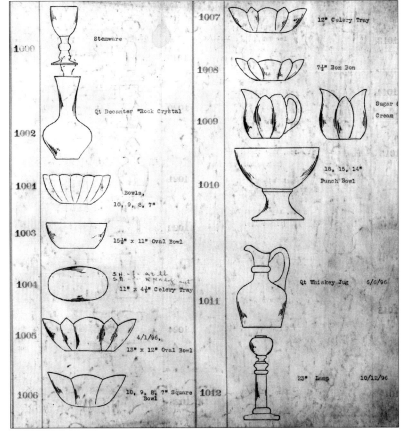

5-47. The items on this page were added in 1896.

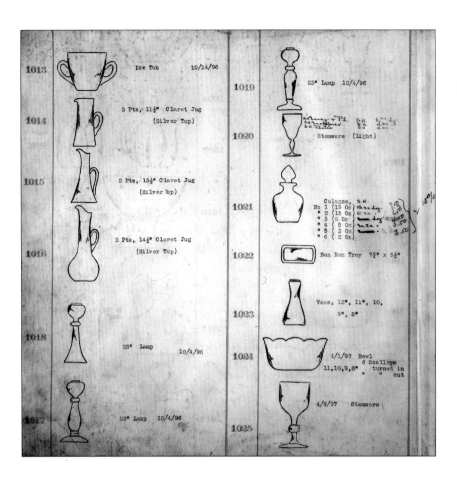

5-48. The punchbowl and stemware at the bottom of this page were added in April, 1897.

cheaper prices. Webb Shaw & Company is listed as supplying 350 and 385 stemware, plain or cut in *New Princess* or *Strawberry Diamond & Fan*. Sèvres blanks were mostly trays, plates, and vases, and Wilkes and Umann supplied mostly stoppers. No other English or Continental suppliers are listed in this book.

The cash books, however, do list other suppliers. For example, in September, 1901, Hawkes paid Dorflinger $4355 for blanks and Corning $3024. Libbey charged $778 and Stevens & Williams $589. Other suppliers of blanks like Wilkes, Union, and Pairpoint received a few hundred dollars or less. The monthly totals for Dorflinger, Corning, and Libbey remained about the same for several years, but the English and European supplies were sporadic rather than monthly. When blanks from Steuben began to be listed, the percentage of Dorflinger and Corning Glass Works blanks dropped sharply and, in 1903 and 1904 respectively, they were phased out. Payment of about $500 a month to Gunthal, the Val St. Lambert agent, can be found for several more years. Unfortunately, these cash book and day book entries tell us nothing about shapes or patterns.

Corning Glass Works also supplied blanks to other cutting firms, sometimes through Hawkes and sometimes directly. Correspondence between Henry F. Spurr of the Boston & Sandwich Glass Company and Hawkes in October 1885, shows that Spurr had ordered fifty-four dozen blanks, mostly of drinking glasses "to patt," plus a dozen oval dishes shaped in a mold supplied by Spurr "in good weight for Star Hobnail Cutting" from the Glass Works.[45] Similar correspondence with C. Dorflinger & Sons concerned ruby hocks ordered several times by the Pennsylvania firm though Hawkes. The first letter says: "What does the Corning Glass Works charge for Ruby plated strait stem hocks. Bowl only plated, leg & foot

45. Henry F. Spurr, Boston & Sandwich Glass Company to Corning Glass Works, October 9, 1885.

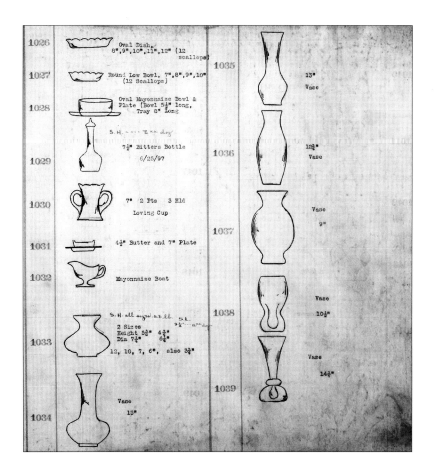

5-49. The oval mayonnaise bowl, #1028, is unusual.

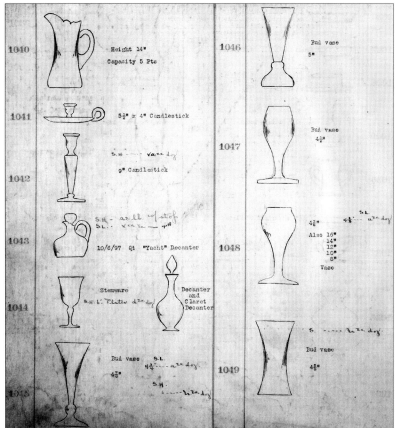

5-50. #1040, the 5 pint pitcher, must have been too heavy to pour from easily when full.

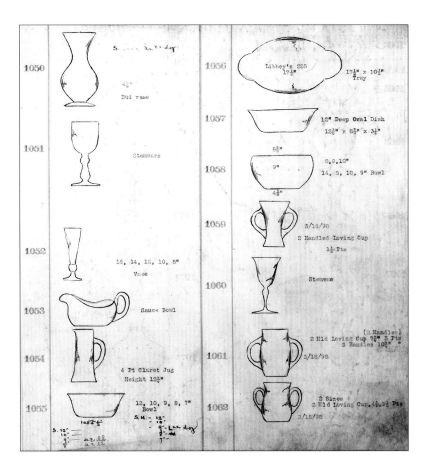

5-51. The blank for #1056, the 17 ½in. bowl, came from Libbey.

flint. We would like to get a few of these in ruby & amber if price is not too high."[46] Apparently Dorflinger placed the order, because in August, 1892, Hawkes wrote, "The Corning Glass Works say they will make the ruby hocks for us on Thursday, and we hope to be able to ship them on Saturday."[47]

In June 1892, Hawkes was apparently getting blanks for McCue and Earl, a New York City cutting shop. "The iron mould for the two bottles which you inquire for, has been made sometime but the glass house people have not yet got around to it, the writer, Mr. Hawkes, asked the foreman of the glass house to give this the preference of everything else, they will do first thing next week." Since John Earl had previously been John Hoare's foreman in Corning, he presumably had connections there so that he could buy glass from Corning Glass Works. As a general rule, the Glass Works did not supply blanks to all comers. Control of the supply of blanks was crucial to controlling the industry.

S. J. Merchant's small cutting shop in Philadelphia had hired some of Hawkes's striking cutters in 1887 and, in retaliation, Hawkes tried to cut off the supply of Merchant's blanks. A letter from Caldwell described the situation: "I beg to submit the substance of a conversation the writer had with Mr. Merchant and which is to be considered strictly confidential... as we would not care to become entangled in any controversy that might possibly arise. Their former source of supply, Dorflinger, has been cut off and they say that they are unable to secure any blanks now, although they are about to make an arrangement with some other glass manufacturer... The cut work that they are doing is from dealers in town buying their own blanks and having Merchant cut them... the blanks can be secured from Dorflinger, Boston & Sandwich, New England and Hibbler Co.

46. C. Dorflinger & Sons, White Mills, to T. G. Hawkes, n.d.
47. T. G. Hawkes & Company to C. Dorflinger & Sons, White Mills, August 23, 1892.

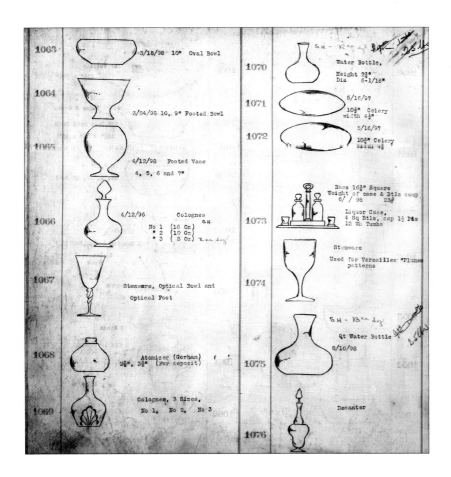

1063   3/18/98 10" Oval Bowl

1064   3/24/98 10, 9" Footed Bowl

1065   4/12/98 Footed Vase
        4, 5, 6 and 7"

1066   4/12/96   Colognes
                   S.H
        No 1 (16 Oz)
         " 2 (10 Oz)
         " 3 (8 Oz)

1067   Stemware, Optical Bowl and
        Optical Foot

1068   Atomizer (Gorham)
        2⅜", 3⅛" (For deposit)

1069   Colognes, 3 Sizes,
        No 1, No 2, No 3

1070   Water Bottle,
        Height 7¾"
        Dia 6-1/16"

1071   5/16/97
        10¾" Celery
        width 4¼"

1072   5/16/97
        10¾" Celery

1073   Base 16¾" Square
        Weight of case & Btls comp.
        6/ /98   23#
        Liquor Case,
        4 Sq Btls, cap 1½ Pts
        12 Wh Tumbs

1074   Stemware
        Used for Versailles "Plumes"
        patterns

1075   Qt Water Bottle
        8/10/98

1076   Decanter

5-52. The liquor set, # 1073, had four decanters and twelve tumblers.

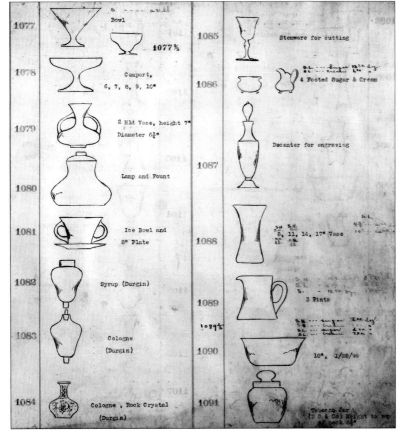

1077   Bowl

1077½

1078   Comport,
        6, 7, 8, 9, 10"

1079   2 Hld Vase, height 7"
        Diameter 6¼"

1080   Lamp and Fount

1081   Ice Bowl and
        8" Plate

1082   Syrup (Durgin)

1083   Cologne
        (Durgin)

1084   Cologne, Rock Crystal
        (Durgin)

1085   Stemware for cutting

1086   4 Footed Sugar & Cream

1087   Decanter for engraving

1088   8, 11, 14, 17" Vase

1089   3 Pints

1089½

1090   10", 1/20/99

1091   Tobacco Jar
        (D C & Co) Height to top
        of neck 6¾"

5-53. #s 1082, 1083, and 1084 were for the Durgin Silver Company for mounting #1091, the tobacco jar was for Davis, Collamore & Company.

123

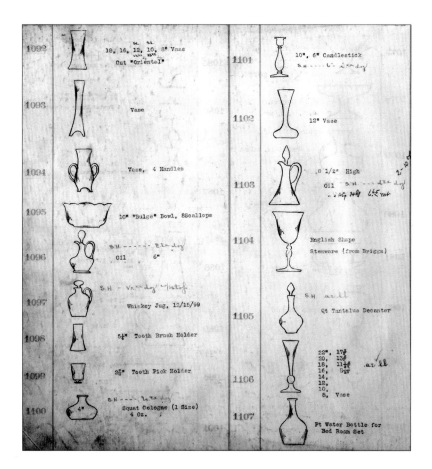

5-54. #1104 is shown as "English Shape Stemware (from Briggs)" which may mean the blanks were imported or that the shape was copied from an English example.

Brooklyn, the last one of which are no doubt the ones that the arrangement is to be made with and who are probably surreptitiously supplying them now.[48]

Hawkes wrote Edward D. Libbey at the New England Glass Works, Henry Spurr at the Boston & Sandwich Glass Company, Frederick Shirley at Mt. Washington, and Louis Dorflinger in White Mills. He received replies indicating that none of them would supply Merchant. Louis Dorflinger replied: "We refused some four months ago to have anything to do with Merchant. We refused to sell blanks to John M. Maris & Company of Philadelphia who wanted them for Merchant. There is no place he can get blanks now excepting in Corning, & we think he is getting them there through Maris & Company in Philadelphia." Hawkes replied that he was positive that Corning Glass Works sold blanks only to Hawkes and Hoare. Frederick Shirley said: "Yours to hand & you can rest assured we shall not sell any blanks to parties named in fact we should be glad if cut glass mfrs would all agree not to sell outside shops. We hear that Mr. Earl of Hoare's has made association with J. McCue of NY does this mean Corning blanks? I trust Mr. H. [Hoare] & yourself can convince Mr. Houghton that it is to his interest to supply only yourselves & I will willingly join all other factories in an agreement not to sell to outsiders if they will not, in fact we continually refuse to do it now."[49]

In practice, this exclusion rule, which would have restricted glass cutting to only a dozen or so firms, was honored only sporadically. As the demand for cut glass grew, it was largely ignored. Occasional correspondence between Hawkes and Hoare indicates that they swapped blanks frequently on a small scale and that Hawkes did so with Dorflinger, Clark, and other nearby glassmakers.

Both the Boston & Sandwich firm in New England, and C. Dorflinger & Sons in

48. J. E. Caldwell, Philadelphia to T. G. Hawkes, January 31, 1887.
49. F. S. Shirley, Mount Washington Glass Company, New Bedford, Massachusetts to T. G. Hawkes, February 3, 1887.

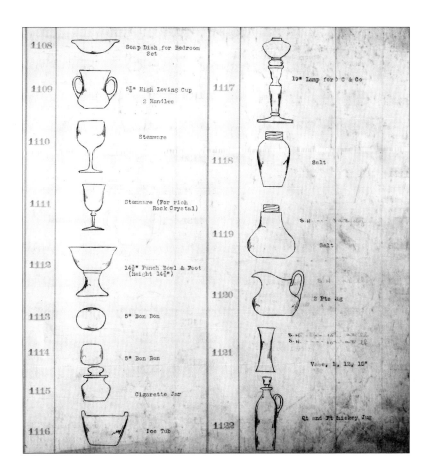

1108		Soap Dish for Bedroom Set
1109		5¾" High Loving Cup 2 Handles
1110		Stemware
1111		Stemware (For rich Rock Crystal)
1112		14⅜" Punch Bowl & Foot (Height 14⅜")
1113		5" Bon Bon
1114		5" Bon Bon
1115		Cigarette Jar
1116		Ice Tub
1117		19" Lamp for D C & Co
1118		Salt
1119		Salt
1120		2 Pts Jug
1121		Vase, 1, 12, 15"
1122		Qt and Pt Whiskey Jug

5-55. The 19in. lamp was for Davis, Collamore & Company.

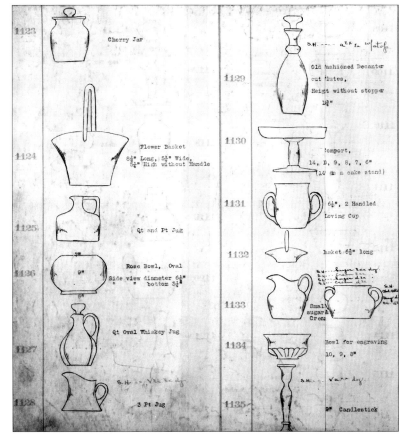

1123		Cherry Jar
1124		Flower Basket 8¼" Long, 5¾" Wide, 5¼" High without Handle
1125		Qt and Pt Jug
1126		Rose Bowl, Oval Side view diameter 6¼" " " bottom 3¼
1127		Qt Oval Whiskey Jug
1128		3 Pt Jug
1129		Old fashioned Decanter cut flutes, Height without stopper 11¼"
1130		Comport, 14, D, 9, 8, 7, 6" (14 as a cake stand)
1131		6¼", 2 Handled Loving Cup
1132		Basket 6⅜" long
1133		Small sugar & Cream
1134		Bowl for engraving 10, 9, 8"
1135		9" Candlestick

5-56. #1125, the jugs, are shapes used by Hoare as well.

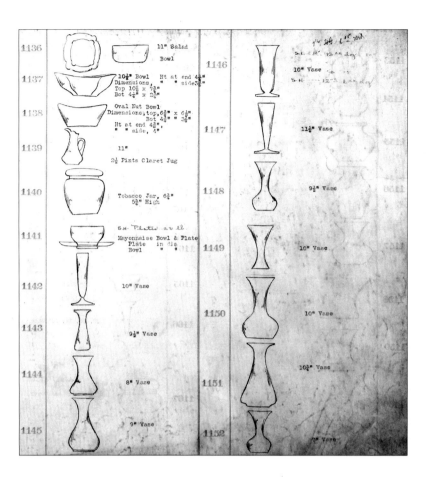

5-57. This page is mostly vases.

White Mills had large blowing rooms and could make their own glass. However, it seems to have been common practice for glass factories to buy blanks from each other. After 1900, the Union Glass Company in Somerville, Massachusetts was the preferred supplier of the largest blanks for punch bowls and vases, probably because they had a shop of blowers who could handle this work. Other companies made specialties of other shapes or types. Hawkes bought "bankers' inks" from Hobbs, Brockunier & Company of Wheeling, in the spring and summer of 1886,[50] supplying the necessary mold, and at the same time he bought inks from the Central Glass Company, also in Wheeling.[51] In 1889, Hawkes received a letter from one of his own former cutters, now working for Dithridge, touting their blanks: "Dear Sir, Knowing that you buy a large quantity of plain Glass & that you like a very fine quality, I thought perhaps the Firm I work for might be able to do some Business with you. I can say that we have some of the Best Glass I ever worked on, if you see fit to order of them I am sure the ware will please you in every particular."[52] There is no indication of whether or not Hawkes ordered Dithridge blanks.

Certain shapes were hard to find, as when the Sandwich firm replied, "I have no tray here similar to sample… have one sent you from factory if on hand there, if not will take some days."[53] Small orders like this were often matchings (that is, replacement pieces for broken objects). In that case, the Hawkes company would write to several other firms in an attempt to find the right color or shape. McCue & Earl wrote to Hawkes for "straight stem Green Hocks, green outside if you can send them by return Express"[54] and Hawkes wrote to Gilman Collamore, a New York City retailer, "We send you today by express prepaid one Amber Hock,

50. Bills from Hobbs, Brockunier & Company to T. G. Hawkes, March 5, May 10, October 30, 1886.
51. Bill from Central Glass Company, Wheeling to T. G. Hawkes, February 19, 1886.
52. R. H. Harrison, Foreman Cutting Dept., The Dithridge Flint Glass Company, New Brighton, Pennsylvania, to T. G. Hawkes, December 12, 1887.
53. Sewall H. Fessenden, Boston & Sandwich Glass Company to T. G. Hawkes, June 9, 1884.
54. McCue & Earl, Brooklyn to T. G. Hawkes, September 20, 1889.

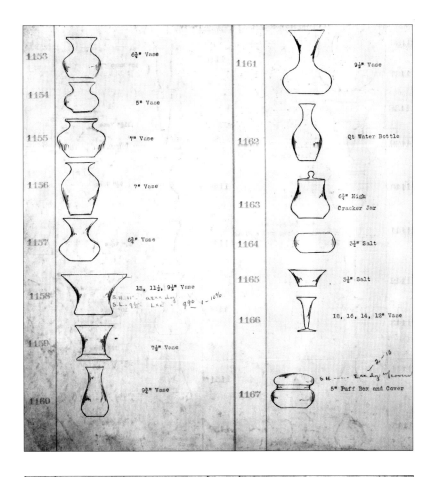

1153	6¾" Vase	
1154	5" Vase	
1155	7" Vase	
1156	7" Vase	
1157	6¾" Vase	
1158	13, 11½, 9½" Vase	
1159	7½" Vase	
1160	9¾" Vase	
1161	9½" Vase	
1162	Qt Water Bottle	
1163	6¼" High Cracker Jar	
1164	3¼" Salt	
1165	3¼" Salt	
1166	18, 16, 14, 12" Vase	
1167	5" Puff Box and Cover	

5-58. The scale of the drawings is unrelated to the size of the objects.

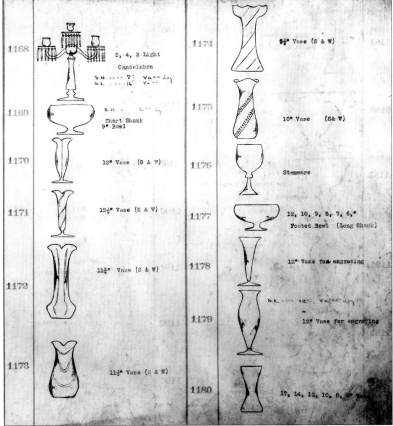

1168	5, 4, 3 Light Candelabra	
1169	Short Shank 9" Bowl	
1170	12" Vase (S & W)	
1171	12½" Vase (S & W)	
1172	11½" Vase (S & W)	
1173	11¼" Vase (S & W)	
1174	9¼" Vase (S & W)	
1175	10" Vase (S & W)	
1176	Stemware	
1177	12, 10, 9, 8, 7, 6," Footed Bowl (Long Shank)	
1178	12" Vase for engraving	
1179	12" Vase for engraving	
1180	17, 14, 12, 10, 8, "	

5-59. #1170 through #1175 are probably blanks from Stevens & Williams.

127

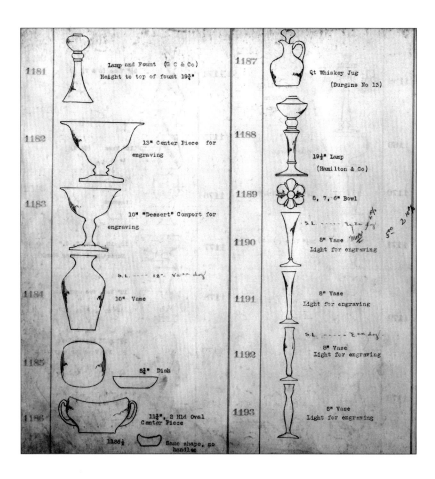

5-60. #1182 is often found with
the Gravic trademark.

55. T. G. Hawkes, Corning to Gilman Collamore & Company New York, November 20, 1888.
56. W. A. Levis for J. E. Caldwell & Company, Philadelphia to T. G. Hawkes, March 24, 1888.
57. McCue & Earl, Brooklyn to T. G. Hawkes, September 19, 1889.
58. John J. Earl, for McCue & Earl, to T. G. Hawkes, October 7, 1889.
59. Invoice, McCue & Earl to T. G. Hawkes, October 24, 1889, marked "Rec. Payment".
60. C. Dorflinger & Sons, White Mills, September 16, 1889.

which we think is your glass, Please send us one dozen to match it by return express."[55] These may have been already cut, if Collamore had a cutter on the premises, but it seems unlikely. J. E. Caldwell wrote to Hawkes, "Can you not purchase Blue Hocks of one of your New York customers?"[56]

In 1889, Hawkes received a request for champagne jugs with ice pockets. Since Corning Glass Works was unable to supply the blank, Tom Hawkes sent the request to McCue and Earl, and received the following reply. "We have sent the Sketch to the Dithridge F. G. Company if the jugs can be made in America they can make them. Hibbler & Company we are sure could not make them."[57] A few weeks later, Earl wrote that Dithridge was having trouble making the jugs[58] but on October 24th, they were shipped and McCue billed Hawkes $10 each for the two jugs.[59] However, at the same time, Hawkes also sent the request to White Mills, and received the following reply: "We return herewith your order and drawing of a Champagne Jug with a pocket in it. We have not got a man in our place who can make this article, and we are therefore obliged to return it to you."[60] It is clear from all of this correspondence that it is rarely safe to make assumptions about where the blanks have been made for any piece of cut glass. Some distinctive pieces, like the jugs with ice pockets, special colors, or very large objects, could only be supplied by one or two firms; however, standard shapes could be ordered from any of several places, and over a period of time they probably were.

One of the techniques which made this multiplicity of blank sources economical was the use of iron molds for shaping the objects. Most researchers have assumed that blanks for high quality cutting were free-blown and shaped only with wooden blocks during manufacture. However, the Hawkes

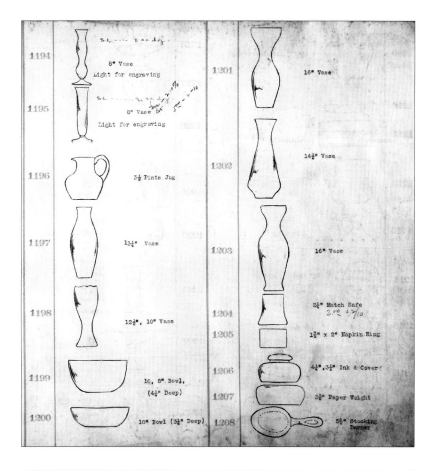

5-61. #1208, the stocking darner, is an unusual item and, if cut, would be hard to use.

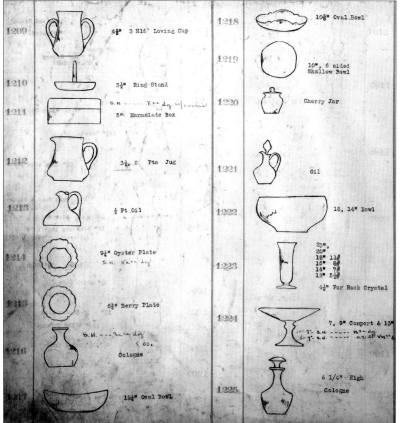

5-62. The 18in. bowl, #1222, is one of the largest shapes Hawkes cut.

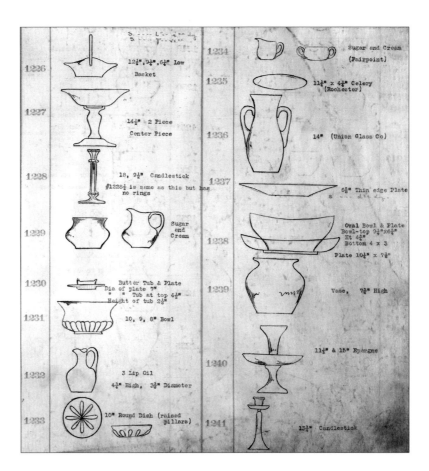

5-63. The centerpiece, #12-27, is found cut in Lorraine pattern (See Figs. 6-19, 6-20); the #1234 set came from Pairpoint, the #1235 celery from Fry and #1236 from Union Glass.

correspondence makes it clear that molds were used extensively from the beginning, and that Hawkes supplied the mold for a specific order and might then send the same mold to another glass house if conditions warranted. Because cheaper cut glassware was made from pressed glass blanks after 1900, Hawkes and some other firms advertised extensively that they used only blown blanks and from that statement, early researchers assumed that free-blown was meant. However, the evidence does not support this assumption. In any case, with the necessity of having stemware and other table pieces of uniform size and thickness, the use of molds makes perfect sense. Sometimes the molds were for special hard-to-make pieces and sometimes for standard shapes. The agent for Ovington Bros., a Brooklyn store, wrote: "Will send you tomorrow a China Dish & Stand & they wish you to have the necessary Moulds made, so that the inside of the Dish, when made will be as large as the outside of Sample, which will make the Dishes full ¼ in more dia. than the Samples. The foot of the Dish I think you will be obliged to make a separate mould for, that you can tell better when you see the Sample, which is an openwork dish. The idea is to carry out the form & Shape as near as possible to Sample, both for Dish & Stand. They want it got up Expressly for them & in that case you will want to charge them for the necessary moulds."[61]

To another customer, Hawkes explained, "To make a square Ice Cream Tray such as you describe, would require a special iron mould which would cost $15.00 extra, and we therefore presume you will not want it."[62] Some of Hawkes' molds were stored at Corning Glass Works which probably had its own molds as well. "We have tried every mould at factory and cannot find anything the right size for

61. F. G. Boughton, for Ovington Bros., Brooklyn, to T. G. Hawkes, January 19, 1882.
62. T. G. Hawkes to Wright, Kay & Company, Detroit, February 28, 1889.

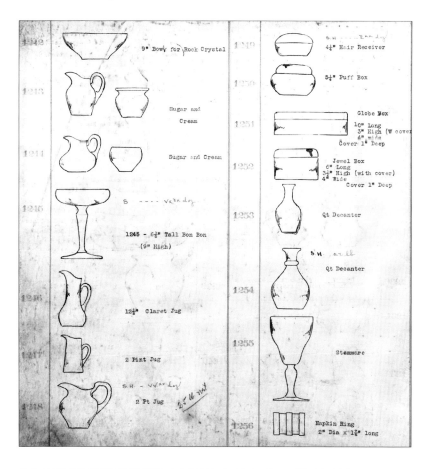

5-64. Note the napkin rings, #1256.

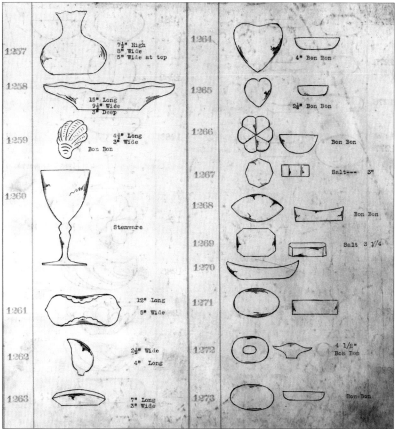

5-65. This page is mostly bonbons.

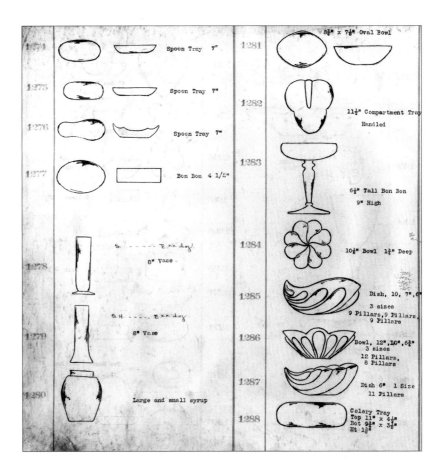

5-66. The pillared blanks at the lower right are unusual.

the blue linings. Will have to make a special mould and it will take about two weeks to get them cut."[63] A letter to Dorflinger underlines the practice of keeping molds at the glasshouse. "We send you this day four iron moulds for Salad Bowls as follows: 1 10 inch, 1 9 inch, 1 8 inch, 1 7 inch No. 700 Round Salad Bowls, the number and size is marked in each mould. Will you please make for us the following: 2 dozen 10 inch to weigh about 8 lbs each, 5 dozen 9 inch to weigh about 6 lbs each... You will please retain these moulds for future orders."[64]

On the other hand, sometimes customers wanted hand made pieces, either to save the expense of the mold or because the finish was thought to be better. Briggs wrote: "Please make for me 1 pair tall glass candlesticks about 12 inches high. Very heavy and of best metal, the cutting to be broad flute, from top to bottom... They may be hand made as it is not worth while to go to the expense of a mould."[65] When one customer wanted a replacement, Hawkes wrote: "Ice Bowls, being made by hand, vary in size, and the only way we can get an accurate fit is to have the bowl returned to us, and we will then make the plate immediately."[66] Some shapes might be made either way, depending on circumstances: "We have received the two 10in. 700 bowls cut Cobweb; these we cut on hand-made blanks having run out of the iron moulded ones. The shape may be a very little different."[67]

Most of Hawkes's molds were made to order by Homer Brooks, a mold maker in New York City, and the process was fairly simple: "We send you to-day by express paid, one wooden model for Cream Tray. Please make us mould for same. We wish this mould beautifully finished on the inside so that when the glass is blown, the dish will come out clear. Take your cast off this model, as in making

63. T. G. Hawkes to McCue & Earl, Brooklyn, August 15, 1888.
64. T. G. Hawkes to C. Dorflinger & Sons, White Mills, September 7, 1888.
65. Richard Briggs, Boston to T. G. Hawkes, October 12, 1885.
66. T. G. Hawkes to Ovington Bros., Brooklyn, October 1, 1888.
67. T. G. Hawkes to Davis Collamore & Co, Ltd., New York, February 25, 1889.

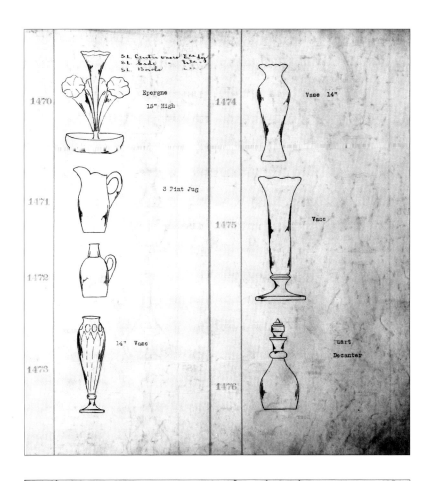

5-67. There is a jump in the numbers here, and some pages in the book may be missing, but the 1470 epergne is a Steuben blank as are #s1471, 1473 and 1474.

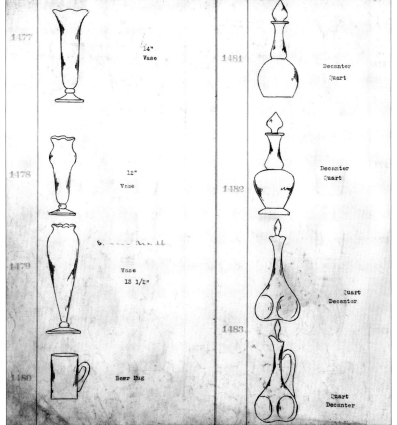

5-68. The first vase on this page is a shape Steuben made; the others are not.

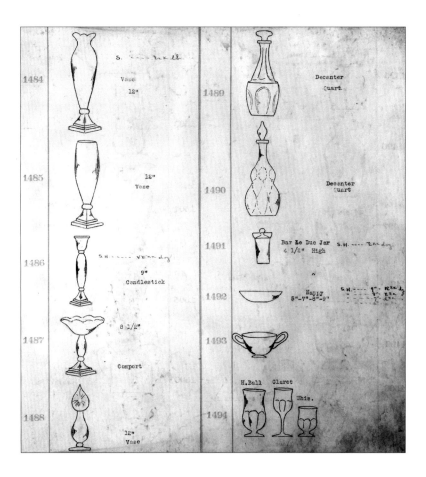

5-69. #s 1484–1487 are Steuben shapes, as is #1491.

the model we have allowed for the shrinkage in iron."[68]

Not all of the molds were smooth on the inside, as the correspondence with Osler and Boulton & Mills, quoted above, specifies that the English firms do not need to bother to finish the mold on the inside. The reason for this is mentioned in a letter to Davis Collamore: "These plates cost us more to cut than Straw. Dia. You will notice they are made in an iron mould, and are smoothed and polished all over, and are all one size and run even; possibly, if we were to make these plates by hand, we would not have to smooth and polish the plain parts all over, and therefore, they would cost some less, but we could not guarantee to give you as nice and even a plate as those we sent you."[69]

However, Hawkes's practice seems to have varied since, in a letter to Dorflinger, he says: "We send you…one iron mould for Cream Tray No. 650. Please make us five dozen suitable for Russian cutting, and five dozen suitable for Straw. Dia. cutting… When you make the Cream Trays, please have the mould kept as hot as possible, as we wish the glass to come out clear."[70]

Most of the blanks made in these molds probably had sheared rims, which was the traditional English way of finishing, but some of them must have used the Continental "blowover" method in which a thin portion of glass protruded above the desired rim and could be easily broken off. This was a faster and therefore cheaper way of finishing the blanks. The men at Dorflinger's shop could finish blanks either way. "Finger Bowl No. 3672 is cracked off not hand finished. In order to get the dozen as light as sample we will have to crack them off,"[71] says one letter. Hawkes replied, "The light finger bowls that you sent us were very satisfactory; when we sent you the sample we knew there was no other way to

68. T. G. Hawkes to Homer Brooks, New York, October 29, 1889.
69. T. G. Hawkes to Davis Collamore & Company, Ltd., New York, April 26, 1889.
70. T. G. Hawkes to C. Dorflinger & Sons, White Mills, November 10, 1888.
71. C. Dorflinger & Sons, White Mills, to T. G. Hawkes, April 26, 1889.

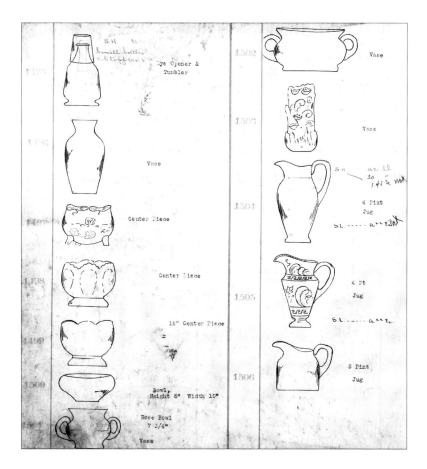

5-70. Only the pitcher, #1504 is a Steuben blank.

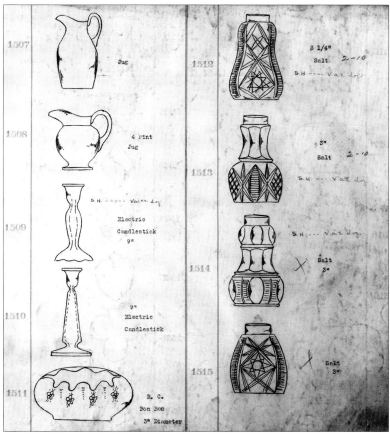

5-71. Only the pitcher, #1508 is a Steuben blank.

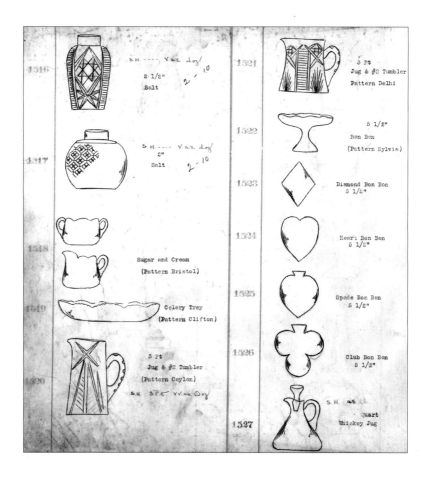

5-72. Only the whiskey jug,
#1527 is a Steuben blank.

make them but in a mould and crack them off."[72]

Hawkes looked into getting his own mold-maker, and sought Dorflinger's advice: "We note what you say about a mould maker, and will make inquiries, and will advise you what we may learn. It seems to us that a very good man for your purpose would be found in some machine shop for railroads. Mr. Brox of Port Jervis has a good man that he got out of the Erie shop, and we would not be surprised if you could find one and that he would suit you very well, and will work at a moderate rate of wages. Most of these mould makers are high priced men."[73]

However, nothing in the archives indicates that Hawkes hired his own mold maker. A number of wooden patterns and plaster casts were in the Hawkes building when it closed. These seem to have been used to record engravings and occasionally to demonstrate cuttings. A letter from Dorflinger says, "We mailed you a plaster cast to show how the necks are to be cut..."[74] but this was not standard procedure. Some of the plasters have a pattern for cutting or engraving drawn on them with a pencil and perhaps these were made in the iron mold and used by the designer to space the pattern. Usually, however, the plaster was an intermediate step between the wooden pattern and the cast iron mold as described in the letters to Boulton & Mills and Osler, above. Hawkes acquired the Sinclaire design archives when that company went out of business, and these included plaster casts of a number of elaborate engraved pieces as well as a few cut pieces. The plaster casts of engraving were apparently made so that if the design was reordered, the engraver had a pattern to follow as well as a drawing.

As indicated in the correspondence quoted above, the Hawkes firm bought a large number of colored blanks from European suppliers in the 1880s. However,

72. T. G. Hawkes to C. Dorflinger & Sons, White Mills, May 6, 1889.
73. C. Dorflinger & Sons, White Mills, to T. G. Hawkes, October 28, 1889.
74. C. Dorflinger & Sons, White Mills, to T. G. Hawkes, June 4, 1889.

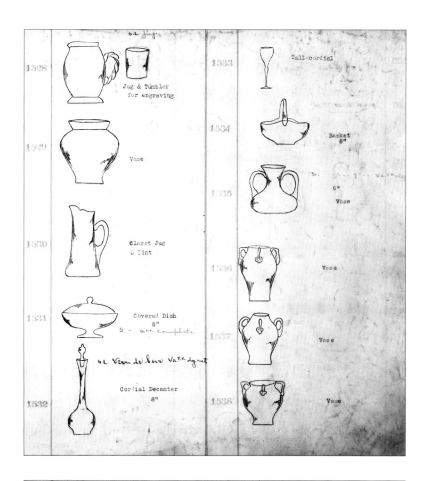

5-73. #s 1528, 1530, and 1532–1537 are Steuben.

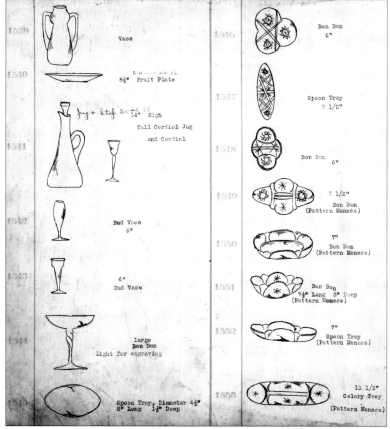

5-74. The vase, #1539, and the jug and cordial, #1541 are both Steuben shapes; the remainder are not.

by no means all of the colored blanks were bought abroad. The orders from Briggs, Caldwell, Davis Collamore, and others do not usually specify a blanks supplier, but it is clear that they ordered colored glass in many more shapes than the stemware blanks which seem to be the most frequently ordered English colored blanks. The orders also sometimes specify solid rather than overlay colors although cased is more common. The 19th century term for this was "plated". To Caldwell, Hawkes said, "We could not promise the green hocks by the time desired as we would have to make a special pot of glass… We will have to wait until we accumulate orders enough to warrant us in making a special pot of glass… We cannot tell when it may be – it may be a month or six months or even longer", and the next week sent the sample green hock to Dorflinger since apparently they could fill the order.[75] Eventually, Caldwell sent the hocks back and asked: "Please let us know when you make Green Glass again, so as we can have hocks made like sample we sent you some time ago. We have been unable to find a factory to make same for us and would like to know at once upon your making green glass."[76] For an order for Collamore, Hawkes explained: "The flower globes, one ruby and one green to flint sample sent would cost $20.00 each. If you wanted the foot plated as well as the bowl, it would be a very difficult job to do, and we question whether it would be satisfactory to you when done; if you will take the foot all flint as sample there will be no trouble about making the rest of it."[77]

A letter from Collamore in 1884 discusses their color requirements for a special order in some detail. "We have an order for a large set…on condition that we get the color of hock glasses as desired. We send by Ex today 2 rose Hocks, #283, neither of which will answer in color. Our customer wishing a more perfect rose color, a third rose sample is enclosed…which you will see is a more delicate shade, less of the purple or deep tone in the color. We think this would do, can you cut us a sample of about this tone of color on the regular 283 blank & 283 cutting. Also can you give us the darker shade of green as sample sent, in a hock glass plated on crystal with crystal stem & foot as the rose color is done, if not the darker shade can the lighter shade of green as sample be treated in that manner. If neither shade of color can be plated on crystal then the next best thing will be the lighter shade of green in solid color for bowl of hock, with crystal stem & foot. A sample of each rose & green is desired…would like the color to show as much as possible round the body… not all cut away. Also that a claret jug will be wished to match the rose Hocks, plated on crystal, stopper the same & cut to match body of decanter, crystal handle, Can you make this large piece of the delicate rose color, also a tall wine bottle to match the green Hocks, of whatever style you succeed in furnishing a sample hock glass of. Stopper in all cases to match cutting of Decanters, not lapidary. The customer as you see is a troublesome one, very strong in her likes & dislikes and the sale hinges upon the colored pieces."[78]

This order was the sort that must have made Hawkes and the glass factory tear

75. T. G. Hawkes to J. E. Caldwell & Company, Philadelphia, February 11, 14, 1889.
76. J. E. Caldwell & Company, Philadelphia to T. G. Hawkes, March 1, 1889.
77. T. G. Hawkes to Davis Collamore & Company Ltd., April 8, 1889.
78. Davis Collamore & Company Ltd, New York, to T. G. Hawkes, Corning, July 18, 1884.

their hair and probably had a small margin of profit. However, Hawkes's ability to get the colored blanks made to order at Corning Glass Works probably was beneficial to his business in the long run. A letter to Dorflinger says: "Please return to us by express, one of the samples of Ruby Hocks, for order 22805; we must have it for size and shape, also for cutting and engraving. The glass-works promises us to make next week, glass specially, for those eight green and eight blue hocks."[79] It is surprising that the glass works would make a pot for so few glasses, but they could probably just make it all up into blanks and hope to sell them later.

Orders of the 1880s were most often for shades of gold ruby, amber, green, and blue with not much description, but "Pomona Green" is specified in one order from Collamore of August 28, 1884, and "Translucent blue" in another of March 12, 1887. Collamore ordered "Peacock Bluc" on May 10, 1889, and Richard Briggs ordered "light amber hocks...to be plated inside" on January 25, 1887. D. B. Bedell, an occasional customer in New York, wanted "Persian Rose and Persian Green" Roman punch cups on December 9, 1889. Where these special names for colors came from is not clear, since the photographic catalogs mention only simple colors.

Hawkes did some repair work for customers; it is not uncommon to find Davis Collamore or J. E. Caldwell sending back a piece which had been damaged at the store before it was sold, with the request to have it cut down or repolished. In one case, Caldwell asked Hawkes to make rose globes out of two broken claret jugs and to cut the top off one tumbler to convert it into a salt; and in another simply asked Hawkes to "Repair the following articles to best advantage..." and sent an assortment of shapes.[80] Hawkes, occasionally, did the same kind of repair work for individual customers but it could not have been very profitable.

Throughout the correspondence of the 1880s, there are scattered complaints about the quality of Hawkes's cutting, or the quality of the blanks. At that time English glassmakers were widely considered to be the best, and a letter from Briggs said: "The glass received from you yesterday is not as satisfactory as usual... It is claimed by my competitors that no American manufacturer will maintain his standard in every respect and I have the hardest work to convince my customers that such is not the case. You have a perfect Knowledge of what makes a perfect piece of cut glass, and I must urge you to see that none other is sent me, under any circumstances."[81] These complaints cluster in 1884 and again in 1889 when Hawkes was apparently having trouble both with his cutters and with his blanks. Collamore complained about the variations in size of the tumblers in the summer of 1884 and Caldwell complained of bubbles in the glass. Briggs wrote: "I must call your attention to the quality of the glass you are sending. The metal is good enough, but the cutters are slighting their work and many of the pieces have bubbles in conspicuous places and deposits of sand in others... I have to compete with three glass factories here and my only way of getting on is to assure and convince my customers that every piece will be perfect. You should adopt

79. T. G. Hawkes to C. Dorflinger & Sons, White Mills, October 18, 1888.
80. J. E. Caldwell & Company, Philadelphia to T. G. Hawkes, December 29, 1891.
81. Richard Briggs, Boston to T. G. Hawkes, March 6, 1884.

some system of more rigid inspection."[82]

Apparently the problem was taken care of, but late in 1888, Hawkes wrote a series of letters to Dorflinger about badly made blanks in which he complained of variations in weight as well as inclusions in the glass: "The ½ pt Tumblers received this morning... We are very disappointed in them...some are so thick and clumsy, that it would be useless to cut them, and a large number of them have big blisters in the bottom. Now unless your shop can do better, please make no more of them, and return us the sample... In package of glass shipped you this day, we send you four of the tumblers, so you can show them to your shop, and also to the man that selects them before shipping. As we remarked to you before, that it is useless to send us any goods except perfect ones."[83]

By the following year, the shoe was on the other foot, and Hawkes received a number of complaints about the quality of his men's work. Mermod & Jaccard wrote from St. Louis in May: "We wish to call your attention to the fact that there seems to be a great deal of carelessness exhibited of late in the goods which are being sent to us. It might be you have come to the conclusion that our people out here are not critical and exacting in what they purchase, but if so, you are very much mistaken... The people with us require just as nicely finished goods as can be found anywhere and we, relying upon your reputation as Hawkes, assure the people that we do give them the choicest of cut glass."[84]

In the same month, Bullard Brothers, jewelers in St. Paul, wrote in much the same vein. In October of that year, Hawkes received a similar letter from Louis J. Dorflinger: "Our New York house has written as follows, 'We are having considerable trouble with the goods from Hawkes. They are not finished as they should be. I wish you would write to him about it.' Will you please give this matter your personal attention...."[85]

In view of Hawkes' recent Grand Prize, it is surprising that he allowed these problems. A letter from Gorham the same month is quite specific about the problems. "We have the 62 small Flasks, We are very sorry but they are not satisfactory. In the first place they are too full of glass, too thick and the outlet is so small that they cannot be used... We doubt if we can use them. If you will fill one with brandy, you will suffer a long while before you will get the brandy out. We would suggest an experiment with it in that way. Our English friends on the other side make Flasks even smaller than this without the objections. We are sorry on your account and sorry because we want the Flasks awfully and we have orders for lots of them."[86]

Since all of the above continued to buy from Hawkes, he apparently overcame the problems. It is quite possible that some of this inattention to detail was caused by the rush to get the Paris glass done and then the resulting orders which followed on the heels of the publicity about the grand prize. For whatever reason, the archives show that the Hawkes firm, like all of the others, was not immune to occasional lapses in quality.

82. Richard Briggs, Boston to T. G. Hawkes, December 5, 1884.
83. T. G.Hawkes to C. Dorflinger & Sons, December 19, 1888.
84. Mermod & Jaccard Jewelry Company, St. Louis, May 24, 1889.
85. L. J. Dorflinger for C. Dorflinger & Company, White Mills, to T. G. Hawkes, October 10, 1889.
86. E. F. Aldrich for Gorham M'f'g Company, Providence to T. G. Hawkes, October 17, 1889.

CHAPTER SIX

Trademarks, Advertisements, and Brochures

Tom Hawkes was one of the first cut glass entrepreneurs to understand the importance of advertising. A number of cut glass makers advertised "to the trade" in the pages of the *Crockery and Glass Journal* and similar papers. However, Hawkes advertised both in the trade papers and in magazines like *Harpers*, *Century*, and the *Ladies Home Journal* in a successful attempt to reach the consumer directly. The Hawkes trademark was the second adopted for cut glass, and the second to be acid-etched on the glass itself instead of printed on a paper label.

The first cut glass trademark seems to have been that of C. Dorflinger & Sons, which appears on their stationery in late 1888 with the notation that the trademark is on a label on every piece. After his success at the Paris Exposition in 1889, Hawkes decided that he should also adopt a trademark. By the summer of 1891 this can be seen in the Hawkes advertisements, although the trademark

HOUSE · FURNISHINGS 40

"The ☞ *Lovers of Cut Glass should be sure to get*

Richest

Cut Glass "**HAWKES' CUT GLASS**"

in the World." *Verdict of the Paris Exposition, 1889.*

THE **DAVIS COLLAMORE & CO. (Limited), EXHIBITORS.**

GRAND PRIZE for the most artistic cut glass at the Paris Exposition this year was awarded over all competitors, foreign or domestic, to the American Manufacturer, **Thomas G. Hawkes,** one of the committee of award being a leading director in the largest cut glass establishment of Europe. Mr. T. G. Hawkes has brought his goods to such a degree of perfection that they stand unrivaled for **Brilliancy, Purity and Design.** Lovers of artistic cut glass will do well to remember that **the richest cut glass produced here or abroad is made by Mr. Hawkes.** The main part of the

PARIS EXPOSITION EXHIBIT of this celebrated firm, as well as a complete assortment for Table Service and Ornamental Purposes (suitable for WEDDING or HOLIDAY PRESENTS), may be seen at the showrooms of

DAVIS COLLAMORE & CO. (LIMITED),

Sole Agents for New-York. **921 Broadway, 151 Fifth Avenue,** } **NEW-YORK.**

6-1. *Advertisement in The Century Magazine, Dec. 1889, p. 40.*   *Courtesy Kurt Reed.*

6-2. *Advertisement in The Century Magazine, 1892. From a clipping in the Hawkes archives with pencilled date. This shows the early trademark on a paper label.*

registration in 1903 says that it had been used since July, 1890. This early mark has two duck-like birds within a trefoil on either side of a fleur-de-lis with the word "HAWKES" above the birds. The mark is within a circular frame and beside it is the notation, "No piece without this trademark is genuine." This trademark was printed on a paper label and affixed to the glass. The trademark printed this way is usually within the circle and although the word "label" is not used in most of the advertisements, the text says nothing about the mark being imprinted on the glass. Libbey's trademark for cut glass was the next one adopted, in 1891, and Libbey's second trademark, the word "Libbey" with a sword, registered in 1896, was the first one to be acid-etched on cut glass.[1] By 1903, the acid-etched trademark had caught on with other manufacturers as well, although Dorflinger continued to use a paper label.

Correspondence with the Homer Lee Bank Note Company, who were also printing business stationery for Hawkes, indicates that they printed the labels early in 1890. They supplied 25,000 labels in gummed sheets and a punch so that the Hawkes packers could cut out the individual labels from the sheets.[2] The same month, Mr. Turner of Davis Collamore & Company was asking, "What do you think of a nice round ticket about ¾ in dia with Hawkes Cut Glass – Grand Prize – Paris Ex – 1889 being put on all your glass before packing up."[3] There is no indication that this was done, however, and the trademark labels printed for Hawkes undoubtedly were used instead. This paper label was in use throughout the 1890s. It was succeeded by the acid-etched mark, which was slightly redesigned and now had "HAWKES" printed under the trefoil, about 1902 or 1903.

The first Hawkes advertisement so far found appeared in the *Pottery and Glassware Reporter*, a trade paper published in Pittsburgh. Hawkes paid $20 for the advertisement to run from June 4th to September 3, 1885 in the weekly paper, obviously hoping to publicize his glassware to his customers, jewelers, and china and glass sellers. The advertisement was simple and it had no art; it said: "T. G. Hawkes, /MANUFACTURER OF/ Rich Cut Glassware, /CORNING, N.Y./ We make a specialty of the finest Rich Cut table glassware. We keep a large assortment of our choicest goods in stock. / Catalogues and price lists furnished on application."[4]

1. Kenneth M. Wilson, *American Glass 1760–1930*, Hudson Hills Press, 1995, II, 843.
2. Homer Lee Bank Note Company, New York, to T. G. Hawkes, January 14, 1890.
3. J. Turner for Davis Collamore & Co. Ltd., New York, to T. G. Hawkes, January 18, 1890.
4. Invoice, *Pottery & Glassware Reporter*, Pittsburgh to T. G. Hawkes, July 1, 1885.

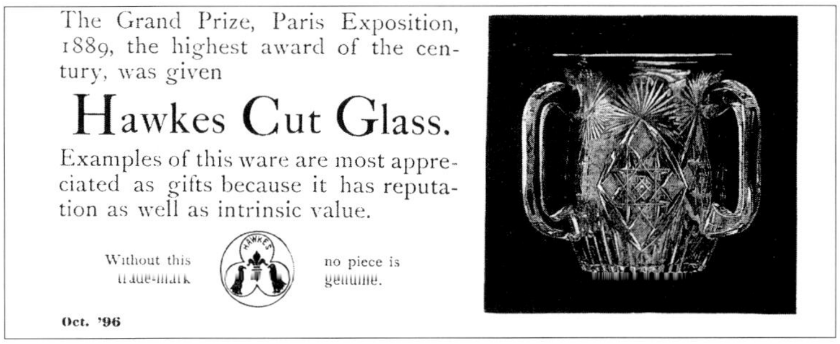

6-3. *Advertisement from The Century Magazine, December, 1896, p. 53. Courtesy Kurt Reed.*

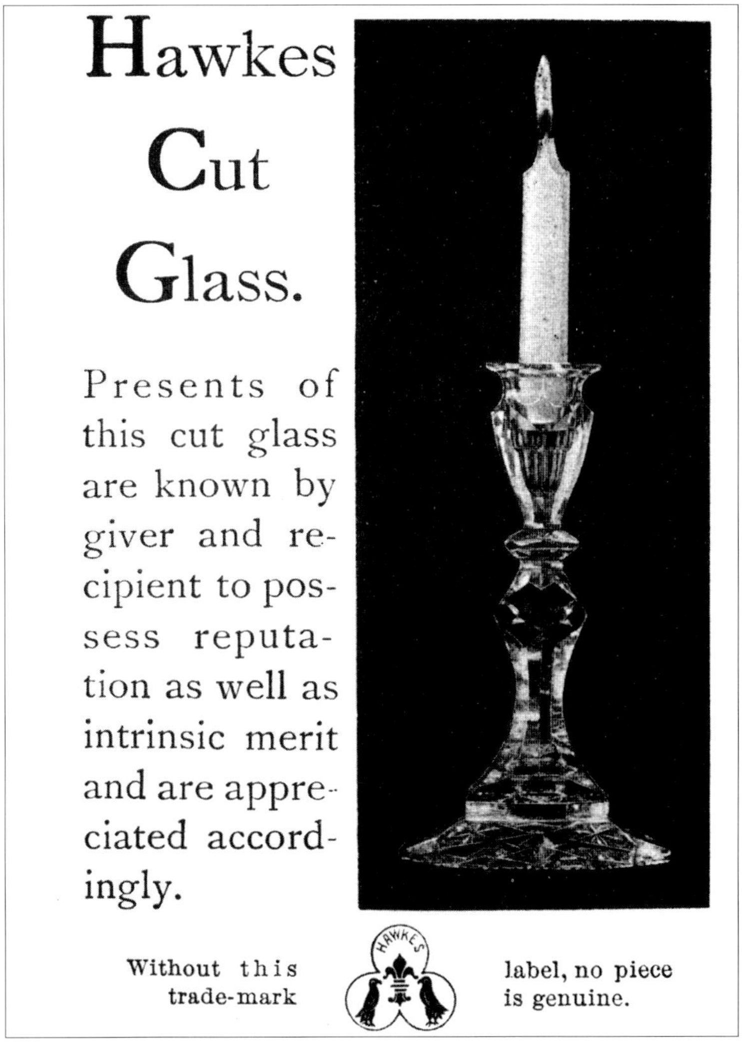

6-4. *Advertisement from The Century Magazine, October 1896, p. 33. Courtesy Kurt Reed.*

In January of 1887, J. E. Caldwell wrote to Hawkes suggesting that part of Caldwell's annual advertisement in the "Philadelphia Blue Book" should be devoted to Hawkes and that Hawkes should pay the $45. cost.[5] The Blue Book came out that June and annually until 1890 it included the Caldwell/Hawkes advertisement, another simple print one. It was a full page, about 4in by 6in, similar in text to that in the trade paper but which in 1889 emphasized "Richly Cut American Glass" and the fact that it was available in Philadelphia only through Caldwell.[6] Caldwell's own newspaper advertisement in 1889 said: "The Exquisite Crystal, CUT BY THOMAS G. HAWKES OF CORNING IS FOR SALE ONLY BY J. E.

5. J. E. Caldwell, Philadelphia to T. G. Hawkes, January 26, 1887.
6. Houston for Caldwell, to Hawkes, June 19, 1889.

6-5. The pattern on this 7in. plate is Lombard.

6-6. This jug is cut in Brazilian pattern.

6-5 through 6-10 are cutouts of advertisements of the early 1890s which are in the Hawkes archives pasted on to a ledger page which was originally used to record sales to J. Caldwell & Company The P & C. refers to Proctor & Collier, the firm which managed Hawkes' printing and advertising.

CALDWELL & CO." and it mentioned that prices were as low as those for inferior goods in other stores.[7]

The emphasis on American cut glass in retail advertisements was growing in the late 1880s but it was certainly stimulated by the Gold Medal Hawkes received at the 1889 Paris World's Fair. From then on Hawkes emphasized the medal in his advertising and other companies mentioned the superiority of American cut glass. Ovington Brothers was a large china and glass retailer in Brooklyn, and advertisements Ovington placed in the *Century Magazine* issues of September 1888 and November 1889 show this increasing emphasis. The 1888 advertisement says, "Some of the cut glass now produced rivals the…ornaments of rock crystal preserved in the royal cabinets of Europe, …and nowhere is it made in such perfection as in America." A year later, the Ovington advertisement says "Rich Cut Glass/Solid Silverware/ The growing demand for Cut Glass has influenced us to devote an entire room, 30 x 80, displaying an unparalleled exhibit of the highest grades of rich Cut Glass." Davis Collamore advertised in the same magazine two years later: "For years we have made a special feature of the best display of home manufactures that were obtainable, with such success that at the Paris Exposition of 1889 we secured for Hawkes' American Cut Glass — Grand Prize… Photographs of Cut Glass sent on application." Regrettably, no photographs accompany these earliest advertisements, but in the summer or fall of 1891, Hawkes began to use both photographs and a trademark in their advertising and to place advertisements for the retail market as well as the trade papers. Clearly,

7. L. Townsend for Caldwell to Hawkes, April 26, 1889.

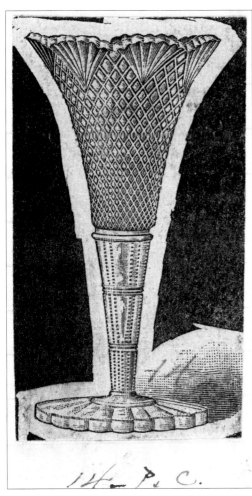

6-7. *This simple trumpet vase is cut in* Strawberry Diamond and Fan *pattern.*

6-8. *This* Lombard *pattern jug has exceptionally deep cutting on the handle.*

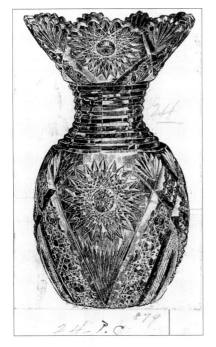

6-9. *This vase is cut in* Chrysanthemum *pattern.*

6-10. *This* Lombard *stemware, on solid stem blanks, is unusual.*

"brand recognition" was assuming greater importance.

By 1891, the Hawkes firm was sufficiently well known that it received a letter from Cyrus Curtis, publisher of the *Ladies Home Journal*, soliciting an advertisement in a special issue to be devoted to wine drinking in fashionable society.[8] Mr. Curtis said, "The tendency towards the use of aerated waters makes the subject of cut glass a matter of special interest to every society woman, and your advertisement in that particular issue would be so thoroughly apropos…" Unfortunately, a copy of the advertisement hasn't been located; if Hawkes took one, it was not on the same pages as the articles on drinking. By October, 1891 or perhaps that summer, the Hawkes firm placed monthly advertisements in *Harpers Monthly Magazine*, *Scribner's Magazine* and the *Century Magazine*, all of which were literary magazines with some advertising. The advertisements were consistent in showing a piece of glass, a line or two of text, a cut of the trademark surrounded by a circle, and the words, "No piece without this trademark is genuine"(the paper label) and "Hawkes Cut Glass" in various type styles. No mention of Corning is made, to avoid confusion

8. Cyrus H. K. Curtis, *The Ladies Home Journal*, Philadelphia to T. G. Hawkes & Co., October 24, 1891.

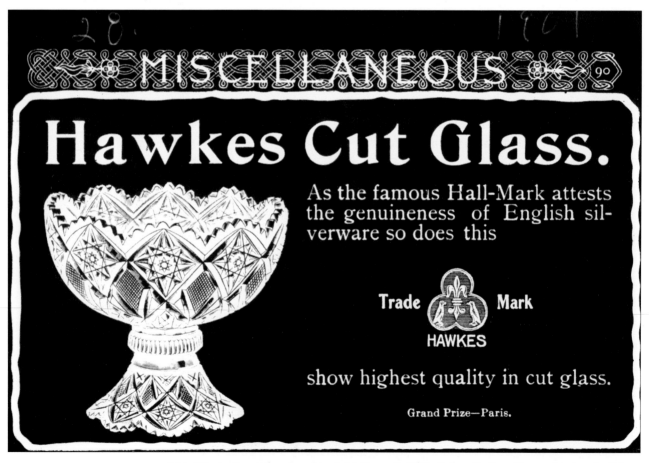

6-11. *This advertisement from the archives is dated in pencil, 1901. It shows the first acid-stamped trademark which seems to have been used briefly about that time.*

6-12. *This advertisement for monogrammed stemware is dated "Dec. 1908".*

6-13. *This advertisement for a rose vase was in a 1908 publication, probably the* Journal.

with Hoare and Corning Glass Works. The patterns shown in these early advertisements are usually the patented ones, *Brazilian, Chrysanthemum, Grecian,* and *Venetian,* although *Imperial* and the cheaper *Strawberry Diamond & Fan* appear, too. By 1891, Hawkes had opened an account with Proctor & Collier, a printing and advertising company in Cincinnati, and the advertisements were placed through that firm, probably for a monthly stipend. By 1901, the account books show monthly payments to Proctor & Collier of $285.00 specifically for advertisements in the *Ladies Home Journal* and the advertisements in the literary magazines were gradually phased out.

In the late 1890s, the Hawkes firm produced its first advertising booklet "HAWKES CUT GLASS" which had a terra cotta sculpture showing a glasscutter on the cover and a picture of the trademark along with a list of patterns made, on the inside. It's impossible to date this exactly, but the design of the cover is very similar to a that of a booklet on Rookwood Pottery, a Cincinnati company which exhibited with Hawkes and Davis Collamore in Paris. The Rookwood booklet was advertised in the December 1896 issue of *Century Magazine* and internal evidence dates the Hawkes booklet to after 1896 and before 1901. The account book for 1901 shows a payment to Proctor & Collier in December for an October printing bill of $463.30 which may be for this book or the second edition of it. On page 21 of the book is a print of the circled trademark seen in the 1890s advertisements with the text, "'Hawkes Cut Glass' invariably bears this trade-mark on a label of this size pasted upon each piece…" It seems likely that the print run of this book was small, because only one copy has been noted so far. The book was intended for Hawkes's customers, the jewelry and china and glassware stores, and it was probably mailed to them in time for the Christmas sales.

A second edition of the book was produced probably between 1901 and 1905.

6-14. The Colonial pattern jug appeared in the Ladies Home Journal in Jan. 1909.

6-15. This advertisement for a fern or flower holder in Constance pattern is dated 1909.

The covers are the same (with the old trademark on the back cover) and the text is nearly the same, but the pieces used as illustrations are different, the list of patterns is somewhat different, and the revised version of the trademark is listed with the words, " 'Hawkes Cut Glass' invariably bears this trade-mark engraved on each piece." It is this trademark, with more hawk-like birds and "HAWKES" below the mark instead of within it, which is found on most Hawkes glass. It was registered in 1905 although it may have been designed earlier.

There was also an intermediate mark, since one advertisement found, dated 1901 and printed in *Century Magazine*, shows a trefoil with the duck-like birds, the word "HAWKES" below, and the text, "As the famous Hall-Mark attests the genuineness of English silverware so does this trade mark show highest quality in cut glass."(Fig. 6–11) This appears on two pieces in the Corning Museum collection[9], and is usually referred to as the "old mark" although it is not exactly the same as the original design on the paper label. I have never seen a trade-marked piece with "HAWKES" within the trefoil at the top instead of below it. As it was registered, the "old mark" of 1903 did not include the word "HAWKES" either within the trefoil or below it, but as it is found on the glass, the name is always there. The Hawkes stationery in use in 1917, when Sam Hawkes wrote to the Smithsonian about his gift to the U.S. National Museum, shows the trademark with HAWKES both within the trefoil and below it, and so it seems that the marks were not as standardized as one would like to think. It is likely that all of the acid-stamped pieces date from after 1900.

Several copies of the second edition of the booklet have survived, and it was reprinted on newsprint by a collectors' club about twenty-five years ago. The illustration of a pot maker also has been published in a book about the Boston & Sandwich Glass Company so it is possible that some of the illustrations in this

9. E. S. Farrar and J. S. Spillman, *The Complete Cut & Engraved Glass of Corning*, Crown Publishers, 1979, p. 71, Ill. 173, p. 117, Ill. 424.

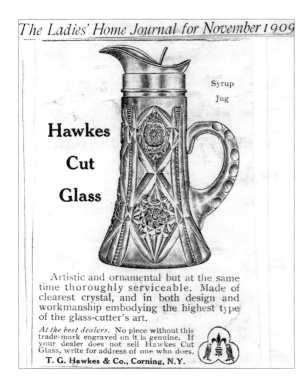

6-16. *This syrup jug in Vermont pattern was used in the Ladies Home Journal in November, 1909.*

6-17. *This monogrammed sherbet cup and plate was advertised in the Ladies Home Journal, in October 1910.*

booklet were generic, provided by Proctor and Collier.[10] Two more advertising brochures were printed in 1904. The covers of these are signed "F.C. '04" and "F.C. '05", indicating that Frederick Carder designed them. One brochure is called, "HAWKES CUT GLASS" and the other is "HAWKES ROCK CRYSTAL AND GRAVIC GLASS." These two books are much smaller in format than the first and they have illustrations of individual pieces, but none of glassmaking or glass cutting. The cut glass booklet has no pattern names, but two of the four pieces shown in the engraved glass book are called simply Rock Crystal Design and the others are engraved in *Gravic Carnation* and *Gravic Chrysanthemum* patterns. The copies of these books in the Hawkes Archives are the only ones so far found, so very few copies seem to have been printed.

The advertisements placed in *The Ladies Home Journal* from 1902, and in *The Jewelers Circular*, a trade paper, are very similar and show a piece of glass, the new trademark with text about it appearing on every piece, and the words, "Hawkes Cut Glass." The location, "Corning, N.Y.", and the full name of the firm, T. G. Hawkes & Co., appear in the trade papers, but not in the *Ladies Home Journal* until 1907. The patterns and shapes show much more variety than in the earlier advertisements, but alas, few pattern names are mentioned. Many of the illustrated pieces are the same as those in the second edition of "Hawkes Cut Glass." *Queen's* pattern shows up in a 1907 advertisement and was probably new around that time; *Pueblo* also appears at this time.

A brochure of about 1905–1910, entitled "Hawkes Glass Services", shows several sets of lightweight stemware with monograms. Four of these are "Optical", which means mold-blown with shallow ribs which can be seen but not felt on the exterior. The plain paneled Colonial pattern is also featured and the brochure invites buyers to consider building a service of glassware in increments over several years, one of the few times when a Hawkes publication stressed economy rather than quality or beauty.

10. I am indebted to Vincent Ortelli for drawing this to my attention.

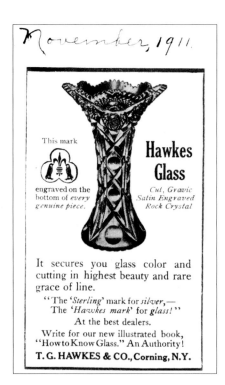

6-18. *This advertisement for a vase was in a November, 1911 publication, probably the Ladies Home Journal.*

6-19. *This centerpiece in Lorraine pattern was advertised by Hawkes around 1905. At least two examples of this design are known, although its large size makes it a rarity.*

In 1910 and 1911, Hawkes produced a series of small brochures, each illustrating a single piece, which were coordinated with the monthly advertising in the *Ladies Home Journal*. Some showed pieces which had been advertised before, but occasionally new patterns are featured, for example, *Starlight* which is shown in a flyer dated December 1, 1911. Only a few of these flyers are dated, but some have the names of jewelry stores, and a notice from Hawkes indicates that jewelers were offered a free supply of flyers with their name if they sent out a mailing. Several of the Gravic patterns are featured in these flyers, along with *Panel*, and a rock crystal engraved pattern called *Renaissance* which was one of Hawkes's most expensive patterns. I had previously thought this pattern dated from the 1920s, but it can now be shown to have been popular a decade earlier.[11] However, although it was no longer in production by the early 1920s, replacement orders were filled and Sarah Hawkes Thornton, Samuel Hawkes's daughter, remembers taking an order for an entire set of this pattern when she worked for her father during the summer of 1925. Most pieces of this pattern, however, can be dated to 1910–1915; Mrs. Thornton remembers that the 1925 set had to be specially made because it had been discontinued for some years.

A Salad or Berry Bowl in *Old English* is shown in an August 1910 flyer with a text which mentions its "18th century charm of line" and by 1914, Richard Briggs's Christmas brochure, which has a page devoted to "Hawkes' American Cut Glass", says "Messrs. Hawkes have this Fall reproduced many of the old English designs, as the Georgian…Adams…Hepplewhite."

In 1911, Hawkes published another, new booklet, "How to Know Glass", which replaced the earlier booklets.[12] The format of the new book is much the same as those of the old, but the illustrations and listed patterns are somewhat different. In 1918, T. G. Hawkes & Company included a copy of this booklet in its gift to the Smithsonian Institution so it was in print for at least seven years, and probably much longer. A study of the advertisements in the *Jewelers Circular*

11. E. S. Farrar and J. S. Spillman, *The Complete Cut & Engraved Glass of Corning*, Crown Publishers, 1979, p. 100, Fig. 332.
12. *Harper's Monthly Magazine*, October 1911.

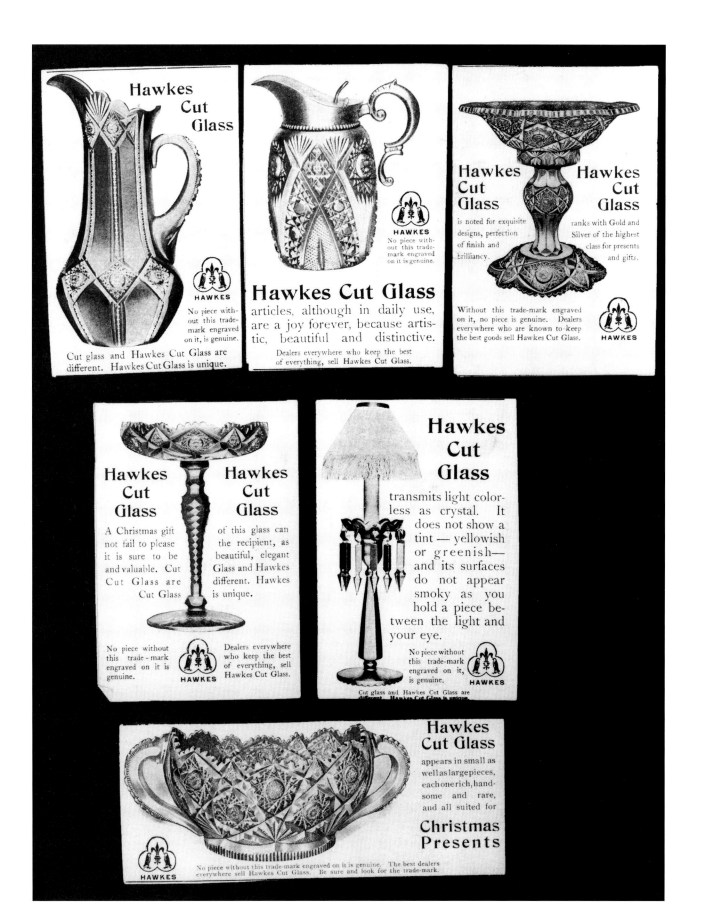

6-21. *Group of advertisements from the Hawkes archives, probably all dated around 1905–1910.*

MAKE May a Money-maker! Set these spring days to working for you by artistic displays of Hawkes Cut Glass.

This is the season when the light, the graceful, the fresh-and-simple particularly appeal.

The Ladies' Home Journal and Good Housekeeping May advertisement opposite shows that we are using this bit of psychology ourselves—

Bound to turn the town's eye "Hawkesward"—with good team action!

Yours very truly,
T. G. HAWKES & CO.
Corning, N. Y.

Good Taste in Glass
The pure crystalline quality that leaves decoration a matter wholly of surface and form is more and more prized.
Hawkes Cut Glass
has extreme delicacy of tone and an elegance achieved by lines of perfect simplicity and grace. It is the artistic choice.
At the best dealers. No piece without this trade-mark engraved on it is genuine. If your dealer does not sell Hawkes Cut Glass, write for address of one who does.
T. G. Hawkes & Co., Corning, N. Y.

6-22. Brochure featuring a compote and distributed in May, 1909.

Easter in Glass
Rarely will you find so happy an expression of whiteness, brilliance and beauty as
Hawkes Cut Glass
Ordinary cut glass may become commonplace as a gift—Hawkes Cut Glass is not the same thing. It is a creation by itself, possessing the elegance that removes certain work in precious metals from the merely "intrinsic" and gives it the value of *art.*
At the best dealers.
No piece without this trade-mark engraved on it is genuine. If your dealer does not sell Hawkes Cut Glass, write us for address of one who does.
T. G. Hawkes & Co., Corning, N. Y.

YOUR CLIENTELE shares the growing custom of Easter gift-giving.

Good! Encourage them by opportune displays of Hawkes Cut Glass.

As we say in our Ladies' Home Journal March advertisement, people feel the harmony between Hawkes purity and Easter sentiment.

That is, they do when it is suggested to them.

A special occasion for attracting new trade lies right here.

Don't let it pass!

Yours very truly,
T. G. HAWKES & CO.
Corning, N. Y.

6-23. Brochure featuring a vase.

Renaissance Goblet in Hawkes Rock Crystal

The Charm of Crystal

The peculiar attraction of a delicate medium handled with daring skill is found in Hawkes Rock Crystal.

Designs showing the play of the glass engraver's wheel are marvels of decorative ingenuity.

No surface offers so beautiful a relief for the well-executed designs as Hawkes Rock Crystal.

In color the perfect, dazzling white admired by connoisseurs; the engraving chastely, exquisitely done; the lines the acme of grace.

The collection of a set in Hawkes Crystal offers a fascinating interest to women and men of taste.

Our display of Hawkes Rock Crystal is rich in beautiful pieces. Come in and study this most artistic of fine glass.

Yours very cordially,

GRAINGER–HANNAN CO.
Detroit, Michigan

6-24. Brochure featuring a goblet in the Renaissance pattern.

Weekly, which appeared in nearly every issue from 1904 until 1930, shows how the Hawkes firm adjusted its product line to suit changing tastes. Until 1911, the illustrated pieces are all heavily cut and the advertisement headline reads "Hawkes Cut Glass." In 1910 and 1911, there are several full-page advertisements touting the quality of Hawkes glass "cut from the solid blank" rather than from pressed blanks. A 20 inch "Alice" vase, a 15 inch *Panel* plate, and a Gravic tray engraved with fruits are shown in these advertisements, which seem to be an attempt to revive interest in heavily cut glass.

By 1915, the advertisements are smaller, the phrase "Hawkes Cut Glass" has disappeared and the tag line is "T. G. Hawkes & Co., Manufacturers of Glassware, Cut, Engraved and Silver Mounted." The advertisement in the September 1, 1915 issue is for "Bridal Veil Glass" which, to judge from the description, seems to be Steuben's Verre de Soie with engraving. The next month's advertisement shows the White House *Russian* service with the line, "The United States Government uses Hawkes Glass" and that seems to be the last time cut glass was shown. Engraved glass is featured for the next decade, most of it rather simple. Engraved auto vases were featured in 1917 and 1918. The advertisement for January 22, 1919 lists Hawkes products as "Cut Glass, Engraved Glass, Rock Crystal Glass,

Hawkes Cut Glass

9-IN. FOOTED FRUIT BOWL

UNEQUALED and unvarying
quality of glass, originality of
design and brilliancy of cut makes
it distinctive—*dependable.*

No piece without
this trade-mark en-
graved on it is genu-
ine. If your dealer
does not sell Hawkes
Cut Glass, please
write us for address
of dealer who does.

T. G. HAWKES & CO., Corning, N. Y.

Distinctive!
Dependable!

These two words designate the kind of
cut glass upon which the most profitable,
permanent business can be built.

Show brilliantly beautiful designs—you
make sales at the best prices by the very
superiority of your display.

Have your line known as absolutely
flawless—you make steady customers of
the most desirable trade.

The unequaled variety of Hawkes designs is being constantly increased. The
Hawkes reputation for unvarying perfection
grows stronger with every piece sold.

The bowl opposite, shown in the February Ladies' Home Journal, is bound to be
a great favorite—is sure to add much to
the prestige of its seller.

Why not order it with the other pieces
you need to fill out stock depleted by holiday business?

Yours very truly,
T. G. HAWKES & CO.

6-25. Brochure featuring a footed fruit bowl in Raleigh pattern.

The *grace* of
glass and its value
as a medium for the
play of light de-
pend upon its *color*—

Hawkes
Cut Glass

is the sought-for,
flawless *white.* Con-
noisseurs will tell
you that this ex-
quisite transpar-
ency and the
Hawkes *cutting* are
the "ne plus
ultra" of glass
art.

At the best dealers. No piece without this
trade-mark engraved on it is genuine. If
your dealer does not sell Hawkes Cut
Glass, write for address of one who does.
T. G. Hawkes & Co., Corning, N. Y.

"Knee Deep in June"

That's the condition our dealers are apt
to be in this month.

There seem to be more matrimony, more
graduating, more "bridge," "showers,"
anniversaries and general celebration what-
not than usual.

More bungalows and big country houses
and modest suburbanettes are going up.

Is it prosperity? Or is it perspicacity?
Both we think. People—larger numbers
of them—are finding that they can afford
the best. Dealers are steadily coming into
line with the theory that it is wisdom, fore-
sight, money in the bank and a number of
other good things to meet this commercial
"uplift" with a representative stock of
Hawkes Cut Glass.

Hawkes, not only because it is the best,
but because its sale is *confined to the jewelry
trade.* No price-cutting competition from
department stores. Therefore, you owe it
to yourself to co-operate with us.

This Ladies' Home Journal ad for June,
seen by every woman within your buying
horizon, *is triply profitable* if immediately
followed by strong local advertising.

Yours very truly,
T. G. HAWKES & CO.,
Corning. New York.

6-26. Brochure featuring a vase advertised in the June and July, 1910 issues of
the Ladies Home Journal.

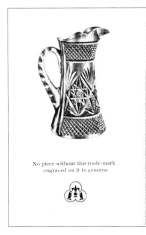

No piece without this trade-mark
engraved on it is genuine

"The Choice of the Connoisseur"

Hawkes Cut Glass possesses qualities of color,
form and surface which have won for it the preference among judges of rare wares.

The decoration of a Hawkes piece is beautifully
proportioned to the lines of the design. It is in
the forms themselves that beauty is chiefly sought
for, in the frank and natural play of line and light.

The changing taste in table glass is happily
reflected by a "Hawkes" group. The delicacy,
grace and exquisite fashioning of Hawkes pieces
when compared with the heavy, uninspiring glass
of the well-loaded table twenty-five years ago,
proves how thoroughly these artists have mastered
the possibilities of their material.

As a *gift* Hawkes Cut Glass is peculiarly desirable, a tribute to cultivated taste. For the adorn-
ment of the home table the touch of refinement,
the glint of beauty secured by even the simplest
design, is a delight to the leisure of the eye.

We shall take pleasure in showing our rich
collection of Hawkes Cut Glass comprising the
latest designs.

HENRY YOSTE
JEWELER
Vicksburg, Miss.

6-27. Brochure featuring a water jug.

Salad or Berry Bowl,
"Old English"

Old English glass long recalled to
connoisseurs the zenith of the glass
designer's art. In

Hawkes Cut Glass

18th century charm of line is en-
hanced by greater richness and craft
in cutting and by a glory of colour
unrivalled among the artistic wares
of the world.

At the best dealers. No piece without this
trade-mark engraved on it is genuine. If
your dealer does not sell Hawkes Cut
Glass, write for address of one who does.
T. G. Hawkes & Co., Corning, N. Y.

August!
"No season slow
Unless made so."

August spells apathy for some lines, but
it plays right into the hand of "Hawkes."

We talk a good deal about *color* in our
ads and rightly, for it's the *sine qua non* of
fine glass and one of *the* beauties of Hawkes.

Consider, then, the dazzling, perfect
white of a Hawkes piece with the vivid
tone of the raspberry, the luscious pink of
a melon, and naturally Hawkes fruit bowls,
canteloupe plates, etc., make a strong appeal to the August imagination.

The current ad in the Ladies' Home
Journal shows one of the most taking
Hawkes designs of the year.

The effect of this ad on your clientele
will be doubly electrical if you continue
the good work with newspaper ads and
window attractions.

Hawkes Glass gains additional character
and elegance by the fact that it is a *jeweler's specialty* and cannot be bought at
department stores.

With cordial wishes for "the golden
month."

Yours very truly,
T. G. HAWKES & CO.

6-28. Brochure featuring an Old English salad or fruit bowl advertised in the
August, 1910 issue of the Ladies Home Journal.

Sterling Silver-Mounted Glass, Decorated Gold Glass, Decorated Enameled Glass,
Auto Vases, Desk Sets, Cigarette Boxes, Monograms, Engraved and Gold
Decorated, Colored Glass, Old English and Irish Glass, Period Glass, Odd
Matchings." Although it is not mentioned in the advertisements until the 1920s,
the block letter, acid-stamped "HAWKES" was in use by 1917, since several pieces
given to the Smithsonian in that year were marked that way.

The trade paper advertisements are headed "Hawkes Glass" with an occasional
subheading "Hawkes Crystal Glass" until July 1924, when the heading was
changed to "Hawkes Crystal." T. G. Hawkes & Company continued to use this
heading for most of their advertising until 1962. Among the oddities in the
1920s advertisements are a silver plate bail handle, guaranteed to turn an ordinary
plate into a more salable sandwich plate or a cake tray, and Hawkes "Lucina
Crystal", "a new form of glassware that has all the soft, subdued dignity of
pottery, yet without sacrificing the luster, sheen and brilliance of crystal." The
decoration was hand-painted and fired, according to the text.[13]

Hawkes "Le Verre de Juane"[sic] or Glass of Yellow, a translucent glassware with
an alabaster-like finish, was mentioned in 1921. Floral designs were to be added
to the vases, but the advertisement does not specify if they are engraved or

13. *The Jewelers Circular,* December 21,
1920.

153

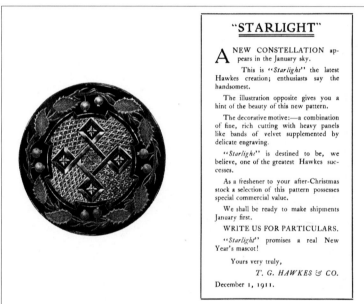

6-29A and B. Two views of a
brochure showing a piece in
Hawkes' new Starlight pattern
introduced in 1911.

enameled.[14] A number of simple patterns are shown in the advertisements, *Laurel*,
Marjorie, *Amy*, *Reo*, *Clermont*, *Sheraton*, *Empire*, and *Kismet* in 1919, *Milliards* in 1920, *Clyde*
in 1921, *Dorcas* in 1922, *Arcadia* and *Lila* in 1923, and *Alpine* and *Newport* in 1924.

In the mid-1920s, Hawkes again produced a series of brochures for customers,
this time showing gold and silver banded tableware with no other decoration
(May 1924); a "Hampton Vase" decorated with engraving and opaque enamels
(June 1924); the new "Killarney Crystal" with green stems and feet and engraved
shamrocks; pieces with golf themes, a mah-jong patterned iced-tea set (March 1,
1924) and the first mention of "Singing Waterford" (July 1, 1925). The Proctor
& Collier Company was still printing the brochures and the advertising was now
being placed in *Good Housekeeping* and *House And Garden*, but not necessarily every
month. Another brochure, probably from about 1924–25, is headed "Hawkes

6-30A. and B. Toupee stand in Starlight pattern. T. G. Hawkes & Company about. 1911–1915, D. 17.8cm.
Courtesy Mr. and Mrs. Lowell Switzer. Crofford photo.

6-32. *Printed advertisement for Hawkes French dressing bottle, about 1915–1925. This was intended for use in a store.*

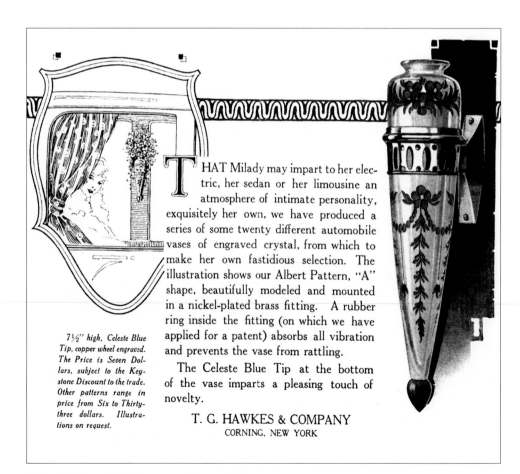

7½" high. Celeste Blue Tip, copper wheel engraved. The Price is Seven Dollars, subject to the Keystone Discount to the trade. Other patterns range in price from Six to Thirtythree dollars. Illustrations on request.

THAT Milady may impart to her electric, her sedan or her limousine an atmosphere of intimate personality, exquisitely her own, we have produced a series of some twenty different automobile vases of engraved crystal, from which to make her own fastidious selection. The illustration shows our Albert Pattern, "A" shape, beautifully modeled and mounted in a nickel-plated brass fitting. A rubber ring inside the fitting (on which we have applied for a patent) absorbs all vibration and prevents the vase from rattling.

The Celeste Blue Tip at the bottom of the vase imparts a pleasing touch of novelty.

T. G. HAWKES & COMPANY
CORNING, NEW YORK

6-33. *Advertisement for Hawkes automobile vases, 1917.*

6-34. *Advertisement for use in a jewelry or department store, about 1925.*

Crystal Glass" and features the patterns R. C. [rock crystal] *Aquila, Sheraton,* and *Satin Engraved Augusta,* probably the three types of patterns Hawkes made, that is polished engraving, cut, and matte finished engraving.

A flyer with the penciled date, August 1, 1925 is clearly aimed at wholesale buyers and mentions that Hawkes will advertise in color in *House and Garden* in October, November, and December. The flyer describes a new 36-piece line of "Singing Waterford," (the re-named Old English line) a dozen new crystal table services, including some in green or blue engraved or with Sterling trim, *Navarre* pattern gold-encrusted crystal, *Gloria, Avalon, Granada, Valencia,* and *Milo* patterns in clear engraved crystal, and *Kashmir* and *Rosalie* patterns in rock crystal.[15] The gold-encrusted and clear engraved pieces start at $1.00 a stem while the rock crystal patterns are only slightly more expensive at $21 and $14.50 a dozen. The green or blue pieces start at $1.00 apiece with gold decoration and at $3.00 with engraving or silver mounting. Locked whiskey bottles with matching glasses, cocktail shakers, ice pails, pocket flasks and single drink flasks seem typical of the 1920s as do smoking accessories, and the brochure also lists a full line of table and gift ware.

One of Samuel Hawkes's more interesting advertising ideas appeared in 1927. An article in *The Jewelers' Circular* describes "One of the Largest Cut Glass Vases in the World" which the firm had just produced: "An American glassmaker, John Lofquist, is known as the strongest man in the glass industry and as a proof of his prowess completed in 1905 seven of the largest glass vases ever turned out by a glass factory. T. G. Hawkes & Co., ...heard of the existence of these vases and immediately began negotiations to possess them... The molten glass which Lofquist had to handle on the end of a blow pipe in shaping this vase must have

15. This brochure was rendered partially illegible by the flood of 1972 and all of the pattern names can't be read.

157

weighed at least 55 pounds. A large part of the time this weight had to be handled "free hand," that is, without the aid of any support for the pipe. The pipe acts as a lever, making it a much greater strain to handle the weight on the end of the pipe than as if a weight of 55 pounds were lifted directly in the hands... H. A. Jacoby, the superintendent of the Hawkes plant, says it is doubtful if so large a vase will again be made for many years to come. The vase... is by far the largest of them all and has been in the process of decoration for some time. The work of decorating has all been done by Corning glass cutting artist in the Hawkes employ. The decoration is by John Demuth and Alexander Perry and the finishing by Nicholas Bach and Paul Ambersone. In order to decorate the vase, a system of pulleys and a portable platform had to be built, as the decorators could not possibly hold and manipulate this heavy article during the process of decoration, The 'Old Singing Waterford' design was used for the decoration. The vase is for American Beauty roses."[16]

A picture of Samuel Hawkes "decorating" the giant vase accompanied the article, and the vase was shown in the next photographic catalog issued by

16. *The Jewelers Circular*, August 17, 1927.

6-35. *Advertisement showing three Hawkes rock crystal engraved patterns, Aquila, Calais, and Dawn, about 1925.*

6-36. *Picture taken for publicity purposes of Samuel Hawkes "working" on the big vase purchased from Union Glass Works in 1927.*

Hawkes. It was 32 inches tall, 10 inches across the top and the price was set at $500. The vase was displayed in the Hawkes showroom for a number of years, and its original printed showroom label is now in the Hawkes archives. Unfortunately, its present whereabouts are unknown, as is the location of the four other blanks which were purchased at the same time. They may never have been cut, since the biggest one didn't sell. Lofquist was a blower at the Union Glass Works in Somerville, Massachusetts and his abilities as a blower were described in a letter from Julian de Cordova to Samuel Hawkes. Cordova closed his company in 1927, and this is probably why the large blanks were available. Lofquist had blown the blank for the gigantic punchbowl which the Tiffany store exhibited in 1904 and the Union reaped a considerable amount of publicity for his skills at that time.[17]

A two inch square booklet printed in the late 1920s is called "What is Glass or HAWKES Crystal Glass versus JUST GLASS" and it seems designed to be given to customers who purchased the glass. The text deals mainly with the formulas for "Hawkes Crystal, Hawkes Ruby, Blue, Green and Amber Glass" as well as with Old Singing Waterford, suggesting that these were the lines the company was pushing hardest at the time.

Late in 1928, a Hawkes advertisement mentions that rock crystal glass has been increasingly popular for several months and that Hawkes has goblets in rock crystal patterns from $14.50 to $500 a dozen, net.[18] The advertisement was repeated several times without illustrations, but by the following February, Hawkes was illustrating his *DuBarry Goblet*, #4091 which retailed for $600 a dozen. The *"DuBarry"* pattern was shown in the advertisements for several months, several times in a full-page advertisements, but it seems unlikely that many sets were sold. $600 may have been the wholesale price since a 1929 advertisement from an unspecified magazine shows the price as $1200 for a dozen goblets. The National Museum of American History has one *DuBarry* goblet, the gift of Mrs. Thornton. If no sets were ordered, this goblet may be the only example surviving.

By 1930, the Hawkes advertisements were again full-page and for several months they featured the "Waterford" patterns. In 1931 a brochure for the Waterford line illustrated the *Munster Waterford*, *Walpole Waterford*, and *Marquess of Waterford* patterns and included the tag line, "Makers of Rock Crystal Glassware for over Half a Century." A companion brochure, in a larger format, is called "The Romance of Beautiful Crystal Glassware" and it illustrates several patterns of rock crystal stemware including *Belvidere*, *Ceres*, *Cavalier*, and *Empire* (see 2-52) as well as the cut *Marquess of Waterford* pattern. The prices range from $30 a dozen for *Ceres* goblets to $500 a dozen for the *Empire* pattern goblets; by comparison, the *Marquess of Waterford* goblets were $114 a dozen. That was the most expensive of the Waterford patterns which seem to have been the only cut patterns advertised around 1930. A final brochure, "Hawkes Crystal Glass" which illustrates the *Waterford York* pattern and the *R. C. Riviera* pattern, but without prices, is probably

17. *China, Glass and Pottery Review*, November 1904; *Somerville Journal*, December 9, 1904, p. 10; *Boston Post*, December 11, 1904, p. 2.
18. *The Jewelers Circular*, February 2, 1928.

6-37. *Advertisement for rock crystal stemware in Corfu (left) and Du Barry (right) patterns. The Corfu is $45.00 for a dozen glasses, the Du Barry is $1200.*

from the late 1930s or the 1940s. All three of the last advertising brochures say "The name Hawkes or this trademark" appears on every piece. However, the use of "HAWKES" on stemware dates from before World War I and the single name mark was commonly used by Hoare and Sinclaire as well.

Hawkes had an agent in San Francisco for a few months in 1910, but that was apparently unsuccessful. In 1920, another was selected and throughout the 1920s the advertisements mention a Pacific-Coast office on Geary Street in San Francisco, and by the end of 1925, a New York office at 542 Fifth Avenue. The New York office was still open in the same location until 1949 and for a good part of that period was managed by Penrose Hawkes, a cousin of Samuel. A Canadian agent in Montreal was also tried for a few months in the early 1920s, but like the West Coast office, he turned out to be too expensive for the amount of business he produced.

Christmas advertisements in November and December, 1932 show rather more elaborate pieces. It is possible that Hawkes prospered for several more years. However, the general picture to be gained from the advertisements and the advertising brochures is one of declining interest in cut and engraved glass, at least on the part of the buying public. Samuel Hawkes was interviewed for the August 29, 1929 issue of *Printer's Ink* and he subsequently reprinted the article for customers. In his article, "Craftsmanship will never be crowded out", he stressed the quality of the Hawkes products and the fact that he chose to keep the company small in order to maintain its quality.

6-20. Centerpiece cut in Lorraine pattern, about 1905. H. 35.8 cm., trade-marked. Courtesy Martin Folb. Folb photo.

6-31. Cardboard advertising stand for a French dressing bottle, and bottle, about 1915–1925. H. (bottle) 19cm. Gift of Otto Hilbert (CMG 75.4.82).

Methods of Selling Glass and Customer Relations

By 1883, Hawkes had established a customer list on which Davis Collamore & Company of New York was his most important customer, closely followed by Richard Briggs in Boston and J. E. Caldwell and Company in Philadelphia. Briggs and Collamore were china, glass, and tableware establishments in the highest price range and Caldwell was a jeweler. For most of the life of the company, Hawkes continued to target jewelers and "china houses" as its principal customers, although the firm did sell directly to some retail customers in Corning and the Corning region. After the establishment of a showroom in New York in 1925, orders were taken in New York as well. By that date, however, Davis Collamore & Company had closed. The firm also sold glass to department stores, especially the upscale department stores like Wanamaker's in Philadelphia, after most of the china and glass houses were closed.

Many of the letters in the 1880s are from customers, mostly in New York state, who wanted to order glassware directly from the factory, a practice which seems to have been customary then. Hawkes usually filled the orders; however, it is clear from the correspondence that in the 1890s, Hawkes generally referred private inquirers to one of the jewelers who carried his line. A number of these steady customers had glass on consignment. Hawkes would send a shipment which he selected twice a year, and the jeweler sent a monthly statement saying how much had been sold and remitted payment. At the same time, many of these retailers were ordering "specials" from Hawkes, so the monthly payments were usually larger than the payments for the consigned pieces.

This was obviously a somewhat risky way of doing business, since customers occasionally defaulted on consigned goods. In the main though, it seems to have worked well for the Hawkes firm during the 1880s and most of the 1890s. Most of the consignment customers had a monopoly of Hawkes goods in their area and most of them were adamant about keeping this exclusivity, especially Briggs and Caldwell. Collamore requested an exclusive arrangement more than once, but Hawkes seemed reluctant to give it to him. Ovington, a Brooklyn competitor, had Hawkes glass on consignment as did the Dorflinger retail store. The following stores had "memo" accounts with Hawkes in the 1880s and early 1890s: D. B. Bedell, New York; M. W. Beveridge, Washington; Richards Briggs, Boston; Bullard Brothers, Minneapolis; Burley & Company, Chicago; J. E. Caldwell, Philadelphia; Davis Collamore & Company Ltd., New York; Gilman Collamore, New York; C. Dorflinger & Sons, New York; Nathan, Dohrmann & Company, San Francisco; Edgar Everett, Troy, N.Y.; John Foote, Cleveland; Jacquard Watch & Jewelry Company, Kansas City; Mermod & Jacquard, St. Louis; John Mitchell, Addison, N.Y.; Phelps & Adams, San Francisco; Joseph Seymour & Sons, Syracuse; Sheaffer & Lloyd, Pittsburgh; Sherwood & Golden, Utica; Uberroth & Company, Bay City, Mich.; Jules Wendell, Oswego, N.Y.; J. T. Wise, Elmira; Wright, Kay & Sons, Detroit. This list is incomplete and Hawkes had many more customers than the ones to whom he extended this courtesy. By the early 1890s, Hawkes had begun to phase the memo business out and when inquiries were made, the letter writers

7-1. Suitcase with samples carried by a Hawkes salesman, probably in the 1930s and 1940s. The samples, see Figs. 7-2 through 7-7, may not have all been in production at the same time as they seem to be from a lengthy time span.

Courtesy Robert F. Rockwell, Jr.

were told that Hawkes no longer operated in this manner. That was a slight exaggeration, however. While Hawkes does not appear to have opened any new memo accounts in the 1890s, he did continue to serve his best customers "on memo" until the end of the decade. An 1888 list of "Goods on Memorandum" has seventeen customers, with amounts ranging from $175.00 for D. B. Bedell to over $2500 for Collamore and $1800 for Dorflinger, all three in New York City.[1] A detailed list sent to Davis Collamore early in 1889 indicates that they had at all times $3000 or $4000 worth of Hawkes glass on hand and since they often paid for it several months after it was bought, they paid the Corning firm several hundred dollars a year in interest on the outstanding debt. Briggs operated the same way and frequently paid Hawkes with "notes" which came due six months later. Most of the other companies settled every month, although they often had to be reminded to do so.

Although there are several references in the letters to a Hawkes catalog, Hawkes did not issue a printed catalog until after 1903, judging from those that survive. The earliest printed catalog, as distinct from booklets distributed to customers, may be the one which says in its introduction that the company was founded "thirty-three years ago", which dates the catalog to about 1913.

The earliest letters make it clear that in the 1880s the "catalogue" was in fact a box of photographs, several sets of which have survived. The photographs were mounted on cards with prices sometimes printed and sometimes entered by hand, and this arrangement made it possible to add and delete items from the line easily. The prices given were retail and stores were advised that they would have a discount of 50% from the prices marked. The box was often mailed to customers who returned them with their orders. Otherwise, the salesmen carried the photographs along with sample pieces when they traveled. In 1887, Hawkes borrowed from Caldwell "photograph books" of Dorflinger, Mt. Washington, and the New England Glass Company, and soon after he produced his own large

1. "Goods on Memorandum", December 28, 1888, letter book, p. 534.

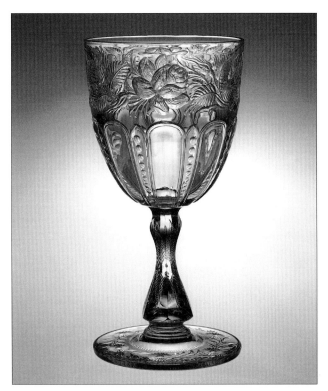

7-2.*Cut and engraved goblet, probably 1920–1930. H. 17cm, trade-marked. Courtesy Robert F. Rockwell, Jr.*

7-3.*Wineglass in Rock Crystal pattern, probably 1930–1940. H. 16cm, trade-marked. Courtesy Robert F. Rockwell, Jr.*

format photographic catalog, which was constantly being updated. This, too, was sent by mail to stores. "We have a catalogue which we can send you, if you desire it, but of course as we keep getting up new goods all the time, it is almost impossible to show them in the catalogue as we would wish. However, our catalogue contains more than two hundred photographs", wrote T. G. Hawkes to a Pittsburgh jeweler.[2] The "office book of photographs", as it was sometimes called, existed in more than one copy and was used by traveling salesmen, although the boxes of photographs seem to have remained in use as well until some time after Hawkes incorporated his business in June of 1890 and changed the name to T. G. Hawkes & Company

When inquiries were received from individuals in the 1890s, Hawkes would refer them to the nearest store handling his glass. "We do not retail, but frequently have visitors, to whom we extend courtesies, and sometimes sell to them but always at an advance [that is, at more than the wholesale price], as a protection to the trade"[3] he explained to one store, which inquired about competition.

In March, 1889, Hawkes solicited a new customer, Wattles & Sheafer of Pittsburgh, with the following letter:

"We wish to introduce our goods in your city, and are desirous of doing so through some prominent jeweler… We address you this to inquire if you have any intention of handling cut glass, and if so, if we could make some arrangement with you… Some of these [Exposition] goods and others we would be willing to consign to you during the winter of 1889–1890 only, and, on the expiration of that time you could return any that you did not wish to keep and have charged regularly. We feel confident that this departure would be to our

2. T. G. Hawkes to Wattles & Sheafer, Pittsburgh, February 11, 1889.
3. T. G. Hawkes to Bayless Bros. & Company, Louisville, Kentucky, September 21, 1892.

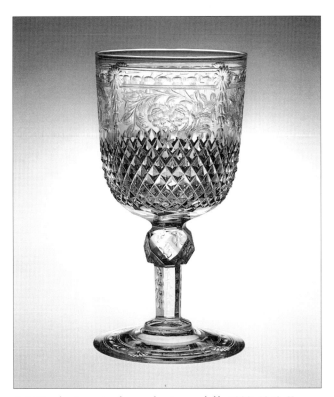

7-4.Wineglass in a cut and engraved pattern, probably 1930–1940. H. 15.5cm, trade-marked. Courtesy Robert F. Rockwell, Jr.

7-5.Engraved goblet, probably 1930–1940. H. 22.5cm, marked "HAWKES". Courtesy Robert F. Rockwell, Jr.

mutual advantage; at least, we are willing to send the goods…and if it proves unsuccessful it would be entirely our loss. We find that jewelers all over the country are going more and more into the fine china and glass business, and with excellent success."[4]

The firm was apparently receptive to this idea, because at the end of March, Hawkes sent a six-page list of goods on memorandum, and the following letter:

"You will notice that we have sent you an elegant assortment of goods and we do not think that any house in Pittsburgh has such an assortment. We shall add a few more pieces from time to time, including some candelabras, until the expiration of our agreement, after which we hope your glass department will be a permanent one. All the goods are ticketed with the number of the shape, size and cutting so that you will only have to put your retail prices on the ticket. Please send report of sales on the first of each month, and give the marginal number of the article, as well as the size, name, cutting and price. We keep the account on a memorandum book, from which your itemized monthly reports of sales are checked off, and then charged up regularly on our sales-book, and a bill sent to you. In displaying cut glass, a great deal depends on the light; a north light is preferable, or a light from overhead. The light should not be very strong, but just sufficient to bring out the lustre of the metal. This point can be determined by experiment. Please do not let any glass men see the display if you can avoid it, as we are constantly annoyed by other manufacturers copying our designs and patterns… Will you please have the glass insured for $1300 and send bill for same to us…"[5]

In the same year, Hawkes received a letter from a German merchant, who asked for a catalog and price list. Hawkes replied that he did not issue a catalog.[6] His

4. T. G. Hawkes to Wattles & Sheafer, Pittsburgh, February 7, 1889.
5. H. P. Sinclaire Jr. for T. G. Hawkes to Wattles & Sheafer, Pittsburgh, March 28, 1889.
6. P. A. Tacchi's Nachfolger, Frankfurt a M. to T. G. Hawkes, June, 18, 1889.

7-6. Two wineglasses in an engraved
thistle pattern, probably
1940–1950. H. 19.5cm.,
18.6cm, both marked "HAWKES".
Courtesy Robert F. Rockwell, Jr.

large book of 200 photographs was probably too bulky to send abroad but it is surprising that he did not wish to encourage this transatlantic trade. Around the same time, he received a letter from Pitkin & Brooks in Chicago inquiring if Burley had an exclusive option to handle Hawkes glass in Chicago, or if Pitkin & Brooks, "Importers & Jobbers" of pottery, lighting, and glass according to their letterhead, could carry it. Mr. Pitkin was anxious to come to Corning to look over the full Hawkes line.[7] According to the note at the bottom of the page, Hawkes replied that only Burley handled Hawkes glass in Chicago. In the light of the foregoing, it is amusing to find Hawkes instructing his salesman to "go into the glass-room of Pitkin & Brooks, and look over the glass, also look at the glass kept by Spalding & Company but do not let either of these houses know that you are in the glass business".[8]

In October, 1889, John Turner of Davis Collamore wrote indignantly: "You must be well aware that Dorflinger's is represented by Wilhelm Graef and Bedell while Tiffany buys from J. Hoare. G. Collamore have been advertising right along until lately, that they kept the English glass at prices as moderate as the American, but superior in quality. Now D.C. & Co. Ltd. seems to be about the only house left without being able to say we are agents for —! You hardly put us in a position to advertise Hawkes' Cut Crystal (although we are doing it) we have not the least encouragement in the Matter... There is no doubt had we been given the exclusive sale of your goods for New York City it would have been far better for you & ourselves. It would have fostered a mutual feeling & have caused some of those smaller Manufacturers to have kept out of our store".[9]

In a subsequent letter, Turner insisted that his store should also have the

7. E. H. Pitkin for Pikin & Brooks, Chicago to T. G. Hawkes, September 2, 1889.
8. T. G. Hawkes to W. H. Bryant, Chicago, August 22, 1892.
9. John Turner for D. C. & Company Ltd., New York, to T. G. Hawkes, October 1889.

exclusive rights to handle Hawkes glass in Brooklyn too, since Ovington was opening a Fifth Avenue store, and Hawkes must have consented as Bedell, Ovington, and Gilman Collamore all dropped out of the customer list shortly after this. Dorflinger (see Chapter 4) continued as a customer in the early 1890s, but if the glass was being sold under the Dorflinger label, Davis Collamore & Company could hardly complain. Early in 1889, an accounting for 1888 shows that the New York store sold $16,000 worth of Hawkes cut glass that year,[10] so it was a customer Hawkes must have been anxious to keep. Not long before, Hawkes had become dissatisfied with the amount of business done in Philadelphia and wrote to Caldwell to complain:

"We think it would pay you to carry a pair of each of these candelabras in stock, our other customers do it, and have sold a good many within the last year, and while Philadelphia ought to be one of our best markets for these goods, our sale in them has practically amounted to nothing… We have been thinking for some time of writing to you in reference to this agreement which gives you the exclusive sale of our glass in Philadelphia, and which practically shuts us out of that market, and we have felt for a long time that our business in Philadelphia was really much smaller than it should be. We know it to be a fact that one of our competitors sells in your city alone between $40,000 and $50,000 worth of cut glass table ware yearly, while our sales for the last three years have averaged less than $12,000,…prices have reached such a low point that our only safety is in doing as large a business as possible."[11]

This competitor was probably Dorflinger. Competitive pricing was always a problem as the stores frequently asked for lower prices, especially on special

7-7.Photograph of H. H. Clinger, one of Hawkes' best salesmen, ready for customers in his room in a hotel in 1905. He is showing cut glass and Steuben, and his photographic catalog is open at the foot of the bed.

10. Thomas S. Whitbeck for Davis Collamore & Company, New York to T. G. Hawkes, January 17, 1889.
11. T. G. Hawkes to J. E. Caldwell & Company Philadelphia, March 23, 1889.

orders. A letter from Burley & Company explains one situation:

"This pair of candelabras was sold in competition with Richard Briggs for $135.00 delivered here in Chicago… The lady brought photographs sent here from Richard Briggs and consulted one of our salesmen. The goods were to be delivered here in Chicago in perfect condition at the price named. We obtained the order through a matter of eloquence in the part of the salesman. This is not the first time we have been placed in a similar position by Richard Briggs and by the Philadelphia people. Of course we cannot ask you to sell us for less than you get for the same article from others who are probably just as good customers as we are, but we do ask you to give us the benefit of your best prices in all cases. We are doing all we can to push your make of goods and advertise your name."[12]

Exactly how Hawkes handled the exclusivity issue is shown in several exchanges with three stores in Minneapolis and St. Paul. Bullard Brothers of St. Paul wrote to Hawkes in January, 1888 requesting a consignment account and mentioned that their chief competition was Dickinson & Company of St. Paul and Minneapolis, which was already a Hawkes customer. Hawkes added Bullard to his list, and explained that the goods sent to Dickinson were a "different class of goods", by which he probably meant cheaper, since in another letter he promised not to send Dickinson any wares cut in "Pillar". Later that year, a firm named Myers requested a sizable order on memo and after Hawkes refused them memo status, their order was canceled. A later letter to W. H. Bryant, Hawkes' traveling salesman, refers to Dickinson as a "bargain house" and cautions Bryant against calling on them as Eustis Brothers would be a preferable Minneapolis outlet.[13] Richard Briggs was particularly fussy about the exclusivity issue. He designed several patterns which could only be sold through his store, the Louis XIV pattern and its variant, which he patented. He also wanted certain shapes in certain patterns reserved for his use and as early as 1884 ordered, "Also do not on any account furnish either of these shapes to any one else in the country,"[14] in reference to some barrel-shaped decanters he ordered in Russian and in Hobnail patterns. Whether Hawkes observed this restriction or not, was not stated. However, the price books show that Collamore, Caldwell, and Burley all had patterns that were exclusive to them.

Letters from Collamore were more inclined to question the prices than the monopoly of shapes and patterns. In 1887, after the store had shown candelabras to a hotelier, they wrote to Hawkes to make sure that he would not quote the customer a wholesale price or do business directly with him.[15] The next year there was a spate of letters about pricing in which Hawkes first lowered prices at the store's request, then defended his pricing policy:

"We are under the impression… that we have varied our prices since we commenced our business with Davis Collamore & Company, less to them, than any other manufacturer in the country. This is a point that we have been very particular about, and have often filled orders for you, when we knew that we were making an absolute loss on the goods, rather than keep changing prices with you often."[16]

12. Martin, for Burley & Company, Chicago to T. G. Hawkes, February 6, 1889.
13. Bullard Brothers, St. Paul to T. G. Hawkes and penciled reply, January 6, 1888; T. G. Hawkes to Bullard Brothers, August 18, September 8, November 20, 1888; T. G. Hawkes & Company to W. H. Bryant, September 3, 1892.
14. Richard Briggs, Boston to T. G. Hawkes, November 10, 1884.
15. Lowndes for D. C. & Company to T. G. Hawkes, January 24, 1887.
16. T. G. Hawkes to Davis Collamore & Company, New York, November 1, 1888.

7-8.Pitcher engraved with a girl in a swing. Hawkes, 1903–1905. H. 38.1cm. Gift of Mr. and Mrs. Thomas P. Dimitroff (CMG 81.4.135). At least three examples of this pitcher are known, and it shows up just to the left of the lamp in Fig. 7-7.

Hawkes then challenged the New York store to order goods from another cutting house and compare the prices and quality. A couple of weeks later he wrote: "We shall be very much pleased to have Mr. Carleton W. Bonfils call on us, and will try and explain to him the difficulties of glass-making, and glass-cutting and show him how hard it is sometimes to fill orders promptly."[17]

In 1886, there was a dispute with Caldwell about pricing: "Mr. Houston's understanding of the agreement made with you this summer was that all S. & Fan goods would be cut at Dorflinger's prices and it was on this basis that we ordered these goods… Messrs. C. Dorflinger & Sons do a large business in Philadelphia, their goods are in every store and with this S & Fan pattern they seem to have struck the popular chord. The prices they have put down, which no doubt assists its reception, and we must meet the demand. It is with no desire on our part to cavil at prices that we have asked for the reductions but because we understood that you would make anything that they could at the same price."[18]

In fact, Caldwell often asked Hawkes for reductions to match Dorflinger's prices. Briggs, in turn, complained that the New England factories tried to undercut his prices and that Hawkes had to help him beat the competition. A Midwestern customer, complaining about prices, said: "We notice that your price of Hobnail Tumblers is $18. We have been paying Meriden Flint Glass Company $15 and the

17. T. G. Hawkes & Company to Davis Collamore & Company, New York, November 15, 1888.
18. J. E. Caldwell, Philadelphia to T. G. Hawkes, January 10, 1886.

Boston Sandwich quote $12."[19] Hawkes usually countered these complaints by saying that his goods were of better quality. When Mermod and Jaccard complained about the price of the *Cobweb* pattern, Hawkes reminded them that it was to replace Dorflinger's *Parisian* pattern in their line and that the prices were comparable.[20]

A letter from a Columbus, Ohio store underlines this competition between the cut glass firms:

"Gentlemen — We have lately been trying to push T. G. Hawk & Co's. cut glass and have stirred up a little competition. The Wedgmere pattern of Libbey's is being pushed by a competitor and advertised rather extensively. We can sell Hawke's glass by comparing color of metal especially with the Toledo ware, and have kept some pieces of their goods for that purpose, but we would like some little card or facsimile of your Paris medal, if you have it, to put in case with glass. Cut Glass is just beginning to sell in Columbus and we intend to sell nearly all of it, but must have clear glass and otherwise perfect goods. If you have any especially good way of showing up the murky or smokey color of glass, we would like to know of it. Would like to have two or three good but small electrotypes of pretty pieces for newspaper work."[21]

The note at the top of the page indicates that Hawkes sent seven electrotypes, probably the same ones which he was using then in the *Harpers* and *Century* advertisements. He had a facsimile of his prize certificate which he could send, but one wonders how he thought the store could show up the murky quality of the Libbey glass.

When Hawkes first started in business, he employed L. G. Boughton, who was headquartered in New York, as his principal agent. Boughton, who also represented Dorflinger, called on the New York stores twice a week and offered to go to Boston and Philadelphia as well, although Hawkes does not seem to have given that business to him. Mr. Boughton sold for crockery firms, but made it clear that he would be happy to devote himself exclusively to Hawkes if the Corning company would put him on salary instead of commission. He had photographs of the glass but not samples, and he found this hampered him. Sometime in the early 1880s the account with Boughton was dropped and by 1888, H. P. Sinclaire, Jr. who had been hired as a book keeper right out of business school in 1882, was on the road as a salesman, although he also continued to oversee the books. His frequent selling trips were described in letters to Hawkes which are far more detailed than those of the other salesmen.

"Arrived in Detroit this (Sunday) morning, but find hotels are crowded on account of the fair, so I will leave tonight for Grand Rapids. You might write from Corning to... [list of area firms] something about as follows, Our Mr. Sinclaire writes us from Detroit, ...that he was unable to secure a room at any of the hotels to display his samples. He will be in Detroit again in about three weeks, when we hope you will be able to look him over."[22]

In an earlier letter, Sinclaire talks about breakage of his samples, which was something of a hazard and asks his employer to check into a special cloth to wrap

19. Rice & Burnett, Cleveland to T. G. Hawkes, February 16, 1885.
20. T. G. Hawkes & Company to Mermod & Jaccard, St. Louis, October 3, 1892.
21. Hasbrook & Byers, Columbus, Ohio to T. G. Hawk & Company February 18, 1893.
22. H. P. Sinclaire Jr., Detroit to T. G. Hawkes, September 22, 1889.

the goods. "I was rather encouraged, however, when I heard that the New England's man broke a large Punch Bowl, and that our friend Mr. Abbott [Hoare's salesman]... had quite a number of pieces broken... Leave for Chicago tonight."[23] To a prospective customer, Sinclaire wrote, "We were in Cleveland with a line of samples, and called at your store, but were unable to see you... A gentlemen in your employ, ...thought that it would be satisfactory if we sent you a line of samples... we thought it best, however, to first write and get your permission to send the goods."[24] During the late summer and fall, he was constantly on the road, visiting first eastern and then mid-western companies. For regular customers, the Hawkes firm sent samples directly to the store and then Sinclaire followed up with a visit to take orders. "We send you today... the new samples... Please open the packages and look the goods over and retain them until our Mr. Sinclaire calls on you..."[25]

By 1892, W. H. Bryant had been hired as Hawkes principal traveling salesman, although Sinclaire still made occasional trips. The cash book payments in 1900–1905 show Bryant as the highest-paid salesman, with H. H. Clinger and four others on the road most of the time.

When Sinclaire or Hawkes deemed a prospective customer unworthy, their replies to requests for catalogs or samples could be crushing. "We do not issue any catalogues, as our goods are only of the most expensive kind. We do not think that you could use them", Sinclaire responded to one such inquiry.[26]

7-9. Showroom at 73-79 W. Market street, Corning, newly redecorated by Tiffany and Company after a 1924 fire.

23. H. P. Sinclaire Jr., Detroit, to T. G. Hawkes, September 15, 1888.
24. H. P. Sinclaire to Messrs. Cowell & Hubbard, Cleveland, October 2, 1888.
25. T. G. Hawkes to Mermod & Jaccard Jewelry Company, St. Louis, September 8, 1888.
26. H. P. Sinclaire Jr. for T. G. Hawkes, to H. L. Buck, Springfield, MO, September 27, 1888.

8-1. The "Edenhall Goblet", engraved by William Morse for T. G. Hawkes & Company about 1912–1917. Steuben blank, 3073. H. 30cm, trade-marked, signed "W.H. Morse". Private collection.

8-2. Detail of one side of "Edenhall Goblet".

CHAPTER EIGHT

The Patterns

The Hawkes company produced a large number of patterns and shapes during its life and a study of the patents, the correspondence and orders, and the catalogs makes it possible to date the "life" of some of these patterns. Apparently, when the company opened the patterns were referred to only by numbers and, since there are no photographs remaining from the earliest days, the pattern "100" (which was a big seller in the first year) is impossible to identify. As detailed in Chapter 10, Richard Briggs, the Boston glass and china dealer, renamed the #283 pattern "*Russian*" and the #284 pattern, "*Moscow*" in 1881. Other customers continued to use the numbers until the mid-80s when most of them were phased out in favor of pattern names.

The Briggs orders for 1882 include the following patterns: *Deep Hobnail, Hobnail, Moscow, Quarter Diamond, Russian, Sharp Diamond,* and *Strawberry Diamond.* In the same year, Collamore Davis & Company ordered patterns 100, 160, 175, 283, and 322 as well

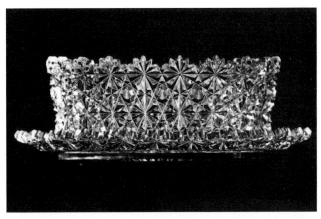

Figs. 8-3 through 8-10 and 8-13 through 8-18, 8-21 through 8-39 are taken from salesmen's sample cards used in the early 1880s. Most of these have printed captions and hand-written prices; they are impossible to date exactly because the company changed the cards as they introduced new shapes and patterns. The prices are retail; jewelry stores received a discount of up to 50%.

8-4. 9in. Salad or Fruit Bowl and Plate cut Russian on shape 112 cost $50.

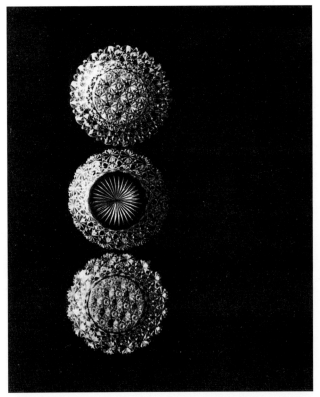

8-3. 7in. Plates in three variations of Russian; 283 and 375 are the same except for the edge finishing and cost $59.50 for a dozen; Star & Hob in the center cost $49.50 for a dozen.

8-5. 6in. Handled Ice Cream Saucers cut in Russian, Hobnail, and Strawberry Diamond patterns on shape 171 cost $90, $56 and $42 a dozen.

as Checker & Square, Quarter Diamond, Sharp Diamond, and Table Diamond. These are not the only patterns Hawkes made in the first three years, but they must represent most of them since Briggs and Collamore were the two largest customers. Most of these patterns were old in 1882. Strawberry Diamond originated in the late 18th century and was extremely popular in the 1820s and 1830s, but never quite went out of style. The other diamond and hobnail patterns all were variations on patterns of the 1850s which had remained popular for three decades and had been produced in pressed glass as well as in cut glass. In addition to the above, the Hawkes firm, like all of their competitors, was cutting "matchings" at the request of customers.

By 1885, there was considerably more variety in the patterns listed and the

8-6. *Pint Cordial Jugs cut in Russian, Hobnail and Straw. Dia. on shape 350 cost $17, $14 and $11 each.*

8-7. *Footed Sugar Bowls cut in Russian, Hobnail and Straw. Dia. on shape 414 cost $17, $13, and $11 each.*

8-8. *The Tankard Jug cut Hobnail on shape 417 came in six sizes ranging from ½ pt. to 4 pints with the price rising from $9.00 for the half-pint to $24.00 each for the largest size.*

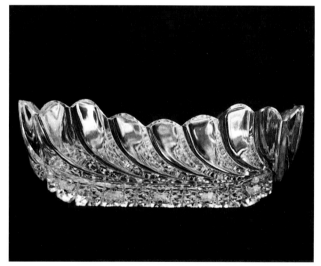

8-9. *The Salad or Fruit Bowl cut Russian and Pillars on shape 420 came in 5 sizes with the prices rising from $14 for a 6in. one to $50 for a 10in. one.*

8-10. *The same shape, cut Russian to the top, had the same price range.*

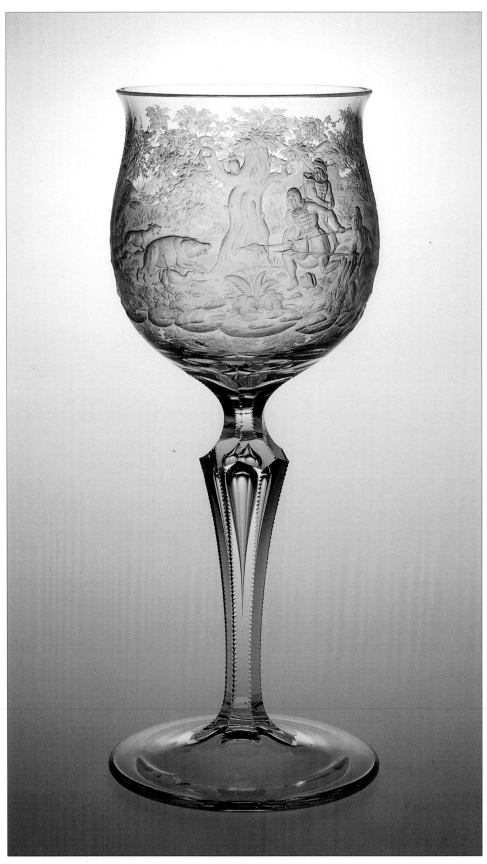

8-11. Goblet on a similar, non-Steuben blank, engraved with a hunting scene, perhaps by Morse, or by another Hawkes engraver of the period, but unsigned. H: 28.1cm. Jones Museum of Glass and Ceramics, Douglas Hill, Maine.

8-12. *Detail of hunting scene goblet.*

numbered patterns had been phased out or named. Examination of the orders from Briggs, Caldwell, and Collamore for 1885, showed that the following patterns were then in production: *Diamond, Fan and Diamond, Flute and Prism, Glasgow, Gothic, Hobnail, Lace Hobnail, Old Pattern* (only Briggs ordered this one, but he ordered it all year long), *Persian, Persian and Pillars, Prism & Cut, Queen Anne, Rolled Pillars, Russian, Russian and Pillars, Russian and Prism, S. & HU* (a pattern ordered chiefly by Caldwell), *Sharp Diamond, Star & Hobnail, Strawberry Diamond, Strawberry Diamond & Hobnail, Thistle, 283 1/2* (perhaps a Russian variant), *322, 643,* and *6424.*

Several of Hawkes's customers ordered patterns which were made exclusively for them. *Louis XIV (see 8-42)*, which was developed for Richard Briggs and patented by him, is the most famous of these, but there were others as well. In 1885, Briggs wrote: "I have seen a very old tumbler and send you today a plaster mould which I have made from it. Will you please make for me one tumbler <u>exactly</u> the same and if the effect is as I wish, I will send you an order for a quantity."[1] By April, Briggs was ordering a full set of samples in different sizes of stemware and had christened the pattern, "*Louis XIV*"; for the next twenty years he

1. Richard Briggs, Boston, to T. G. Hawkes, March 3, 1885.

179

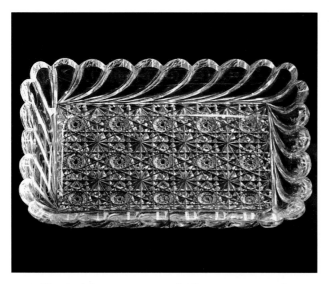

8-13. *The 504 dish cut in Persian and Pillars pattern came in four sizes from 8in. to 11in.; all cost $220 each, a tremendous price, but the Pillars were very difficult to cut.*

8-14. *The Cream Jug cut in Russian, Hobnail or Straw. Dia. on shape 425 cost $8.50, $7.50 and $5.50 each.*

ordered it in quantity, usually with a monogram. In 1889, Briggs paid Hawkes to have his lawyers patent the pattern, with the patent assigned to Briggs, not Hawkes. In one letter, Briggs says, "I would be obliged if you would put one of your 'patent applied for' tags on each piece."[2] On October, 1888, Hawkes was preparing a special "*Peacock*" pattern for Briggs, but apparently this never went into production. In the mid-eighties, Briggs wanted a "*Thistle*" pattern and Hawkes produced several samples, but when this was added to the line it was not exclusive to Briggs.

Hawkes's first design patent, in 1882, was for the *Russian* pattern. It was five years before he patented another design, perhaps because the 1882 design patent had not protected the *Russian* pattern or its name from use by other companies. Hawkes had ordered tags from a printer in 1889 with the words "DESIGN PATENT" in an arc at the top of a circle, "APPLIED FOR" in the center and "HAWKES" in an arc at the bottom.[3] Two years later, Hawkes was using circular tags which said "DESIGN PATENT" across the top, "HAWKES" across the bottom and had the "NO 18301" in the center.[4] He may have printed these tags for more than one pattern, but only one sample tag has survived. Exactly why Hawkes patented the designs of some patterns and not others is not known.

Getting the patent approved was not a rubber-stamp process; one confusing patent drawing in the correspondence from Knight Brothers, a firm of patent attorneys used by Hawkes, turned out to show a pattern designed by Benjamin Davies and assigned to L. Straus & Sons.[5] The examiners apparently felt that *Brazilian*, as originally designed, was too close to this, and Hawkes modified it slightly and resubmitted it.[6] Hawkes normally sent pieces of the new pattern to Washington where a draftsman employed by Knight Brothers did drawings to accompany the description. "We send you today…one claret glass — our new pattern, but with some of the work left off, as on certain shapes, especially the smaller pieces, stemglass, finger bowls, etc. we find we cannot put all the pattern on without crowding it," said Mr. Hawkes. Eventually, photographs replaced the draftsman's drawings.

2. Richard Briggs, Boston, to T. G. Hawkes, May 25, 1889.
3. T. G. Hawkes, to E. A. Wright, Philadelphia, March 15, 1889.
4. H. B. Taylor, Cuba, New York, to T. G. Hawkes, November 20, 1889, enclosing patent label.
5. A. C. Revi, *American Cut & Engraved Glass*, 1965, illustrates this pattern, p. 113.
6. Knight Bros., Washington, D.C. to T. G. Hawkes, April 8, May 10, 1889; T. G. Hawkes to Knight Brothers, undated but around May 1, 1889.

8-15. *The 4 Pint Champagne Jug cut Russian with hollow diamond neck on shape 454 cost $36 each.*

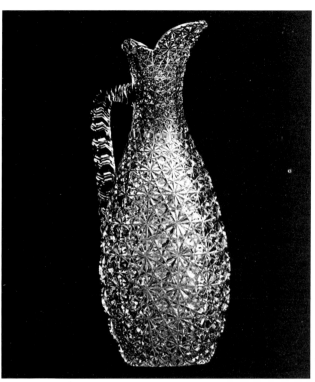

8-16. *The 4 Pint Champagne Jug cut Russian to the top on shape 454 cost $50 each.*

8-17. *The 4 Pint Champagne Jug cut Russian on shape 481 cost $36.*

8-18. *Quart Whiskey Jugs engraved with birds and foliage on shape 490 cost $15 each.*

8-19. Goblet cut in Buckle pattern, T. G. Hawkes & Company about 1910–1920. Ht.14.2cm. Gift of Harold Williams in memory of Hettie Williams (CMG 92.4.26).

The design patents ran for three and a half, seven, or fourteen years, according to the fee the patentee elected to pay, and they were not renewable, according to Hawkes's lawyers. Between 1882 and 1896, Hawkes patented sixteen patterns, a small fraction of his total, and there is no indication of how he selected which patterns to protect. Certainly, *Brazilian*, *Chrysanthemum*, *Russian*, and *Venetian*, all of

8-20. *Goblet with gilt and enamel decoration similar to the one in the Smithsonian shown in Fig.8-160. Probably 1915-1925. H. Hawkes collection.*

which he patented, were his best-selling patterns in the late 1880s and early 1890s; there are more orders for them than for the other patterns by far. The pattern Dorothy Daniels called "*Maltese Cross*", patented Sept. 2, 1890, on the other hand, does not appear under that name (or any other name that I could find) in any orders or in any of the early catalogs, so it must not have been a good seller.

8-21. *Quart Claret Jugs engraved with birds and foliage on shape 596 cost $15 each.*

8-22. *Quart Decanter cut Russian on shape 499 cost $31.*

Hawkes patented *Russian* for seven years, some of the others for three and a half, but from 1889, the term was always fourteen years.

That Hawkes was inventive, and always looking for new ideas, is shown by lengthy correspondence in 1887 and 1888, in which it becomes clear that he joined with Robert Haines in an attempt to develop a corrugated glass shell for a light bulb. Hawkes and Haines were successful in patenting this idea as an "Improvement in Incandescent Electric Light Bulbs" (Patent No. 372, 313, granted Nov. 1, 1887), but then they discovered after much trial and error that the Edison company found the shape "a failure, as the lines throw shades. We also find that these bulbs are very apt to break, and are very brittle."[7] Not long after, Hoare developed his cut glass "Light Radiator" which was a cover for an electric bulb; obviously the new lighting technology was on everyone's mind. A letter from Caldwell asks "Do you cut incandescent electric light bulbs and at what price."[8]

The question of who created the designs for the Hawkes firm is also answered in a letter in the archives:

"We will send you next week a bowl cut in our new pattern, Coronet for which we have just received a patent... We are sorry we will not be able to send any more new designs this year but Mr. Hawkes who attends to all the designing is in Europe, and will not be back until the middle of September when it will be too late to get up anything new."[9]

By 1888, most of the earlier, simple diamond-based patterns had disappeared and Hawkes had begun to introduce his new patterns in the style collectors today call "brilliant cut". (When it was being produced, it was called "rich cut glass"; the term, "Brilliant Period glassware" was popularized by Dorothy Daniel.) Patterns introduced by 1888 include *Block, Brilliant, Chinese, Coburg, Cobweb, Double 6424 and Prisms, Empress, Gothic and Silver Diamonds, Grecian, Grecian & Hobnail, Hollows,*

7. Francis R. Upton for Edison Lamp Company, Harrison, N. J. to T. G. Hawkes, March 13, 1889.
8. J. E. Caldwell & Company, Philadelphia to T. G. Hawkes, November 8, 1889.
9. T. G. Hawkes & Company to [illeg] & Herter, San Francisco, August 3, 1892.

8-23. *Salad or Fruit Bowl with Plate cut Russian on shape 502 came in three sizes ranging from $40 for an 8in. one to $60 for a 10in. one.*

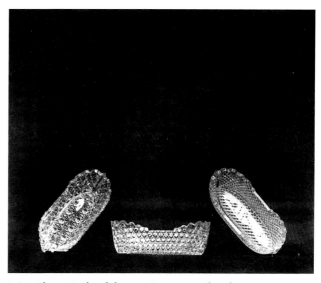

8-24. *Olive or Bonbon dish cut in Russian, Hobnail or Straw. Dia. on shape 533 cost $17, $13 or $11 each.*

8-25. *The 4 pint Champagne Jug cut Russian on shape 503 cost $36.*

8-26. *Honey Dish cut Russian on shape 534 varied in size from 7in. to 9in. and in cost from $13 to $21.50 each.*

Japanese, Lapidary, Large Hobnail, Large Russian, Large Strawberry Diamond, Lustre, Mirror Block, Mitre & Fans, Passion Flower (candlesticks only), Pillars, Pillars & Lace Hobnail, Pillars & Plain Star, Pillars & Rich Star, Pillars & Silver Diamond, Princess (first ordered Jan. 3, 1887 by Collamore)[10] Princess & Hollows, Princess & Prisms, Prisms, Rock Crystal, Roman, Russian & Stars, Russian & Hobnail, Serpentine & Russian, Serpentine & Strawberry Diamond, Silver Diamond Star, Spiral Twist, Straight Pillars and Hobnails, Strawberry Diamond & Fan (an old variant of

10. Davis Collamore, New York, to T. G. Hawkes, January 3, 1887.

185

8-27. The 535 dish, cut in Persian pattern came in five sizes from 6in. to 10in. and varied in price from $15 for the smallest to $32 for the largest.

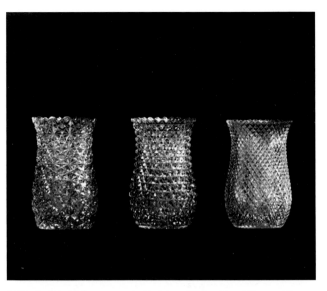

8-28. English celery vases cut in Russian, Hobnail and Straw. Dia. on shape 538 cost $19, $13 or $11 each. They were called "English" because of the vase shape which was old-fashioned by American standards.

Strawberry Diamond), and *Victoria*. This is a tremendous increase in the number of patterns made, and it is not surprising that Hawkes turned to a photographic catalog to replace the boxed set of cards; he needed a larger format.

Hawkes patented nine patterns in the four year period between 1887 and 1890 and this gives some idea of how rapidly the patterns proliferated. These include *Russian & Pillar* and *Grecian* in 1887, *Old-Fashioned Hobnail*, *Star Rosette* and *Princess* in 1888, *Brazilian* in 1889 and *Venetian*, *Maltese Cross* and *Chrysanthemum* in 1890. Most of these are fairly complex and expensive patterns, but *Princess* and *Old-Fashioned Hobnail* are simpler and cheaper. The former, patented May 8, 1888 (no. 18,301) was misidentified as *Devonshire* by Dorothy Daniel in 1950 and that error has been perpetuated by succeeding authors. Now that more catalogs are available, it is possible to see that the pattern identified in the catalogs as *Princess* is the one patented in 1888. This is confirmed by the fact that there are orders for *Princess* pattern beginning in 1887, but none for *Devonshire*.[11]

Venetian must have been introduced in 1889, because it is included in Hawkes's display at the Paris Exposition. The other new patterns in the Paris exhibit were *Plaid* (which may have been used only for lamps), *Stars & Lace Hobnail*, and #3708. A somewhat surprising letter to Dorflinger that year says, "We have changed the name of our new pattern from Venetian to Brazilian."[12] This leaves us in some doubt as to what Hawkes sent to Paris, since *Venetian* is named on the shipping list, but *Brazilian* is not. However, there were several orders for *Brazilian* in the spring of 1889, so it is likely that both patterns were in production that year. Most of the patterns listed above were produced throughout the 1890s. The Hawkes archives include orders only until 1893, but the 1890s catalog, advertisements, and the two editions of the turn of the century brochure show some of these patterns and

11. Bill Evans, "Desperately Seeking 'Devonshire'", The Hobstar, Nov.16, No.9 (June, 1994), pp.1, 6-9.
12. T. G. Hawkes to C. Dorflinger & Sons, White Mills, March 26, 1889.

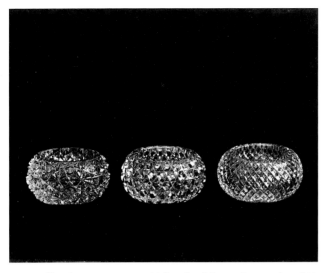

8-29. *Table Salts cut in Russian, Hobnail and Straw. Dia. on shape 540 cost $8, $6 and $4.*

8-30. *Quart Decanter and Claret Jug cut Russian on shape 546 cost $33 and $36 each.*

8-31. *Salad or Fruit Bowl cut Persian on shape 551 came in three sizes from 8in. to 10in. and ranged in cost from $28 to $46.*

8-32. *The Salad Bowl with Spoon and Fork cut Russian on shape 552 cost $55 for the 9in. size and $65 for the 11in. one.*

a good many more. The patterns introduced in the early 1890s include *Chrysanthemum, Coronet, Fancy Prisms, Imperial, New Princess, North Star, Norwood,* and *Valencian.* An 1893 letter from Hawkes to a retailer in Indiana lists his principal patterns and their prices. *Grecian* and *Chrysanthemum* were the most expensive patterns at $42 per dozen for goblets, *Venetian* was next at $25, and *Cobweb, Russian,* and *Thistle* all cost $18 per dozen, *Brazilian* and *Norwood* cost $16.50 per dozen, and *Strawberry Diamond and Fan* was the least expensive at $10 per dozen goblets. "We do not print a price list of our line, but the above covers all the principal patterns. In case you are in need of anything at any time, we will be pleased to send you our office catalogue, by express, prepaid, from which you can make a selection"[13] wrote Hawkes.

After 1895, the pace at which new patterns were introduced increased and by 1901 *Aberdeen, Alpine, Cairo, Clarence, Constellation, Cut & Engraved, Devonshire, Fancy Star,*

13. T. G. Hawkes & Company to Geo. H. Wheelock & Company, South Bend, October 1, 1893.

8-33. *The 10in. Flower Vase cut Russian on shape 553 cost $56.*

8-34. *The 11in. Flower Vase cut Russian on shape 555 cost $58. A 10in. one was $48.*

Feathers, Festoon, Florence, Kensington, Lorraine, Lombard, Monroe, Nautilus, Nelson, New York, Nos. 1–9, Old English, Oriental, Penrose, Savoy, Versailles, Windsor and *Yeddo* were added to the line. Most of these patterns remained in the line until about 1905 when it appears that all but a few were gradually phased out between 1905 and 1910.

A comparison of the 33 patterns listed in the first edition of *Hawkes Cut Glass* with the 31 listed in the second edition show that just in that brief time between the two printings (two to five years, just before and after 1900), only a third of the patterns are the same. *Argyle, Berkshire, Kimberley, Madison, Portland, Tunis,* and *Washington* are all patterns listed in the second edition of the brochure, but not illustrated there or anywhere else as far as I am aware. Some of these patterns were probably very short-lived and if they did not sell, they were withdrawn in a year or less. While it was undoubtedly true that Hawkes would also cut special orders of their own early patterns up until World War I; as a practical matter, the early richly cut patterns like *Brazilian, Grecian,* and *Venetian* were rarely produced after 1910. Daybook entries for April, 1904, show at least twenty of the patterns of the 1890s still in production, but *Imperial* and *Chrysanthemum* are the only early patterns which are known to have remained in production after 1910, since they appear in a fragmentary catalog along with *Panel* and *Willow,* the patterns patented in 1909 and 1911. After 1910, Hawkes reused *Grecian, Persian, Princess, Roman,* and *Venetian* as pattern names; in fact, a third *Venetian* pattern was put into production in the 1920s.

The mid-teens "Price Book" has entries for *Alpine, Kensington, Lorraine, Penrose* and *Versailles,* as well as later patterns, but since there are no illustrations, one can not be certain that these are the original 1890s patterns and not reuses of the name.

8-35. *The 10 ¾in. Flower Vase cut Russian on shape 560 cost $66. A 9 ¾in. one was $50.*

8-36. *A 12in. Salad or Fruit Bowl and Plate cut Russian on shape 561 cost $70.*

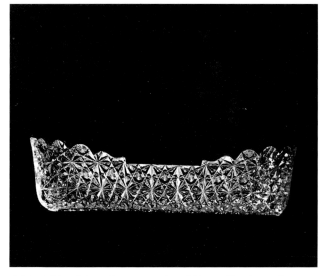

8-37. *A Celery dish cut Russian on shape 582 was 12in. long and its price was recorded in code.*

8-38. *Table Bells cut in Lace Hobnail, Hobnail or Straw. Dia. cost $7.50, $6.50 and $5.50.*

Examination of the catalogs in Corning's collection, most of which are undated, but several of which seem to have come between about 1905 and 1915, confirms the view that many of the patterns of those years were short-lived. The exceptions to this were the *Panel* pattern and *Queens* pattern, both of which are found often enough to show that they were made over a longer period of time. Both of these patterns, along with *Raleigh* and *Sonora*, are listed in the "Price Book".

The earliest gravic patterns, which seem to have been quite successful, were very heavily engraved, often with polished engraving. What distinguished the earliest gravic floral patterns from the contemporary rock crystal patterns was the style of engraving, not the technique. The later gravic patterns are simplified, with matte flowers and polished leaves.

In the mid-teens, Thomas Hawkes added a silver department and started two cheaper lines of glassware which he marketed as "Signet" and "Edenhall." Many of the "Edenhall" pieces were silver-mounted, and all were probably very simply

8-39. *A five-Light Candelabra 19in. high and 15in. wide cost $150.*

8-40. *A 22in. Kerosene lamp cut in Star & Hobnail pattern on shape 634 lacks its price on this card which seems to come from a set dating from about 1887–1890.*

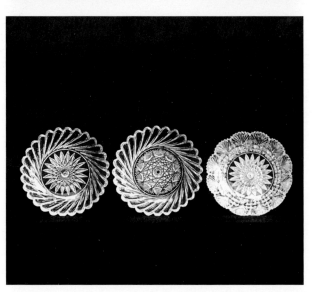

8-41. *6in. Ice Cream Saucers were available in Princess, Pillars and Rich Star and Pillars and Plain Star about 1887–1890.*

engraved. There are no illustrations for any Edenhall patterns in the Hawkes Archives, although the "Number Book" has line drawings of the shapes. There may have been only one basic Edenhall pattern.

The one remaining "Signet" catalog shows a limited range of patterns, mostly with simple engraving. The remaining evidence for these two lines is scanty and both seem to have been phased out by 1918. Signet was set up as a separate company somewhat like Steuben, although its products were sold along with those of the main firm. A few pieces of glass have turned up with the Signet trademark, "SIGNET" in a banner across a cloud-like pattern, but only one marked "Edenhall" piece has been reported.

8-42. *Cordial, wineglass, tumbler and plate in Louis XIV pattern, made by Hawkes for customers of Richard Briggs, Boston, usually on Baccarat blanks. ca. 1885–1900. H. of tallest: 9.8cm. Gift of Thomas Dimitroff and Bill Melanbacher (CMG 91.4.11A–D).*

The name of the Edenhall line was undoubtedly inspired by William Morse's Edenhall goblet which was engraved in the mid-teens (see pp. 174-175). This was kept as an exhibition piece by the firm and was shown at department and jewelry stores from 1917 to 1940, but eventually it was sold to a private collector in the 1960s (Figs. 8–1, 8–2). Morse was a gifted engraver, and the piece is beautifully done, although Samuel Hawkes's claim that it was second only in importance to the British Museum's Portland Vase is perhaps a little overstated.[14]

An examination of the glass given to the National Museum, Smithsonian Institution by the Hawkes company in 1917 and 1918 gives a good idea of what was then being made, although the gift also includes some historical designs no longer in active production. The first shipment of glass was sent to the Smithsonian on May 22, 1917, and included the following pieces:

10in. Plate, Cut & Engraved [Rock Crystal style, engraved by W. H. Morse]
Champagne Jug, Satin Engraved
10in. Plate cut Pillars and Rich Rock Crystal [Coronation pattern]
Decanter Very Rich Rock Crystal
10in. Plate Cut & Engraved Peacock
Covered Urn Plated Ruby glass over Crystal, Handsomely Engraved and Polished

14. Exhibition catalog, T. G. Hawkes & Company n.d. but has inserted letter dated 1940.

8-43. Bowl cut Alpine on shape 346 cost $30.

8-44. Bowl cut Old English on shape 346 came in four sizes ranging from 7in. to 10in. in diameter and cost from $13 to $26 each.

Figs.8-43 through 8-48 are from a Hawkes catalog dating from about 1900. Pieces in these patterns probably do not have Hawkes trademarks but would have had paper labels.

10in. Plate showing 1st Process in Glass Cutting (Marking Design)

10in. Plate showing 2nd Process in Glass Cutting (Design Roughed In)

10in. Plate showing 3rd Process in Glass Cutting(Design Smoothed Out)

10in. Plate showing 4th Process in Glass Cutting (Design Polished and Finished)

Vase Exact Reproduction Saracenic Glass of XV Century

10in. Plate Rich Mitre Cutting [Revere pattern]

Reproduction Ancient Alexandrian Rock Crystal Goblet

10in. Sculptured Glass Plate [Gravic Iris pattern]

Cut & Engraved Goblet as furnished to the Executive Mansion in Washington [Russian]

10in. Plate Rich Mitre Cutting [Venetian pattern]

Reproduction Old English Covered Comport Period about 1790

10in. Plate Rich Mitre Cutting [Russian pattern]

Reproduction Old English Covered Urn Period about 1790

10in. Plate Rich Mitre Cutting [Chrysanthemum pattern]

Colonial Cut Candlesticks

Engraved Sterling Silver Mounted Flower Basket

Cut and Engraved Sterling Silver Mounted Bowl

Enamel and Gold Decorated Goblet

Rich Paste and Gold Decorated Service Plate

Fern Dish Engraved Glass Sterling Silver Mounted

Royal Purple Engraved Glass Vase with Gold Plated Sterling Silver Base

The "Saracenic" glass and the "ancient Alexandrian goblet" are certainly handsome, but they are hardly authentic reproductions; still, it is interesting to note that Samuel Hawkes had already seen the increasing lack of interest in richly cut glass and was trying new ideas. Not many years later, the "Old English" line was renamed "Waterford".

A second, smaller shipment was sent to the Smithsonian on October 11, 1917 with a further seven pieces, as listed below:

Vase, Corinthian

Vase, Chelsea Bird

Decanter Pillars & Fleur De Lys

8-45. *Plate cut Oriental on shape 350 came in five sizes ranging from 7in. to 15in. and cost from $14 to $60.*

8-46. *A 20in. 5 light Candelabra cut Brazilian on shape 758 was also made in four and three light versions.*

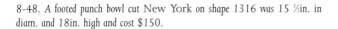

8-47. *Bowl cut Cairo on shape 1185 cost $16.*

8-48. *A footed punch bowl cut New York on shape 1316 was 15 ½in. in diam. and 18in. high and cost $150.*

8-49. *Cologne bottle with silver top engraved in Rock Crystal pattern.*

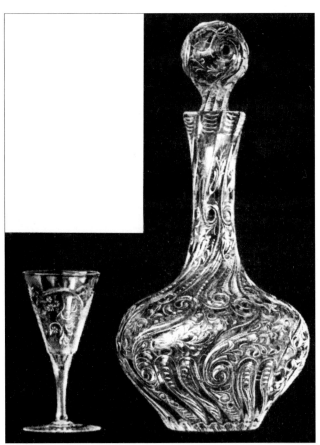

8-50. *Decanter and wineglass engraved in Rock Crystal pattern.*

Figs. 8-49 through 8-56 are taken from the earliest Hawkes brochure, printed about 1896–1898 for distribution to customers. These pieces originally had paper labels with the Hawkes trademark and do not have an acid-stamped mark.

Green Cased Claret Jug, Silver Mtd.
Oval Box China Astor
10in. Bowl Rich Cut
L/S 3106 Frame Millicent

Most of these pieces are illustrated here (Figs. 8–152 through 162), although a few of them were unfortunately not available for photography. The "Saracenic" vase is colorless, with cut panels and engraved polished flowers on a matte background. The "Colonial" candlesticks are simple columns with panel cutting. The silver-mounted flower basket is exactly like one shown in an early catalog[15] except that the glass insert is colorless. The fern dish is a plain oval dish with light floral engraving. The amethyst vase has molded vertical ribs and a simple silver foot. The "Corinthian" vase is olive green with a darker foot; it has an unpolished base and it looks both unfinished and of poor quality. It might be another attempt at an ancient reproduction, deliberately left rather crudely finished. The green-cased claret jug is very simply cut, the dresser box is gravic engraved in the familiar *Astor* pattern and the richly cut bowl is of the type collectors today call "blown out" bowls. The last named and several of the 10in plates must have been out of production at least a decade before they were given to the National Museum. In 1918, a third shipment was sent which included more gold enameled plates and an amethyst cased cut and engraved jar, Fig. 8–162. It is astonishing to see the enameled and gilded goblet and plate and the "Venetian style" ribbed pieces in this group, as both styles of decoration had been thought to date from the mid-1920s or later. A further large group of drinking glasses,

15. Estelle S. Farrar and Jane Shadel Spillman, *The Complete Cut & Engraved Glass Of Corning*, Crown Publishers, 1979, p. 109, fig. 379.

8-51. Humidor in Cobweb pattern.

8-52. Trumpet vase in a simple diamond pattern.

8-53. Cologne, cruet and syrup pitcher in Venetian pattern showing how the design was adapted to different shapes.

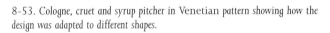

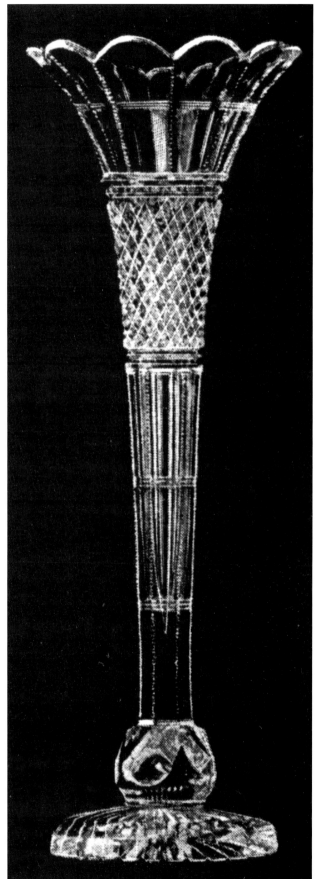

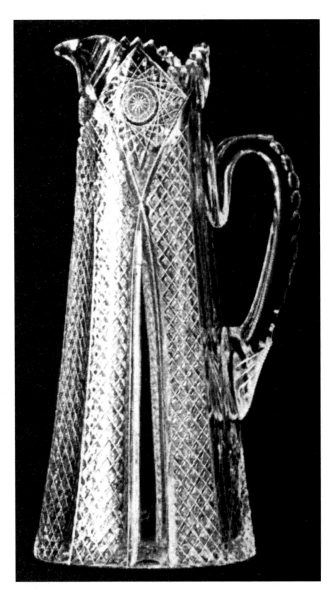

8-54. Tankard Jug labelled Aberdeen.

8-55. Tantalus set with two decanters.

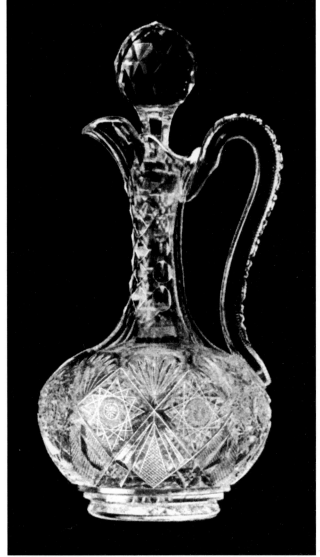

8-56. Claret jug cut in Monroe pattern.

8-57. Alberta, Mildred, Ormond *and* St. Regis *are shown.*

8-58. Canton, Flutes and Greek Border, Puritan *and* Raleigh.

part of the company's collection of samples, was given to the National Museum of American History by Samuel Hawkes's daughter in 1965. These document a number of special orders, but most of them unfortunately have never been photographed.

Figs. 8-57 through 8-72 are from a Hawkes catalog of about 1909 to 1913 which showed no prices.

Shapes and Uses – Special Types

The orders contain passing references to specific shapes by names which were apparently familiar to everyone. Richard Briggs frequently illustrated his orders with small line drawings which enable us to identify some of these. Handled custard cups looked exactly like the standard punch cups, Roman punch cups were often conical. "Mattoni" dishes were straight sided ovals made in several sizes, which may have been named after a worker at the Sandwich factory, where the term was in use by the 1870s.[16] "Canton" bowls were straight-sided, and square and "India" bowls were bulbous rather than straight-sided but square. A "Tiffany" water bottle was bulbous and flat-bottomed, while a "Webb" decanter had a pear-shaped body. "Mitchell" goblets were straight-sided and usually intended for engraving, but not cutting. "Church" goblets were apparently another shape, but they were not illustrated.

Sometimes the references are to certain shapes with limited uses. "The four celery trays you will please cross off as they were ordered February 3rd, & the celery season being over would not be of any good to us", said Davis Collamore in one letter.[17] Lamps, which Hawkes never made in considerable quantities, were apparently a slow seller. In 1888, Hawkes offered lamps cut in *Plaid* pattern at a substantial discount to Burley and Company: "We find that Glass Lamps are very slow sale. The cheapest lamp we make is no. 645 cut in Star & Hobnail price $40."[18] Davis Collamore ordered half a dozen glass spoons "to match china sample" in 1889, but there's no evidence that those were regular sellers.[19] Caldwell asked, "Have you any small pieces of glass that would do for Toothpick holders, or would your 544 Mustards without lids do? Send us three or four in different cuttings with prices in next package."[20] In another letter, Davis Collamore ordered two dozen "Egg glasses" cut in *Strawberry Diamond* and in *Hobstar*, both with "S/B"[21] (Abbreviations which refer to the shapes in these documents

16. Kirk J. Nelson, "Introductory Note to the 'c. 1874' Catalog and Price List," *The Acorn*, vol. 3, 1992, p. 15.
17. Davis Collamore & Company, New York, to T. G. Hawkes, June 21, 1882.
18. T. G. Hawkes to Burley & Company, Chicago, September 4, 1888.
19. Davis Collamore & Company, Ltd. New York, to T. G. Hawkes, February 28, 1889.
20. J. E. Caldwell & Company, Philadelphia, to T. G. Hawkes, October 8, 1888.
21. Davis Collamore, New York, to T. G. Hawkes, September 29, 1887.

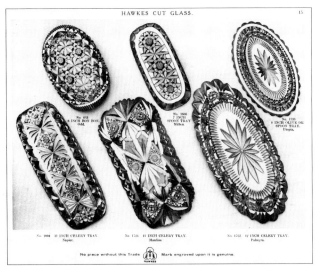

8-59. Manlius, Milton, Napier, Odd, Palmyra and Utopia.

8-60. Canton, Mars, Rio, Sonora and two different Odd patterns are shown.

8-61. Alberta, Caroline, Kaiser, Odd, Othello and Weston patterns are shown.

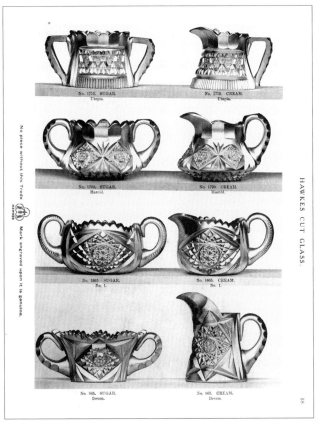

8-62. Sugars and creamers in Devon, Harold, No. 1 and Utopia are shown.

8-63. Caroline, Celeste, Hero, Kaiser, Odd, Queens and Teutonic are shown.

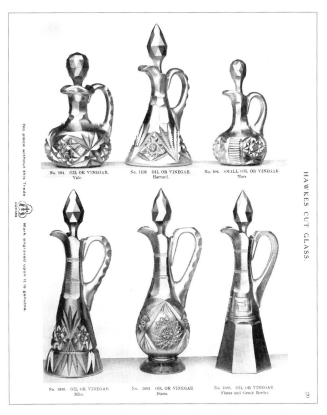

8-64. Cruets in Diana, Flutes and Greek Border, Harvard, Mars, Milo and Yale.

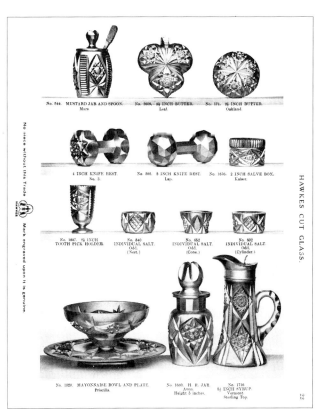

8-65. Accessories in a variety of patterns. The toothpick holder is unusual.

8-66. Vases in Borneo, Cuba, London, Mocha, Queens and St. Regis.

8-67. Vases in Brighton, Flutes and Greek Border, Grant, Rathbone and Queens.

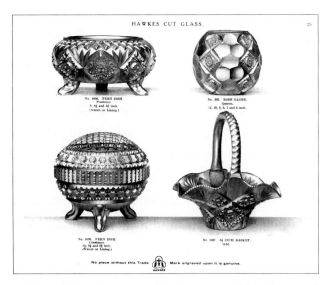

No. 1696. FERN DISH.
Prudence.
9, 8½ and 6½ inch.
(Screen or Lining.)

No. 685. ROSE GLOBE.
Queens.
12, 10, 9, 8, 7 and 6 inch.

No. 1696. FERN DISH.
Constance.
9½, 8½ and 6½ inch.
(Screen or Lining.)

No. 1467. 8½ INCH BASKET.
Odd.

No piece without this Trade Mark engraved upon it is genuine.

8-68. *Fern dishes in Constance and Prudence, a rose globe in Queens and an Odd basket.*

No. 1728. 10 INCH CHEESE AND CRACKER DISH.
Gravic Cosmos.
(Satin Finish.)

No. 200½. 11 INCH SANDWICH PLATE.
Gravic Cosmos.
(Satin Finish.)

No. 1677. 5 INCH BERRY DISH.
Gravic Cosmos.
(Satin Finish.)

No. 1726. BOWL.
Gravic Cosmos.
(Satin Finish.)
9, 8, 7 and 6 inch.

No. 390. BOWL.
Gravic Cosmos.
(Satin Finish.)
10, 9 and 8 inch

No. 100. 8 INCH NAPPY.
Gravic Cosmos.
(Satin Finish.)

No piece without this Trade Mark engraved upon it is genuine.

8-71. *An assortment of glass in Gravic Cosmos pattern.*

No. 1584. 8½ INCH BON BON.
Satin Engraved.

No. 1133. SUGAR.
Satin Engraved.

No. 1133. CREAM.
Satin Engraved.

No. 1587. 7 INCH TALL BON BON.
Satin Engraved.

No. 1611. 8½ INCH CANDLESTICK.
Satin Engraved.

No. 1102. 8 INCH VASE.
Satin Engraved.

No. 1668. No. 2 COLOGNE.
Satin Engraved.

No piece without this Trade Mark engraved upon it is genuine.

8-72. *An assortment of satin engraved glass.*

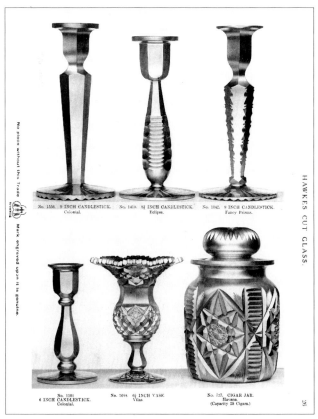

No piece without this Trade Mark engraved upon it is genuine.

No. 1556. 9 INCH CANDLESTICK.
Colonial.

No. 1419. 8½ INCH CANDLESTICK.
Eclipse.

No. 1042. 9 INCH CANDLESTICK.
Fancy Prisms.

No. 1101. 6 INCH CANDLESTICK.
Colonial.

No. 1688. 6½ INCH VASE.
Vilas.

No. 727. CIGAR JAR.
Havana.
(Capacity 25 Cigars.)

8-69. *Colonial, Eclipse, Fancy Prisms, Havana and Vilas pieces.*

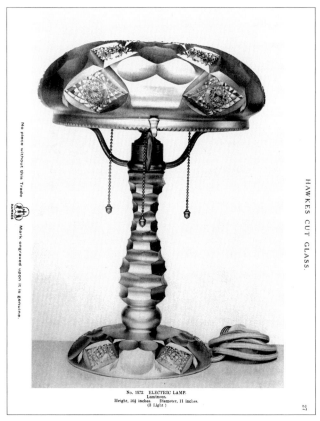

No piece without this Trade Mark engraved upon it is genuine.

No. 1572. ELECTRIC LAMP.
Luminous.
Height, 16½ inches. Diameter, 11 inches.
(2 Light.)

8-70. *An electric lamp in Luminous pattern which is closely related to Queens.*

200

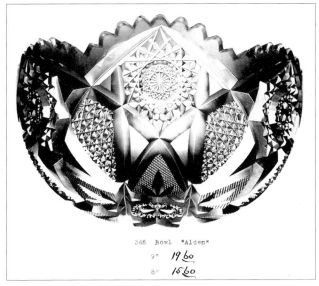

8-73. Alden pattern bowl on shape 346 was available in two sizes.

8-74. Aztec pattern was very simple and inexpensive.

Figs. 8-73 through 8-89 are from a catalog of the early teens.

are S/B for star bottom, SS for straw stem, PE for plain edge, S/S for shell scallop, F/S is fan scallop (these are rim finishes), and LF for low footed.)

Table bells were in the regular line in only a few patterns although they could be specially ordered. "We use the bowls of broken hocks and clarets for these bells, as we have before explained to you, but as we had none in stock cut Russian, we sent the nearest thing we had. We can cut a bell specially for you if you wish, but it would be considerably more expensive, as we only put these bells in at these prices to get rid of our broken hocks, etc. Please let us know if we shall do so or shall we wait until we have some more broken hocks cut Russian? It may be some months before we do though."[22]

Sometimes the special order was even stranger, as when Briggs asked for "SS Wines and round bowled clarets to be made very light, as the customer expresses it <u>thin as paper</u>."[23] Hawkes's scribbled reply stated that he could make it if Briggs sent samples. In another letter, Briggs asked for tumblers in *Louis XIV* shape but cut to match "one of the English tumblers I sent you". The enclosed sketch shows a tumbler with a flared top and engraved flower stems and leaves in a vertical format.[24] Briggs also asked for samples of this pattern in stemware so that he could take orders for it, because he wanted a pattern similar to *Louis XIV* but less expensive. It might well be difficult to distinguish these tumblers, as sold by Briggs, from their English models.

The letters also frequently referred to objects returned to Hawkes to be repaired or cut down into something else. Sometimes the customer made a special request and sometimes the end result was left to the ingenuity of the Hawkes cutters. Matchings were also requested and it is probably these which account for the occasional pieces in older patterns which turn up bearing the HAWKES acid-stamped signature which was adopted after 1910. The *Buckle* pattern, which was originally cut in the 1850s when it seems to have been popular in pressed glass, was made by a number of firms, Dorflinger among them, but several pieces are known with Hawkes signatures (Fig. 8–19). All of the pieces that I have seen have the "Brooklyn star", a type of foot used on some early Dorflinger pieces, but this

22. T. G. Hawkes & Company to Davis Collamore & Company, Ltd., New York, September 27, 1892.
23. Richard Briggs, Boston to T. G. Hawkes, February 12, 1887.
24. Richard Briggs, Boston, to T. G. Hawkes, October 8, 1888.

8-75. Baron pattern bowl was much less expensive than Alden.

8-76. Bedford pattern bowl was $12 in the 8in. size.

8-77. Berlin water jug and tumbler.

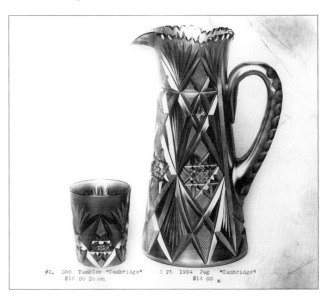

8-78. Cambridge water jug and tumbler.

8-79. Carnot bowl, 6in. in diameter was $5.00.

8-80. Clarendon bowl, 7in. in diameter was $6.00

202

8-81. Pint jugs in Clement and Bruce were $6 and $7.

8-82. Sugar and creamer in Clyde pattern were $3.50 each.

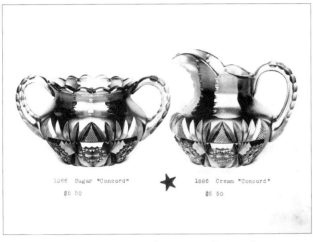

8-83. Sugar and creamer in Concord pattern were $5.50 each.

8-84. Corinthian pattern bowl, was $13 for the 8in. size and $16 for the 9in.

8-85. Cromwell pattern bowl was $5.50.

8-86. Dayton pattern whiskey jug and tumbler.

8-87. Dolphin pattern sugar and creamer.

8-88. Ella pattern bonbon was $1.50.

8-89. Edwin pattern bowl was $4.50.

is neither an indication of date or of origin. A letter from Bullard Brothers to Hawkes specifies that the *Russian* pattern tableware made for them should have the foot cut in this star and fan design and includes a rubbing of it to show Hawkes.[25] This foot design, therefore, cannot be taken as a guarantee of either date or origin; in all likelihood, other makers used it as well. Other examples of this type of work include a cut urn in the Sandwich Museum which has a lid supplied by Hawkes in the 20th century (Fig. 8–151), and small wineglasses in early 19th century style in the Jones Museum.

Pattern copying was always a problem, even in the case of the patented patterns. Hawkes's competitors copied his patterns, especially *Russian*, and he was accused by several of them of pirating. Frederick Shirley, of the Mt. Washington Glass Company, was particularly diligent in watching for this sort of thing. Shirley sent out a circular in 1885 to other glass makers warning that he would sue those who infringed his patents and the cover letter to Thomas Hawkes can only be classified as rude:

"Dear Sir: Yours duly to hand & noted had you confined yourself to the truth we should not have replied but can certainly show you several instances where you have copied & not originated & therefore presume you have lacked the brain

25. Bullard Brothers, St. Paul to T. G. Hawkes, November 9, 1889.

8-90. Bowl in Emperor pattern.

8-91. Creamer and sugar in Estelle pattern.

8-92. Creamer and sugar in Glenwood pattern.

8-93. Creamer and sugar in Helene pattern.

power which you seem to have it believed you have such an excess of. We use ours so much that we still have room for suggestions from others."[26]

Unfortunately, Hawkes's reply is not in the correspondence. A couple of years later W. H. Lum, who was Shirley's agent in New York, complained to Davis Collamore that Hawkes 547 celery tray was too similar to his patented "Lum" celery and Hawkes decided to stop making it. In 1888 and 1889, Shirley complained that Hawkes was cutting his "Mirror Block" pattern. Hawkes's first reaction was negative: "We beg to state that you are mistaken when you say that you originated this Mirror Block pattern; it is one of the oldest patterns that we know of, Mr. John Hoare has drawings of the same pattern cut on heavy Decanters thirty years ago by the firm of Gould & Hoare of South Ferry, Brooklyn."[27] However, after a number of letters back and forth, Hawkes decided it was not worth the trouble to keep cutting the pattern. Shirley seems to have threatened Dorflinger at the same time as Hawkes replied to White Mills: "Some time ago we stopped all communication between Shirley and ourselves as we do not consider him responsible. He is perfectly willing to make agreements almost any day, and break them the next; we do not have any dealings with such concerns."[28]

Other letters in the files are from customers asking Hawkes to copy someone

Figs. 8-90 through 8-114 are from an undated catalog of the mid-teens.

26. F. S. Shirley, Mt. Washington Glass Company, to T. G. Hawkes, October 6, 1885.
27. T. G. Hawkes to F. S. Shirley, Mt. Washington, October 2, 1888.
28. T. G. Hawkes to C. Dorflinger & Sons, White Mills, April 28, 1889.

8-94. *Water jug and tumbler in Homer pattern.*

8-95. *Creamer and sugar in Irene pattern.*

8-96. *3 ½ pint jug in the Old English line on shape 2126.*

8-97. *3 Pint jug in the Old English line on shape 2124.*

29. T. G. Hawkes & Company to Davis Collamore & Sons, Ltd. New York, June 8, 1892.
30. T. B. Clark & Co, Honesdale to T. G. Hawkes, March 24, 1887.
31. Richard Briggs, Boston to T. G. Hawkes, August 1, 1888.

else's shapes or patterns, usually to match a customer's set. One letter from Hawkes to Davis Collamore explains that he would not supply a catalog to a retailer in Marion, Indiana, because he was convinced that the retailer wanted it for Dithridge & Company who had just opened a shop in Marion and probably wanted to copy his designs.[29] This seems to have been carrying worries about competition a little far. However, correspondence between 1887 and 1889 has more than one instance of complaints to Hawkes and from Hawkes to others. T. B. Clark complained about copying the *Czar* pattern in 1887;[30] Richard Briggs ordered tumblers, finger bowls and water bottles cut in "libby's victoria pattern" in 1888 and Hawkes did not refuse the order.[31] In that case, Libbey may have been

8-98. 3 Pint jug in the Old English line on shape 2122.

8-99. 3 Pint Jug in the Old English line on shape 2123.

8-100. Cruet in Palermo.

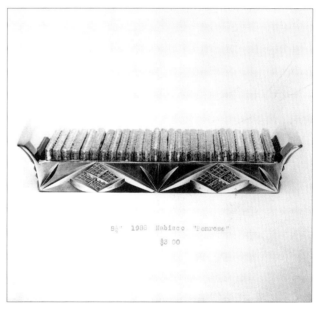

8-101. Cracker container in Penrose.

busy moving from East Cambridge to Toledo and unable to fill the order. There were several controversies with James Hoare who seems to have had a temperament something like Frederick Shirley's. In one exchange, James Hoare wrote to Hawkes that he had seen John S. Earl of McCue and Earl trying to sell "those turnover celery trays" to a customer in New York. When Hawkes wrote to Earl to complain, he replied "would say that when anyone says that we are selling a celery tray like yours they say something that is very far from the truth."[32]

A year later, Hawkes wrote to Hoare: "We notice that you have ordered ten dozen of our no. 547 Celery trays. Some time ago you said that you had to have a few made for Tiffany & Co. and we consented. We understand you claim that

32. J. Hoare & Company to T. G. Hawkes, June 6, 1887; McCue & Earl, Brooklyn, to T. G. Hawkes, June 8, 1887.

8-102. Bowl in Phoenix pattern.

8-103. Sugar and creamer in Regina pattern.

8-104. Bowl in Renfrew pattern.

8-105. Drinking set in Richfield pattern

8-106. Sugar and creamer in Sevres pattern.

8-107. Bowl in Selma pattern.

8-108. Sugar and creamer in Thelma pattern.

8-109. *Water jug and tumbler in Tiger Lily pattern.*

8-110. *12in. Vase in Trellis pattern.*

8-111. *Individual sugar and creamer in Trilby pattern.*

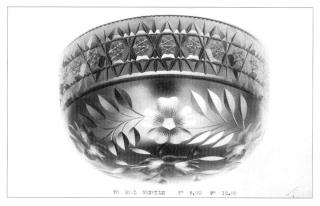

8-112. Venetian pattern bowl. *This is the second Hawkes Venetian pattern.*

8-113. *Westfield pattern pitcher and glass for grape juice.*

8-114. *Winifred pattern sugar and creamer.*

8-115. Adonis bowl cost $5.00

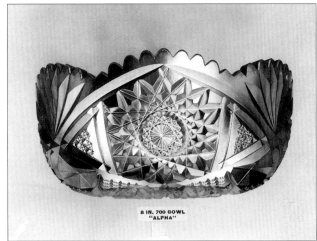

8-116. Bowl in Alpha pattern.

8-117. Jug and tumbler in Arabic cost $24.00 and $34.00 a dozen.

8-118. In Ceylon, whiskey jug cost $17.00, tumblers $16.00 a dozen and highball glasses $33.00 a dozen.

Figs. 8-115 through 8-131 are from a Hawkes catalog of about 1910–1915 with handwritten prices.

other people are making this shape which is not true. Will you inform us if it is your policy to make agreements and then break them the next day? Unless you give us some satisfactory explanation... we will write to Tiffany & Co. and ask if it is necessary that we should furnish them with our designs and patterns through the firm of J. Hoare & Co. We wish you to distinctly understand that we consider your conduct in this matter as highly reprehensible, and a clear cut case of piracy and breaking your word."[33] James Hoare replied that the order to the Glass Works for ten dozen celery trays was a mistake, but "The Balance of Your letter sounds like the prattle of some over Grown School boy, an amateur in Business anything but showing up wonderful Brains and I have no time to answer or Comment on such Trash."[34] A week later, Hoare wrote again to say that one of his employees had just returned from working for McCue and Earl in Brooklyn where he had been working on the identical celery. This time, Hawkes wrote to Earl, enclosing a sample celery and the letter from Hoare. Earl replied as before, saying that he did not make this celery and that he had not employed the cutter from Hoare at

33. T. G. Hawkes to J. Hoare & Company January 15, 1889.
34. James Hoare to T. G. Hawkes, January 16, 1889.

8-119. Cut & Moss Rose jug cost $30.00; the matching tumblers were $40.00 a dozen.

8-120. Cut & Water Cress jug cost $20.00; the matching tumblers were $36.00 a dozen.

8-121. Everett sugar and creamer were $6.50 each.

8-122. Gibson oval bowl was $14.00.

all. The end result was a handsome apology from George L. Abbott, Hoare's partner and a week later, an order from Hoare to Hawkes for "½ Doz. blanks of 'The' Celery tray," so apparently all was forgiven.[35] Considering that these men were all well-acquainted, the whole controversy seems faintly ridiculous.

Two months later, a New York customer wrote to say that he had seen in Neil's Dry Goods store on 6th Avenue "your 547 Celery Tray cut Russian with John Hoare's Label on it." This time, Hawkes had someone from Davis Collamore purchase the celery, complete with label and then sent it to Hoare with a letter complaining about the location rather than about Hoare's cutting. "We have been very particular in never selling Macy & Co. or any other cheap dry goods house any of our glass, no matter what price they are willing to pay for it, and you can readily see that it is a difficult task for us to explain to our customers who are willing to pay us our price for our goods how they can meet this kind of competition. We also send you yesterday's New York Tribune showing O'Neil's advertisement where they make special features of crystal glass at low prices. We

35. J. Hoare & Company to T. G. Hawkes, January 23, January 28, February 8, 1889; T. G. Hawkes to McCue & Earl, Brooklyn, January 23, 1889; McCue & Earl to T. G. Hawkes, January 25, 1889.

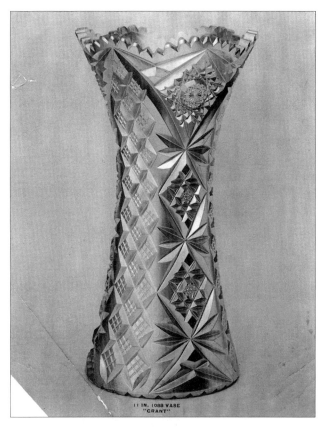

8-123. Grant *vase was* $13.00

8-124. Huron *claret jug was* $12.00

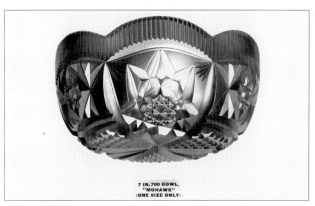

8-125. Mohawk *bowl was* $5.50

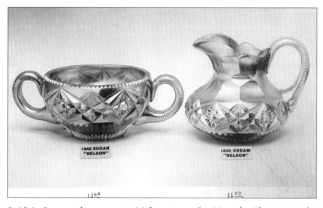

8-126. Sugar and creamer in Nelson were $4.00 each. This is not the Nelson patented in 1897, but a reuse of the name.

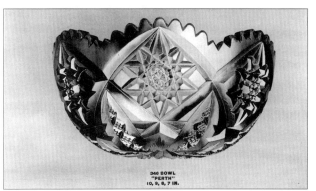

8-127. Bowl in Perth pattern cost from $6.50 to $14.00 depending on size.

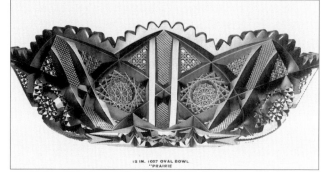

8-128. Oval bowl in Prairie pattern cost $27.00.

8-129. Jug in Pueblo pattern was $30.00.

8-130. Bowl in Puritan pattern was $12.00.

8-131. Sugar and creamer in Ruskin pattern were $5.00 each.

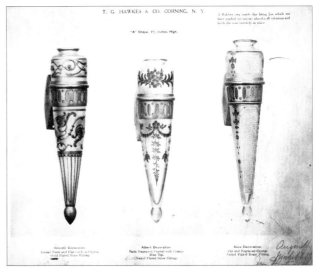

8-132. Page from a Hawkes catalog of automobile vases, dated 1917.

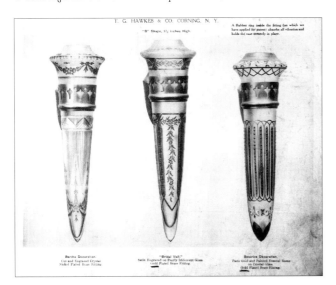

8-133. Page from a Hawkes catalog of automobile vases, dated 1917; the Bridal Veil glass was Steuben's *Verre de Soie*.

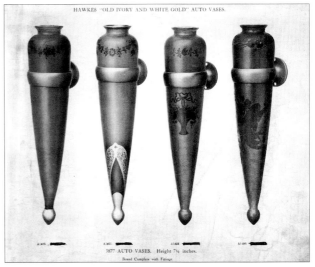

8-134. Page from a Hawkes catalog of automobile vases, dated 1917.

8-135. *Water jug and tumbler in Calliopsis pattern. Signet Glass Company.*

8-136. *Water jug and tumbler in Empire pattern. Signet Glass Company.*

8-137. *Water jug and tumbler in Rose of Sharon pattern. Signet Glass Company.*

8-138. *Lily bowl and holder in Rose of Sharon pattern. Signet Glass Company.*

Figs. 8-135 through 8-148 are pages from a Signet Glass Company catalog of about 1915, the only one known. Some Signet pieces had a trademark, but possibly the marking was not consistent since only a few marked Signet pieces have surfaced. The sugar and creamer in 8-149 have the Signet trademark No prices are given in the catalog, but Signet was a cheaper Hawkes line.

36. T. G. Hawkes to J. Hoare & Company April 12, 1889.

scarcely believe that these goods have been sold to the above party with your consent, we rather think that they have procured the goods in some underhand way…"[36]

There is no further correspondence about the celery tray, so eventually the problem was solved. It must have been a popular shape if everyone wanted it. This is the only reference to a Hoare label, but it raises the possibility that Hoare, like Dorflinger and Hawkes, used a paper label in the 1880s and 1890s.

The proper way to deal with a customer's request for someone else's pattern is shown in an exchange of letters between Burley & Company, who ordered a number of pieces of "Parisian pattern such as Dorflinger gives that name to", and Hawkes. The Corning firm filled the order, assuming that Dorflinger would not object, since it was a small one. A couple of months later Hawkes wrote to Dorflinger to get their permission to fill another small order of *Parisian* for another

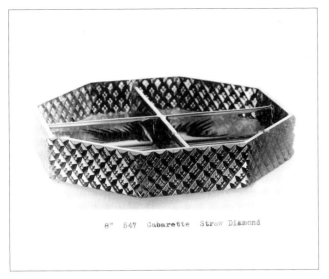

8-139. *Cabarette in Strawberry Diamond pattern. Signet Glass Company.*

8-140. *Water jug and tumbler in Wild Rose pattern. Signet Glass Company.*

8-141. *Vase with airtwist stem in Wild Rose pattern. Signet Glass Company.*

8-142. *Compote with airtwist stem in Wild Rose pattern. Signet Glass Company.*

8-143. *Satin Engraved sugar and creamer. Signet glass Company.*

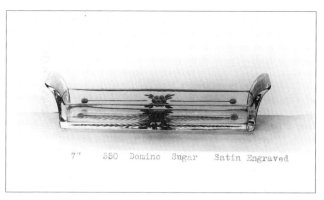

8-144. *Satin Engraved Domino sugar holder. Signet Glass Company.*

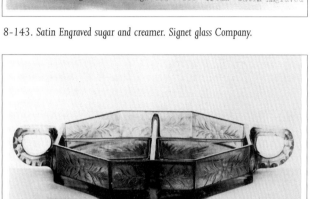

(*Above*)8-145. *Satin Engraved Cabarette. Signet Glass Company.*

(*Right*)8-146. *Satin Engraved Cologne. Signet Glass Company.*

(*Below*)8-147. *Satin Engraved French Dressing Bottle. Signet Glass Company.*

(*Below right*)8-148. *Satin Engraved basket. Signet Glass Company.*

8-149. Sugar and creamer in
Calliopsis pattern. Signet Glass
Company, 1913–1918.
Acid-stamped "SIGNET" with
cloud-like background. Ht. of
creamer 7.7cm. Gift of Mr. and
Mrs. F.S. Earnshaw (CMG
85.4.88AB).

8-150. Candelabra in Deauville
pattern, possibly from the Edenhall
line, T. G. Hawkes & Company
1914–1918, H: 20.3cm. Gift of
Marilyn J. Barker (CMG
90.4.123).

8-151. Colorless cut urn with ruby lining. Replacement ruby lid made by T. G. Hawkes & Company, probably about 1910–1920, acid-stamped "HAWKES" on lid. Ht. 63cm. Gift of Mrs. Russell Alger, Sandwich Museum.

37. Burley & Company, Chicago to T. G. Hawkes, November 12, 1888; T. G. Hawkes to Burley, November 14, 1888; T. G. Hawkes to C. Dorflinger & Sons, February 14, 1889; C. Dorflinger & Sons to T. G. Hawkes, February 15, 1889.

customer, and that duly granted, filled the second order as well.[37]

Sometimes only the name of the pattern was a problem, as when Hawkes inadvertently used the same name as Straus for one pattern and decided to change it rather than provoke controversy. At the same time, he wrote to Dithridge suggesting that they should not have named their patterns *Princess* and *Brazilian*. Hawkes continued to use these pattern names, but Dithridge may have done so as well; not much is known about their products. Clearly, the issue of pattern copying was a sore point with most manufacturers, but the design patents do not seem to have offered much protection, except when backed up with irate letters.

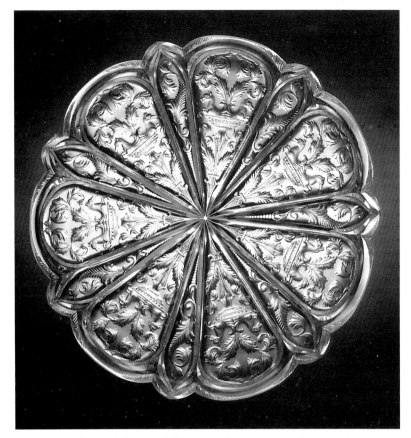

8-152. Cut and engraved plate, signed "W.H. Morse". D. 28cm. Gift of T.G. Hawkes & Company to the U.S. National Museum, May 22, 1917. N.M.A.H, Smithsonian Institution.

8-153. Satin engraved champagne jug. H. 40.6cm. Gift of T. G.Hawkes & Company to the U.S. National Museum, May 22, 1917. N.M.A.H., Smithsonian Institution.

8-154. Plate cut pillars and rich rock crystal (Coronation pattern). D. 28cm. Gift of T. G.Hawkes & Company to the U.S. National Museum, May 22, 1917. N.M.A.H., Smithsonian Institution

8-155. Plate cut and engraved peacock. D. 28.5cm. Gift of T. G. Hawkes & Company to the U.S. National Museum, May 22, 1917. N.M.A.H., Smithsonian Institution.

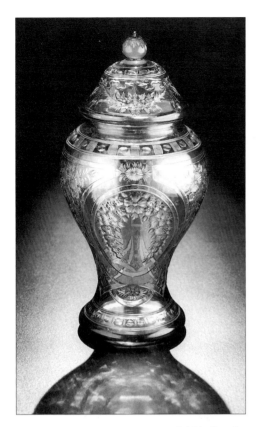

8-156. *Covered urn, ruby cased over colorless glass. H.28cm. Gift of T. G. Hawkes & Company to the U.S. National Museum, May 22, 1917. N.M.A.H., Smithsonian Institution.*

8-157. *Plate with rich mitre cutting (Sevres pattern). D. 28cm. Gift of T. G. Hawkes & Company to the U.S. National Museum, May 22, 1917. N.M.A.H., Smithsonian Institution.*

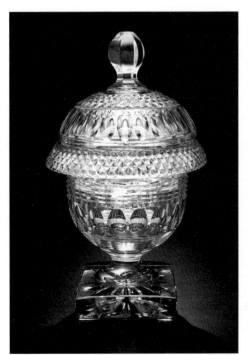

8-158. *Reproduction Old English covered urn. H.33cm. Gift of T. G. Hawkes & Company to the U.S. National Museum, May 28, 1917. N.M.A.H., Smithsonian Institution.*

8-159. *Cut and engraved sterling silver mounted bowl. D.22.8cm. Gift of T. G. Hawkes & Company to the U.S. National Museum, May 28, 1917. N.M.A.H., Smithsonian Institution.*

8-160. Enamel and gold decorated goblet and plate, H. of goblet 16.6cm. Gift of T. G. Hawkes & Company to the U.S. National Museum, May 28, 1917 (goblet) and June 27, 1918 (plate). N.M.A.H., Smithsonian Institution.

8-161. Decanter cut Pillars and Fleur de Lys and vase cut Chelsea Bird. H.(decanter) 31.5cm. Gift of T. G. Hawkes & Company to the U.S. National Museum, Oct. 11, 1917. N.M.A.H., Smithsonian Institution.
8-162.Covered jar, amethyst cased over colorless glass, cut and engraved. H. 9cm. Gift of T. G. Hawkes & Company to the U. S. National Museum, June 27, 1918. N.M.A.H., Smithsonian Institution.

CHAPTER NINE

The Paris Exposition

In 1888, the Hawkes cut glass business was sufficiently prosperous that Thomas Hawkes could afford to try something new. He was approached by the firm of Davis, Collamore & Company, his major customer in New York City, with the suggestion that Hawkes should prepare a large display of cut glass which Collamore would send to the upcoming Universal Exposition in Paris, which promised to be the biggest World's Fair of the decade. Collamore was a prominent glass and china house and this was a major opportunity for the comparatively new Hawkes firm. The only other objects in the Collamore display would be an equally large section devoted to the art wares of the Rookwood Pottery Company of Cincinnati, for which Collamore was the exclusive New York outlet.

Exactly when Hawkes decided to join forces with Davis Collamore and Company is not clear, but it must have been early in 1888, as Hawkes spent the summer preparing glass to send. On December 26, 1888, Carleton W. Bonfils, a principal in the New York firm, sent Hawkes an enthusiastic letter saying "We have a splendid space allotted us in the middle of the building, something like this"[1] and he drew a diagram showing that Collamore, Gorham, Tiffany and the Meriden Britannia Company would occupy the four corners of a square court. All three of the other firms may have exhibited some silver mounted cut glass, but the largest display of glass was certainly that of Collamore and Hawkes. During the next three months, the Hawkes firm sent daily letters to their blanks suppliers, to their silver suppliers and to Bonfils concerning the exhibit. A letter to Gorham in January is typical:[2]

"We send you to-day by express, a sample ruby jug. Please make us four handsome sterling tops suitable for same. In making the tops please carry out the same curve in the spout of the top, as there is in the neck of our jug if you think it advisable. Two of these tops are to be used on two cut ruby jugs... and the others... the same size and shape but green."

Hawkes also sent samples of a punch ladle and a salad fork and spoon and ordered three of each, all in different patterns, to be chosen by Gorham, and large and small ice bowl rims and handles of which he ordered two each. "All of these goods are intended for our exhibit at the Paris Exhibition. We will leave the design, etc. to your Mr. Wilmeson as his taste in such matters would be much better than ours.... We must have these goods not later than Feb. 15."[3] A week later, Louis Dorflinger wrote that they "have received the Punch Bowl mould and will have a try at it very soon."[4] Although the Exposition was not mentioned in that letter, there was a considerable amount of correspondence about the extra-large punch bowls that the Dorflinger factory was making for Hawkes. On January 23 Hawkes wrote "We are very anxious to get one or two of the large Punch bowls but are well aware that these are difficult to make. We are very anxious to make a few. If you can succeed in doing so, please send us a couple."[5] The next day Dorflinger responded, "We are making special preparations to make your large Punch Bowl and will advise you in a day or two what success we have."[6] On February 4, Dorflinger wrote that they would schedule production of the punch

1. Carleton W. Bonfils for Davis, Collamore & Company, New York City, to Thomas G. Hawkes, December 26, 1888.
2. T. G. Hawkes to Gorham Mfg., New York, January 4, 1889.
3. Ibid.
4. C. Dorflinger & Sons, White Mills, to T. G. Hawkes, January 11, 1889.
5. T. G. Hawkes to C. Dorflinger & Sons, White Mills, January 23, 1889.
6. C. Dorflinger & Sons, White Mills, to T. G. Hawkes, January 24, 1889.

9-1. *Hawkes display before it was packed for Paris. The Venetian and Large Hobnail pattern punch bowls are in the foreground and the silver-mounted jugs in the rear.*

bowls the following Monday[7] and on February 8, Louis Dorflinger wrote: "Referring to the large punch bowl. We made a special effort and considerable expense to secure some extra fine material for our best metal to make this work. We have tried several pots of this metal and it is very fine."[8] On February 11, "Large punch bowls are making. four now in the kiln. Will write you particulars tomorrow."[9] Two days later, he wrote: "We send you today by express one of the large punch Bowls. This weighs 33 lbs. We found we could not blow these bowls in your mould as it was impossible to get the glass blown up a uniform thickness so we made them by hand and so far as shape and size is concerned you will find them all right but the metal is not, it has not color enough."[10]

On January 24, Hawkes wrote cheerfully to Bonfils: "Some of the Exhibition goods are commencing to come in from the shops finished and we must say that they are really beautiful. Most of the goods that we are getting up are new designs expressly for this occasion and we must say that they exceed all our former efforts; they are costing us a great deal of money but of course you understand that we wish to send glass second to none. What we want is the medal. It will be impossible for us to get all the goods finished in time for shipment by the 2nd of

7. C. Dorflinger & Sons, White Mills, to Thomas G. Hawkes, February 4, 1889.
8. C. Dorflinger & Sons, White Mills, to Thomas G. Hawkes, February 8, 1889.
9. C. Dorflinger & Sons, White Mills, to T. G. Hawkes, February 11, 1889.
10. C. Dorflinger & Sons, White Mills to T. G. Hawkes, February 13, 1889.

March, still we will have a good portion of them done by that time. We are making quite a large quantity of goods. Please let us know if you have ordered the cases, etc. and have all other necessary arrangements made and what arrangements have you made for the glass that we cannot get finished by the 2nd of March."[11]

On February 2nd, an alarmed Bonfils wrote "Have heard that Tiffany & Company will make a special feature at Exposition of Hoare's glass silver-mounted… Closed contract last night with Allard & Company for fittings, furnishings & c. He guarantees to have everything ready by April 1st and it will be very elegant, as Expo opens May 5th you see we will have plenty of time to arrange goods."[12] And in another letter the same day he said, "We will have a very handsome case for the Ice Cream Set made of antique oak, with lacquered brass trimmings, it will have a drawer in it…" and described the "considerable" paperwork deemed necessary for goods sent to the Exposition.[13]

Hawkes responded: "We have known for some time that J. Hoare & Co. are getting up some clarets, etc. for silver mounting for Tiffany's Exhibit at Paris. We do not think that we need be in the least worried about Tiffany or J. Hoare & Co. Our exhibit will be exclusively rich cut glass with some few pieces mounted in silver to give tone to the exhibit, and when you get it all arranged with the taste that we think you are going to display in the matter, we are under the impression that there will be nothing better at the Exhibition. For our part, we are not sparing time or money to make it go."[14]

By mid-month, Bonfils had sent the paperwork to Hawkes for signature and was urging him to number all of the objects and to let him know when he would have a shipment ready.[15] Goods were to go at the expense of the U.S. government in February and on March 2 and 9th; but anything sent after that would be at the expense of the shipper. Hawkes replied that he would have nothing ready to go in February but would have the bulk of his glass ready by March 2.[16] At the same time, he was telling some of his customers that due to the urgency of the Exhibition work, he could not fill their orders.[17]

He also wrote to Gorham to urge them to hurry with the silver mounts for the Exhibition and he complained that, because of their delay, he would not be able to have fitted cases made for the silver-mounted pieces.[18] Apparently, the manufacture of the cases was fairly rapid, because on February 19, Hawkes wrote to the American Morocco Case Company in New York to order cases for a large footed punch bowl and two decanters, one globe-shaped and the other straight: "For the large punch bowl and foot… make two brass bound wooden cases lined with the finest quality of white satin, wood same as in ice cream set case just received, or if you have a different wood which is equally handsome we would prefer it, as it would give a variety, Cases to have a place to hold the ladle. For the large globe decanter and stopper, make a wooden brass bound case to hold two decanters, case to be lined with White Satin. For the straight decanter [the same]. We also send you three glass bowls, and one salad spoon and fork. Make a brass

11. Signed copy, T. G. Hawkes to Carleton W. Bonfils, January 24, 1889.
12. C. W. Bonfils for Davis Collamore & Company, New York to T. G. Hawkes, February 2, 1889.
13. C. W. Bonfils for Davis Collamore & Company, New York to T. G. Hawkes, February 2, 1889.
14. Signed copy, T. G. Hawkes to C. W. Bonfils, February 4, 1889.
15. C. W. Bonfils for Davis Collamore & Company, New York to T. G. Hawkes, February 12, 1889.
16. T. G. Hawkes to C. W. Bonfils, New York, February 14, 1889.
17. T. G. Hawkes to Eustis Brothers, Minneapolis, February 14, 1889.
18. T. G. Hawkes to Gorham Mfg. Company, Providence, February 19, 1889.

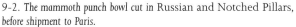

SHOW ROOM OF - T. G. HAWKES, CORNING, N. Y.
GLASS SENT TO PARIS EXPOSITION 1889.

SHOW ROOM OF - T. G. HAWKES, CORNING, N. Y.
GLASS SENT TO PARIS EXPOSITION, 1889.

9-2. *The mammoth punch bowl cut in Russian and Notched Pillars,
before shipment to Paris.*

9-3. *Grecian pattern punch bowl from the Hawkes shipment.*

bound wooden case for each of these bowls and make a place in each case to hold a spoon and fork… We want these just as soon as you can get them out as they are for our exhibit at Paris… Please advise by return mail when you will send these."[19]

A couple of days later, Hawkes was informing the company that one of the three punch bowls was 9 ½ in. high and the other 10 ½ in. and they were not sure of the height of the sample sent so the three cases had to be adjusted accordingly.[20] So much for quality control.

In a letter to Somerville P. Tuck, the U.S. Commissioner to the Exposition, Hawkes asked about shipping dates and explained, "We are making a much larger and handsomer exhibit than we first anticipated, and although we have been working on it more or less for over six months, we even now find that we are pressed for time."[21]

When the American Morocco Case Company was slow in shipment, Hawkes wrote to insist on delivery to Corning and said: "We wish you to bear in mind that we want you to give us first class work do not wait to get them all finished, ship them two or three at a time. We want two cases for large punch bowls… If these cases are satisfactory to us we shall probably order several more for different articles immediately."[22]

Meanwhile, the Dorflinger company inquired about the cutting of the punch bowls; they wanted to see a finished version. "Won't you send one to Murray Street we will no doubt sell it for you as we have sold all the large ones we have."[23] Hawkes replied that he would be happy to cut a large punch bowl for the Murray Street store, but that the blanks had not yet arrived in Corning and needed to be

19. T. G. Hawkes to American Morocco Case Company, New York, February 19, 1889.
20. T. G. Hawkes to American Morocco Case Company, New York, February 21, 1889.
21. T. G. Hawkes to Somerville P. Tuck, Esq., New York, February 22, 1889.
22. T. G. Hawkes to American Morocco Case Company, New York, February 22, 1889.
23. C. Dorflinger & Sons, White Mills, to T. G. Hawkes, February 25, 1889.

traced.[24] Since this was only a week before the first shipment, the cutters must have been gnashing their teeth at the delay. By February 28, they were able to report that the punch bowls were in Corning: "They are very satisfactory to us and we consider them as good a piece of glassmaking as we ever saw."[25]

Somewhat surprisingly, Davis Collamore next inquired about the disposition of the award if they should get it. To whom would it be made out?[26] Hawkes replied indignantly: "If any medal is awarded we are to have it as that is what we are exhibiting for. We are now finishing up an extra large punch bowl and a pair of nine light candelabras and a few other pieces. In all about $1000.00 worth but we cannot give an exact date when they will be finished. Keep us posted on the latest date we can send them.[27]

The initial Hawkes shipment was sent to the American Commissioner in New York March 6, 1889, just in time for the March 7 shipment. Hawkes's letter to Davis Collamore says: "We enclose invoice of glass sent to Paris today. There are some more pieces to go in a few days: A large punch bowl to cost from $300 to $400, two 9 light candelabras, samples of stem ware and a few other pieces. Glass sent today we consider very fine."[28] The entire shipment consisted of eleven packages which held a total of 213 pieces plus the lined cases for some of them. The list follows:

Package no. 1 held eight fitted cases for two punch bowls, one ice cream set, three bowls and two decanters. These were the cases made by the American Morocco Case Company the previous month and they were valued at from $27 to $40 each.

Package no. 2 held four punch bowls, two 15in. ones in *Venetian* and *Large Hobnail* on shape no. 497, (see Fig. 9-1) a 14in. one in *Lustre* pattern on shape no. 497, and a 13in. one in *Cobweb* pattern on shape no. 212. These were priced at $136., $128., $100. and $40., respectively.

Package no. 3 had two 5-light candelabras priced at $75. each and two 4-light ones for $45.

Package no. 4 had two large 3-light candelabras at $35. each, two small 4-light candelabras at $40. each, two extra arms and eighteen drops (doubtless in case of breakage) and a 13in. 433 bowl in *Princess* pattern at $30 and a 12in. 897 bowl in *Empress* pattern at $27.

Package no. 5 had seven bowls in varying sizes:

12in. 462 bowl in *Empress* at $27.

11in. 391 bowl in *Russian & Sharp Pillars*, at $27.

10in. 346 bowl in *Russian & Sharp Pillars & Stars*, at $25.

9in. 346 bowl in *Russian & Sharp Pillars & Stars*, at $20.

8in. 346 bowl in *Russian & Sharp Pillars & Stars*, at $15.

10in. 700 bowl in *Russian & Sharp Pillars & Stars*, at $25.

10in. 346 bowl in *Stars & Fans & Lace Hobnail*, at $ 25.

Package no. 6 had eleven bowls in varying sizes and patterns:

9in. 346 bowl in *Stars & Fans & Lace Hobnail*, at $20.

24. T. G. Hawkes to C. Dorflinger & Sons, White Mills, February 26, 1889.
25. Signed copy, T. G. Hawkes to C. Dorflinger & Sons, White Mills, February 28, 1889.
26. 26 W. H. Lowndes for Davis Collamore & Company, New York, to T. G. Hawkes, March 13, 1889.
27. T. G. Hawkes to Davis Collamore & Company, New York, March 17, 1889.
28. T. G. Hawkes to Davis Collamore & Company, New York, March 6, 1889.

9-4. *Another view of the Hawkes display in Corning, showing the Grecian pattern ice cream set at right.*

8in. 346 bowl in *Stars & Fans & Lace Hobnail*, at $15.

11in. 462 bowl in *Empress*, at $21.

9in. 463 bowl in *Empress*, at $14.

9in. 463 bowl in *Princess*, at $14.

9in. 463 bowl in *Russian*, at $14.

13in. 365 bowl in *Grecian*, at $25.

10in. 365 bowl in *Cobweb*, at $18.

9in. 365 bowl in *Cobweb*, at $15.

8in. 757 bowl in *Cobweb*, at $10.

8in. 757 bowl in *Grecian*, at $15.

Package no. 7 had twenty pieces including the thirteen-piece ice cream set which had its own fitted case.

458 Ice Bowl with silver rim in *Princess* pattern, at $30.

700 Ice Bowl with silver rim in *Princess* pattern, at $32.

458 Ice Bowl with silver rim in *Grecian* pattern, at $ 38.

765 Ice bowl with silver rim in *Grecian & Hobnail*, at $40.

14in. 651 tray in *Grecian* pattern at $30.

a dozen matching. 7in. 375 plates at $72. (see Fig. 9-4)

217 tray in *Japanese* pattern, at $21.

217 tray in *Grecian & Hobnail*, at $20.

13in. 651 tray in *Grecian*, at $18.

Package no. 8 had sixty dishes and plates, mostly in 6in. and 7in. sizes, although there were two 12in. 196 dishes in *Grecian* and *Grecian & Hobnail*. The other patterns in that package were *Persian & Pillars*, *Pillars & Silver Diamonds*, *Russian & Pillars*, *Russian*,

Hobnail, and Princess. These patterns were cut on blank shapes 196, 420, 563, 658, 702, 116, 178, 238, 372, 373, 374, 376, 379, and 426 and they ranged in price from $3.50 to $14.00, although most of the pieces were close to the lower end of the range.

Package no. 9 had forty-seven pieces, again mostly in smaller sizes, but including celery and spoon trays and sugars and creamers as well as dishes. The patterns cut were Hobnail, Grecian, Grecian & Hobnail, Russian, Princess, Empress, Persian & Pillars, and Cobweb, except for the sugars and creamers which were in Strawberry Diamond & Fan, and Stars & Lace Hobnail. The prices for these ranged from $3.50 to $12.

Package no. 10 was of more interest, as it had five pairs of decanters, including the two to go with the fitted cases. These were a pair of 601 Decanters in Pillars & Lace Hobnail at $25 each and a pair of 600 Decanters in the same pattern at $27 each. There were also a pair of large globe decanters in pattern 3708 for $33 each and a pair cut in Pillars at $25 each. The last pair of globe decanters was cut in Large Deep Hobnail, and was priced at $22 each.

Package no. 11 had seventeen silver-mounted pieces for which the mounts had been ordered from Gorham. These included a 458 green champagne jug cut in Roman pattern for $200, another with a different silver rim for $155, and two similar ruby ones for the same prices. There was also a pair of 418 green wine bottles cut in Grecian & Hobnail for $35 each and a pair of 418 ruby wine bottles cut in Grecian for the same price. There were three punch ladles cut in ¼ Diamond, Pillars & Lace Hobnail and Silver Diamond & Pillars for $30 and $25 each and three pairs of salad servers for $40 and $36, cut in ¼ Diamond, Pillars & Lace Hobnail, and Silver Diamond & Pillars.

The extensive list given here shows that there was no engraved glass shown and nothing in Chrysanthemum pattern, although that has been widely published as a "Paris Exhibition" pattern. In fact, the Chrysanthemum pattern was not patented until the following year and it probably was not designed until after the exhibition.

Fortunately, photographs as well as the list of the Exhibition glassware survive. Thomas Hawkes was extremely proud of his firm's glassware and he arranged to have a photographer take photographs of the glass in the showroom in Corning. The photographs were taken just before the shipment, and were labeled "SHOW ROOM OF T. G. HAWKES SHOWING GLASS SENT TO THE PARIS EXHIBITION, 1889"(Figs. 9–1–9–5). They show a considerable amount of stemware and tumblers on the shelves although none is listed on the invoice. However, some was sent later in the summer. A Grecian pattern punchbowl also appears, although none is on the list.

The second consignment left Corning March 26, 1889, for shipment with the final government lot on March 30.[29] This consisted of three cases, one holding two 9-light candelabras priced at $135 each, spare parts for them, and a set of stemware in Grecian pattern on 385 line blanks: one each goblet, saucer champagne, claret, wine, flanged sherry, rose hock, green hock, and a ⅓ Qt.

29. List dated March 26, 1889, Hawkes Archives.

SECTION OF SHOW ROOM AT CORNING, N. Y. SHOWING A PORTION OF THE CUT GLASSWARE SENT TO THE PARIS EXPOSITION, 1889, BY T. G. HAWKES & CO., FOR WHICH THE GRAND PRIZE WAS AWARDED.

9-5. *A view of the Hawkes glass in Corning, published in a trade journal.*

tumbler were sent at prices ranging from $25 to $42 a dozen. The complete place setting was valued at $22.33.

The second package had the 18in. punch bowl on the Dorflinger blank, 497 shape, cut in *Russian & Notched Pillars* and priced at $300. (Fig. 9-2) The third package had a 646 handled and footed lamp with dome shade cut in *Plaid* pattern for $66, a 7in. 493 cheese plate and cover in *Large Deep Hobnail* for $23, a 498 cracker jar and cover in *Large Deep Hobnail* for $16.50, a 4 Pt. 457 Jug in *Large Deep Hobnail* for $15 and another in *Grecian* for the same price, a 6in. 485 rose globe cut in *Pillars* for $7.50, another cut in *Large Deep Hobnail* for $7. and three 636 candlesticks cut in *Cobweb*, *Passion Flower* and *Russian* for $6.50 each.

On April 11, a letter from Collamore reported Bonfils' complaint that the shipment did not include any cut glass lamps and requested that the Hawkes firm make up at least two and send them to Paris at Collamore's expense. Mr. Bonfils was also shocked at the $200 price tag on the silver-mounted champagne jugs.[30] Hawkes replied that the: "price for the colored champagne jugs mounted in silver is $200.00 each and at this price we did not commence to get our money back on them, we broke six of them when they were almost finished in trying to cut under the handles, and we got discouraged several times and thought about giving the job up, but we had invested so much money in them and the silver for them had been all ordered, that we kept cutting them until we succeeded in getting four good ones. The Gorham Mfg. Co. charged as high as $86.00 each for the silver that went on them. We had to make a special pot of green glass to make them which cost us $100.00 so you can readily see that we are out of pocket on the goods."[31]

30. Davis Collamore & Company, New York, T. G. Hawkes, April 11, 1889.
31. Signed copy, T. G. Hawkes to Davis Collamore & Company, New York, April 12, 1889.

Hawkes also asked Mr. Bonfils to cable from Paris if he needed more glass to fill the space. "We have so much money invested in this exhibit, that we do not wish to make a failure", said Hawkes, "and if putting in a little more will be any benefit but we are of the opinion that our competitors will find it very difficult to produce anything any better, or even as good, as the exhibit we have sent …"

On April 23, the New York office of Davis Collamore transmitted a message from Mr. Bonfils in Paris that he needed information on the glass to answer visitors' questions intelligently and to say that if Hawkes had any more outstanding pieces, he should send them and Bonfils would add them to the exhibit.[32]

The French public was enthusiastic about the American glass and a front page article in the New York Times on May 8 on the American exhibits singled out Hawkes for special praise: "The exceptions are grouped together in the four corners of the open spaces in the centre of our section. These are occupied by Tiffany, the Meriden Britannia Company, the Gorham Manufacturing Company and Davis Collamore & Co. of New-York. Only the second and last have their exhibits yet in order, but Tiffany's show will be in many respects the most notable in the whole exposition. Davis Collamore & Co.'s exhibit attracts admiring attention by reason of the collection of Rookwood pottery from Cincinnati, and still more by the wonderful show of cut glass from Hawkes, at Corning, N.Y. The products of this little village factory are marvels to the French glass cutters and already are striking features of the exposition."

On May 10, Davis Collamore wrote that Mr. Bonfils had written that "Webb has forty (40) patterns of stem ware on show at Paris" and that he was anxious to have Hawkes send as many stemware samples as possible at once. He also suggested that Hawkes send "that line of sample goblets which you made for us a few years ago and which were returned to you . . we mean those with polished pillars, rock crystal &c.… We trust that you will see that they cannot expect to sell any stem ware against Webb unless they have a good line."[33] Hawkes did send more stemware samples; there are letters about shipping, but unfortunately, there is no detailed list of the additions. Bonfils and John Turner, his assistant, continued to write home from Paris to order more glass, including two additional lamp shades cut in Plaid pattern, colognes and decanters, and a Russian pattern jug as well as a dozen champagne glasses cut in Grecian pattern. These seem to have been ordered at the exposition and they were sent for immediate delivery to customers in Paris.

On June 10, another article in the New York Times mentioned the Hawkes exhibit again. "To return to the four corners in the centre. I had supposed, in my earlier enthusiasm, that the cut glass from Corning was something unrivaled, but a study of the English section showed similar work quite as remarkable, though on the whole, perhaps, no better."

A third story in the Times, from the June 30 paper, was more complimentary: "At the opposite corner from Tiffany is the Davis Collamore & Co. exhibition of

32. W. H. Lowndes for Davis Collamore & Company, New York, to T. G. Hawkes, April 23, 1889.
33. C. Murray for Davis Collamore & Company, New York, to T. G. Hawkes, May 10, 1889.

9-6. *View of Davis Collamore & Company's exhibit in Paris showing the Hawkes display with the Plaid pattern lamp and the large punch bowl at the rear.*

porcelain, pottery and glass. The Hawkes cut glass, made at Corning, is already a familiar artistic interest to visitors and to the trade, who admire its extreme whiteness of coloring, its delicacy and clearness of cut, and its depth. The ice cream service and salad bowls would not be appreciated here, for they are too heavy for the passing round of the French service, but the punch bowls, and the sherry wine carafes, the claret ruby Roman jugs especially are so many useful delights. The consequence is that already the larger portion of the exhibit has been sold. The glass celery dish is a novelty, and it will be the fashion next season. The great sensation, however, has been the cut glass lamps with the chimney to match and the monster shades corresponding. Nothing of this kind was ever seen here before, and the Parisiennes have gone wild on the subject. All the titled names of France are about represented on the visiting cards attached to the articles disposed of and conspicuous is the Princess Gortchakoff, wife of the Chamberlain of the Czar."

Hawkes received a letter from an official of Gilman Collamore, another New

York customer, who said that he had seen the exhibit in Paris. "Your goods at the exposition have attracted much attention from English Manufacturers. I don't think Continental people care for heavy glassware."[34] If the *Times* article was correct, he was wrong.

On August 1, Collamore sent a list of fifteen more cut glass bowls in 9in. and 10in. sizes in various patterns which they were sending to Paris and they ordered twenty-one more to be sent as soon as possible.[35] The first fifteen included pattern number 6424 (the only pattern in the shipment not previously sent) and the writer requested that the remaining twenty-one not duplicate any in the first shipment. On August 12, Collamore's agent transmitted an order for an 11in. 591 salad bowl cut in *Russian and Sharp Pillars* which was wanted in Paris by September 1.[36] Another order was sent to Corning September 4, but its contents have been lost;[37] it seems to have been the last order received in Corning, which is not surprising given that the exposition closed in October.

Hawkes was not slow to take advantage of the favorable publicity he was receiving. The August 1, issue of the *Pottery And Glassware Reporter* included a double-column width advertisement for "Thomas G. Hawkes, / CORNING, N.Y. / Richly Cut Glassware. / DEALERS VISITING THE / PARIS EXPOSITION / WILL FIND OUR EXHIBIT TO BE OF SPECIAL INTEREST."

By October 1, the awards were announced and Thomas Hawkes had received a cable from Paris announcing that he had won a Gold Medal. The *Corning Journal* rejoiced with him, announcing: "This is a great compliment to the excellence of the work done at their cutting shop, and is a good advertisement for Corning. It will doubtless lead to largely increased orders for cut-glass and thus add to the number of employees. On Monday evening, Mr. Hawkes was serenaded at his residence by the Fall Brook Band and there were several hundred people present. Thomas S. Pritchard introduced Mr. Hawkes who heartily thanked his friends for their congratulations. Remarks were made by C. F. Houghton, John Hoare, and A. Gaylord Slocum. There was much cheering throughout."

The actual medals were not manufactured in France until after the exhibit closed, and Hawkes received his the following January. He immediately ordered colored lithographed certificates which he supplied to his customers to display with their Hawkes cut glass. The Troy, New York paper carried an advertisement by Tappin's Diamond Palace the first week in October which claimed the prize for "Corning Cut Glass" and said that a display of Hoare's glass "duplicates of those cut for the Paris Exposition" could be seen at Tappin's. Edgar Everett, a Troy glass and china dealer sent Hawkes the advertisement and wanted to know if Hoare had had an exhibit in Paris.[38] Hawkes's reply has not been preserved, but it is unlikely that he was pleased; he took pains in his advertising for the next twenty years to have "HAWKES CUT GLASS" in large letters at the top of the copy and "Corning, N.Y." in much smaller letters at the bottom. Apparently Houghton and Hoare continued to advertise somewhat misleadingly, because a Collamore letter of January 16, 1890 refers to this issue. "Glad to get your letter in reference to

34. T. G. Martin for Gilman Collamore, Union Square, New York, to T. G. Hawkes, June 20, 1889.
35. C. Murray for Davis Collamore & Company, New York, to T. G. Hawkes, August 1, 1889.
36. G. Murray for Davis Collamore & Company, New York, to T. G. Hawkes, August 12, 1889.
37. C. Murray for Davis Collamore & Company, New York, to T. G. Hawkes, September 4, 1889.
38. Edgar W. Everett, Troy, New York, to T. G. Hawkes, October 10, 1889.

9-7. *View of Davis Collamore & Company's exhibit from another angle.*

Houghton matter. We will come out all right, it is very poor policy to go against the truth. The Grand Prize is yours and at this end of the Route will do all we can to force matters… Am making a fine display of the Paris Prize Glass."[39]

The display may have included the large punch bowl, since Collamore sent it back to Hawkes for repair December 12, 1891, saying: "This chipping occurred at the Paris Exhibition when the plaster ornament fell on the table where the bowl stood. As the bowl is sold, please return it to us as soon as possible."[40] The customer to whom Collamore referred was James J. Hill, the railroad magnate, who had just completed a luxurious mansion in St. Paul, Minnesota. An identical punch bowl was given to the Minnesota Historical Society by Hill's great-grand-daughter, and photographs show it in the Hill house early in the 20th century. The James J. Hill papers (in the James Joseph Hill Reference Library in St. Paul) include Collamore's invoice to Mrs. Hill for the punch bowl which cost $300. Although Dorflinger did supply Hawkes with two blanks, only one was sent to Paris and there's no indication that the other was ever completed.

Since much of the original display had been sold in Paris, the pieces shown in

39. Sereno D. Bonfils for Davis Collamore & Company, New York, to T. G. Hawkes, January 16, 1890.
40. F. B. Russell for Davis Collamore & Company, New York, to T. G. Hawkes, December 12, 1891.

9-8. *A The exposition punch bowl cut in Russian and Notched Pillars. D. 45cm; ht. 35cm. Minnesota Historical Society, gift of Elizabeth Peyton (grand-daughter of James J. Hill); Peter Latner photograph.*

41. Signed copy, T. G. Hawkes to Richard Briggs, Boston, March 25, 1889.
42. Order form for Richard Briggs, Boston, H. P. Sinclaire, Jr. to T. G. Hawkes, September 13, 1889.
43. Jules Henrivaux, "La Verrerie", *Revue des Arts Decoratifs*", Numero December 1889, Vol. 10, No. 6, p.175.

New York may have included duplicates cut later by Hawkes. Richard Briggs, Hawkes's Boston outlet, wrote inquiring about duplicates and was informed that Hawkes had not had time to cut duplicates of most of the items.[41] Briggs had admired the Paris display but his order of September 13 included a "sample globe Decanter cut large deep sharp diamond same as ones in Webb's exhibit."[42]

Among the other American glass exhibitors, only John LaFarge's stained glass received much attention; it was awarded a gold medal. The largest display of table glass was in the stand of Thomas Webb and Sons of England. Much of this was cameo glass, including the Great Tazza (now at The Corning Museum of Glass) and several other multi-layer pieces, as well as some smaller pieces which seem to have been sent to Tiffany's in New York for later sale. Jules Henrivaux, who wrote a long article on the glass shown in 1889, reported that Webb's crystal was "perfectly white and perfectly cut" and the display included both cut glass and rock crystal engraved glass.[43] Baccarat and J. & L. Lobmeyr did not exhibit and the

9-9. The Prize certificate which Hawkes printed to distribute to retailers of his glass for their displays.

9-10. The Gold Medal which was awarded to Thomas G. Hawkes at the Paris Exposition of 1889.

Bohemian glassmakers sent mostly colored wares. Thus, Hawkes's medal was certainly an honor — especially for a new, small American firm — but it was not won against great competition. Only Webb could have come close. In fact, fifteen grand prizes were awarded to glass firms in 1889, six of which went to French firms. Hawkes won the only American Grand Prize for glass and Webb the only English one.[44] The only other American exhibit of cut glass was by Henri Froment, of Nogent-sur-Marne, France and New Orleans. The origin of his glass is unknown, but Froment seems to have been a dealer rather than a manufacturer.

One Englishman, in his official report, said: "America had only one firm exhibiting (viz, Messrs T. G. Hawkes, Corning, N.Y.) They had a very beautiful and brilliant exhibit of cut glass in great variety. This has never been done, or attempted to be done, by the Americans before, but of course this does not come under the title of excellence of work, only as regards cutting. The exception to this, so far as I could see, was a very large punch bowl, which was well made, measuring fourteen inches deep, eighteen inches diameter and standing upon a hollow foot. The cutting was pillar twist, which refracting the rays of light, equaled in brilliant effect anything in the building. This firm also exhibited some very fine cut jugs and goblets, which in my opinion, were very good indeed. The color of the whole of this exhibit was uncommonly good, and the cutting very superior. If the Americans continue to progress in this beautiful art as they are evidently doing, Englishmen will have to be put on their mettle to beat them."[45]

The same critic also reported on Webb's display: "The exhibit of Messrs. Thomas Webb & Sons of Stourbridge, was beyond all criticism. The color was that of the diamond: colorless, yet reflecting more light than it received; this was a contrast to the French cut work." However, the Grand Prize awarded to Webb, like that given to Hawkes, was for the total exhibit, not for any one piece, pattern, or type of glass. Awards at expositions were almost always given for a manufacturer's entire exhibit rather than for a single piece of glass. The articles about the Webb exhibit tended to dwell on the extraordinary cameo glass and to give only a passing mention of the cut tablewares.

All in all, Tom Hawkes must have felt that the medal, and the attention given to his exhibit in Europe, justified the trouble and expense of participation. Certainly, the Hawkes firm continued to proclaim their Gold Medal in catalogs and advertisements for the next seventy years, and they never exhibited in a World's Fair again — one Grand Prize was enough.

44. Ministère Du Commerce de L'Industrie et des colonies. *Liste des Récompenses*, Paris, Imprimerie Nationale, 1889.
45. "Glass at the Paris Exposition". *Crockery and Glass Journal*, December 5, 1889, p. 144.

Special Orders – for The White House and others

Around 1898-1900, Thomas Hawkes published a small booklet for his customers, "HAWKES CUT GLASS", which discussed the method of making cut glass, his World's Fair gold medal, his patterns, and some notable orders, including those for the White House and George W. Childs. The booklet reprints a letter from Richard Briggs of Boston, dated June 17, 1885, to Hawkes which says: "I have taken an order for a large service of glass in the 'Russian' pattern, from our newly appointed minister to St. Petersburg, …I am especially desirous that this shall be the finest service of glass that was ever made, as it is to be used at the famous State Dinners where the most distinguished people of all nations will see it, and I can assure you that no opportunity will be lost to inform the guests where it was made, by the representatives of this country."[1]

There has been some speculation that the pattern (undoubtedly Hawkes's most famous pattern, then and now) was even named "Russian" because of this order or because of a reported order from Count Bibesco, the Russian minister to

1. *Hawkes Cut Glass*, n.a., n.d. pp.27-28.

10-1. *Sample goblet from the service made by T. G. Hawkes & Company for the* White House *in 1937. H: 15.5cm. Gift of T. G. Hawkes & Company (CMG 51.4.534).*

10-2. Sample ruby-cased wineglass made by Thomas Hawkes for the White House in 1885 or in 1900, both years in which ruby-cased glasses were ordered. H: 11.9cm. Private collection, originally purchased from Hawkes in the early 1960s.

10-3. *Pair of cologne bottles engraved with horses, made as a wedding gift for Ellen Rogers of New York in 1883. H: 18.1cm. (CMG55.4.62AB).*

Washington at the same time. However, no evidence of any kind has been found to support the story of the Russian ambassador ordering a set, and Briggs' letter makes it clear that the pattern was already named when it was ordered by the minister from St. Petersburg. In fact, Briggs himself was responsible for the name. The pattern was designed by Philip MacDonald, a cutter, and was patented by Hawkes in 1882 with no mention of a name. However, a letter in the Hawkes Archives from Wm. L. Briggs of the Boston firm says: "As in my establishment I have so many patterns of glass. It is very confusing to my employees to remember the different cuttings by their numbers so I will kindly ask you in future in both invoicing goods and receiving orders to call the two following patterns by these names. the number 283 pattern to be called the 'Russian' pattern, the number 284 pattern to be called the 'Moscow' pattern."[2]

This letter is dated September 14, 1881 and the patent date is June 20, 1882, so the pattern was in production a year before it was patented. By the summer of 1882, other customers were using the name "Russian" instead of the number. The first order for the #283 pattern yet found in the Hawkes archives is from Davis Collamore, January 11, 1881, about ten months after Hawkes began his own business. However, it's possible that the pattern was already in the line in 1880.

George V. N. Lathrop of Michigan was officially appointed as Envoy Extraordinary and Minister Plenipotentiary of the United States to Russia on May 13, 1885 and he seems to have ordered the glass from Briggs on his way to take up his new posting, which he finally reached in August. Briggs sent the full order to Hawkes on September 5 and ordered a service of tumblers, wines, champagnes, clarets, finger bowls, hocks "3 or 5 colors", ice cream plates, 2 pair quart decanters, 1 pair handled claret flagons, 1 pair champagne jugs, one half dozen water bottles, two ice cream trays, six bonbon trays in pairs, all to be in "*Russian*" pattern. "I shall leave the whole matter in your charge, only asking you to realize the great importance of every piece being not only perfect but elegant. Please do not give the destination of these goods any publicity at present. I would like it at the earliest moment possible as they write me they shall need it in October."[3] A later letter indicated that "I would say in regard to the set of St. Petersburgh glass that I do not care to have the bottom of the feet cut Russian. Please use your very best taste with regard to the shapes of each piece for I think that the success depends largely upon having elegant forms."[4] The glass was apparently shipped in the fall and it was used by Lathrop for several years, but whether he brought it back with him, or left it in Russia for the next minister is not known.

An article in *Good Housekeeping* in 1886 described G. W. Childs' Philadelphia mansion in detail, including the dining room with his: "crystal bowl, fifteen inches in diameter and nearly as high, used for flowers. This and its companion in another city are the finest pieces of glass yet made by any American manufacturer, and for beauty and perfection of cutting they are unexcelled by the best Baccarat ware. The work was done by Thomas Hawkes, the great-grandson of the Mr. Hawkes who first introduced cut glass into England. The profusion of crystal upon the table in the shape of exquisite carafes, compote, fruit and bonbon stands, low and high, and with or without silver bases, is a revelation of the stage to which glass-cutting is carried in the United States. It awakens fresh pride and interest in the artists and artisans in our own land to see these choice productions in a place where only the best things of their kind are used."[5]

The illustration which accompanies the article shows a *Russian* pattern two-part punch bowl in shape #497. The two fifteen inch bowls which went to the 1889 Paris Exposition were cut on this shape. We know that Childs' example was made

2. Richard Briggs, Boston to T. G. Hawkes, September 14, 1881.
3. Richard Briggs, Boston to T. G. Hawkes, September 5, 1885.
4. Richard Briggs, Boston to T. G. Hawkes, September 8, 1885.
5. Mdme. Poole, *Good Housekeeping*, May 15, 1886, pp.1-5.

10-4. *Advertising card showing the crystal bed made by Hawkes for Oliver Brothers of Buffalo and exhibited at the Pan-American Exposition in Buffalo in 1901.*

in 1883, because a trade journal mentioned the bowl in that year, "The Corning Glass Company have made a cut glass punch bowl 16 inches in diameter for G. Washington Childs... of Philadelphia. It is said to be the largest glass bowl ever made."[6] Unfortunately, the order must have been placed with Corning Glass Works rather than directly with Hawkes as there is no correspondence about it in the archives except for a letter from J. Caldwell & Company which says, "We are to have the Punch Bowl that was presented to Geo. W. Childs of this city placed here in Exhibition. Is it your work? And who presented it to him, I have not yet seen it."[7] Later, the same writer asked "How much for a duplicate of the Childs Punch Bowl and how long a time...to make it."

The reply, scribbled on the margin, was $75 for a bowl in pattern #283 and $25 more for the case,[8] and a few days later Caldwell wrote: "Please cut for us one large Punch bowl 'Russian' exactly like the one presented to Mr. Child excepting that we want no space left for initial. Cut 'Russian' all over - diam. of bowl 16in. height of bowl & Std. about 9in. This we have promised in two weeks as per your letter."[9] It is interesting to see that the factory designation for the pattern was still "283", although the customer knew it as Russian.

This obsession with size was common in the late 19th century and as soon as one outsize piece was made, another company would try to make a larger one. Hawkes's largest bowl at the 1889 Paris Exposition was an 18 inch punch bowl, cut in *Russian and Notched Pillars*; John Hoare's punch bowl exhibited at the Chicago World's Fair of 1893 was 24 inches in diameter[10], as was the one which the

6. "Business Memoranda," *American Pottery And Glassware Reporter*, December 6, 1883, p.12.
7. J. E. Caldwell & Company Philadelphia to T. G. Hawkes, October 28, 1883.
8. J. E. Caldwell & Company Philadelphia to T. G. Hawkes, November 2, 1883.
9. J. E. Caldwell & Company Philadelphia to T. G. Hawkes, November 6, 1883.
10. *Corning Daily Journal*, June 3, 1893.

Libbey Glass Company produced in 1904 for the St. Louis Fair. These were both dwarfed, however, by the 27 inch punchbowl, 30 inches high which was cut by John Earl of McCue and Earl on a Union Glass Company blank for Tiffany and Company in 1904 for exhibition at the company's new store.[11] Of all of these big bowls, only Libbey's, now in The Toledo Museum of Art, is known to have survived.

To whom the bowl "in another city" belonged is not presently known, but at least one 16inch punch bowl in this 497 shape is in a private collection. It is cut in *Russian* pattern and engraved with a vignette of a sailing yacht, "Montauk", and the name of Commodore Platt of the New York Yacht Club. The Childs bowl and its twin were also written up in the *Pottery Gazette*, an English trade paper which reported, "the two are the finest pieces yet made by any American manufacturer, and for beauty and perfection of cutting they are unexcelled."[12]

The Hawkes firm undertook two elaborate commissions which were gifts for William H. Vanderbilt, but since no orders for them, or discussion of the decoration, survives in the archives, it seems likely that, like the Childs punch bowl, the orders were placed with Corning Glass Works and the cutting was ordered by C. F. Houghton from Hawkes. Fortunately, both of these commissions were fully described in the local paper:

"A pair of elegant Toilet bottles were presented by Austin Lathrop, Jr, May 8, to W. H. Vanderbilt, on the occasion of his sixtieth birthday. The bottles were made at the Corning Glass Works, and were engraved at the cutting shop of T. G. Hawkes. There were several beautiful designs, consisting of a steamer in full sail, the telegraph and a railroad scene. The engraving was remarkably skilful and perfect and Mr. Vanderbilt expresses his grateful satisfaction and high appreciation of the superior workmanship. It must be very gratifying to know that among the various manufactures for which Corning is noted, it produces work in the glass line, which cannot be surpassed in the country."[13] Austin Lathrop was a local Corning businessman who was interested in railroads. According to another *Journal* story, the engraving on the bottles cost $100.

The second Vanderbilt commission, also connected with railroads, was an engraved punchbowl: "An elegant piece of glassware, a punch bowl sixteen inches across and ten high, was sent from T. G. Hawkes' cutting shop, last week, to William H. Vanderbilt, of New York, late President of the New York Central and Hudson River Railroads. The cost was five hundred dollars, and it is a present from Gen. George J. Magee, of Watkins, President of the Fall Brook Company's Railroads, as a testimonial of his appreciation of the co-operation of Mr. Vanderbilt in securing the construction of the railroad from Corning… This bowl was made at the Corning Glass Works, and the cutting was done at the Glass Cutting Shops of Mr. Hawkes, under his direction; the work occupying four months of time… The bowl is cut in deep lustre cutting, making it appear like dazzling clusters of diamonds. Around the body of the punch bowl are four polished panels, superbly engraved, representing different railroads and coal

11. *China, Glass and Pottery Review*, November 1904.
12. *Hawkes Cut Glass*, p.27.
13. *Corning Journal*, June 16, 1881.

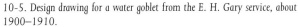

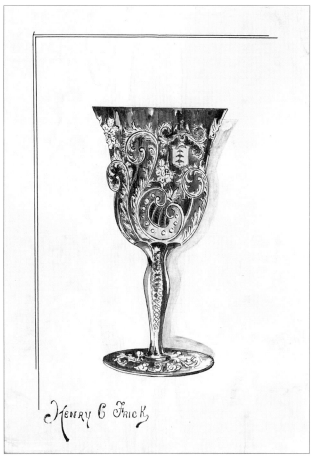

10-5. Design drawing for a water goblet from the E. H. Gary service, about 1900–1910.

10-6. Design drawing for a water goblet from the H. C. Frick service, about 1900–1910. Most of this service is still in the family, but some can be seen at the Frick home, Clayton in Pittsburgh.

scenes. The first panel is engraved to represent the large iron railroad bridge, over Watkins Glen, with Vanderbilt's private car, the "Vanderbilt" drawn by a Fall Brook coal company engine, over the bridge. The second one shows perfectly the Fall Brook coal company's coke ovens at Tioga, Pa. The third panel represents Falling Springs, one of the grandest scenes on the Jersey Shore, Pine Creek & Buffalo railway. On the fourth panel is engraved a large coal breaker and train of coal cars, representing a place of interest on the Philadelphia and Reading railroad. All of the scenes have been engraved from photographs and are beautiful illustrations of art, natural and interesting. The bowl stands in a handsome plush case lined with velvet and gold.[14]

It is likely that the bowl was cut in *Russian* pattern or *Hobnail* with the engraving in four panels, each about five or six inches across. Unfortunately, both of the Vanderbilt presents have disappeared although, with such complete descriptions, it should be possible to recognize them if they ever turn up. One wonders what John Hoare thought of these elaborate commissions going from the Glass Works to Hawkes, while his own firm still occupied space in Corning's building.

During the summer of 1885, Tom Hawkes received his first order for glassware from the White House. Colonel John W. Wilson, commissioner of public buildings, wrote M. W. Beveridge, a Washington retailer, for the names of glass manufacturers who could provide replacements for the Executive Mansion state

14. Corning Journal, June 28, 1883.

service. Beveridge replied: "Below please find address of Glass Manufacturers as requested. Should you require any Table ware for White House I should be please to furnish it from any of the factories as low as you can get it from them. Yours very truly, M. W. Beveridge."[15] His letter listed C. Dorflinger & Sons, Boston & Sandwich Glass Co, New England Glass Works, Mt. Washington Glass Works, and Corning Glass Works as possible suppliers of glass ware. Had the order gone to Corning Glass Works, John Hoare's company would have done the cutting.

The day before Beveridge's reply arrived, Wilson had received this proposal from Hawkes, who happened to be in Washington at the time (Beveridge was one of his customers) and who must have heard about the possibility of an order. "I will furnish the following Glassware... equal in every prospect in quality of glass, workmanship, etc. to samples, for the following prices:

4 Dz	Finger Bowls to sample	$	25.00 Dz
3	Champs		23
4	Clarets		21
4	Goblets		25
4	Roman Punch Glasses		25
4	Brandies		18
3	Rine Wines		23
6	Madeiras		23
4	S. Sherries		18
3	White Wines		22
2	Burgundies		21
6	Ice Cream Plates		23

Very Respectfully yours, T. G. Hawkes, Rich Cut Glass Manufacturer, Corning, New York." He gave as his references his largest customers at the time, Davis Collamore & Company of New York, J. E. Caldwell & Company of Philadelphia, Richard Briggs of Boston, and the Gorham Manufacturing Company of Providence.[16] The prices Hawkes quoted were unusually low, and by the time Wilson received Beveridge's letter with its list of possible suppliers he had already decided to buy the glass from Hawkes, although the order he placed was much smaller than Hawkes had proposed.

"July 29, 1885

...

Please deliver at the Executive mansion in this City the following cut glass to be made in the best manner and similar to samples to be furnished you by the Steward at the Mansion.

3 doz. finger bowls

2 doz. Champagnes

3 doz. Clarets

3 " Goblets

3 " Roman Punches

5 " Madeiras (Red)

15. National Archives, Office of Public Buildings and Grounds, Record Group 42, Letters Received, M. W. Beveridge to Col. John Wilson, July 28, 1885.
16. National Archives, Office of Public Buildings and Grounds, Record Group 42, Letters Received, Thomas G. Hawkes to Col. John Wilson, July 28, 1885.

10-7. *Pitcher engraved with a double portrait and dated December, 1901. H. 25 cm. Private collection. Although unsigned, this is probably the work of H. W. Fritchie or Hiram Rouse, Hawkes engravers. It is very similar to the pitcher Fritchie did of President and Mrs. McKinley in the same year, and Rouse engraved a self-portrait on another pitcher the following year.*

3	”	Sherries
1	”	White Wine (Red)
5	”	ice cream plates

The glass should be delivered as soon as convenient and certainly by October 1."[17]

Because Colonel Wilson ordered less glassware than Hawkes had suggested, the order came to only $640. It was delivered in October. This was an important commission for Hawkes, and he was not slow to publicize it. When the glass was delivered an article appeared in the *New York Sun* and this was copied in a trade paper and in the Corning newspaper:

"EXECUTIVE CUT GLASS

A GLASS Company at Corning is now manufacturing a set of table glassware for the White House. The fifty dozen pieces ordered include for the most part what is called stem ware, i.e. goblets, tumblers, decanters, liqueurs, lemonades, etc.

17. National Archives, Office of Public Buildings and Grounds, Record Group 42, Letters Sent, Col. John Wilson to T. G. Hawkes, July 29, 1885.

The light glasses are for the most part gold, ruby or amber ware. The order also includes Roman punch glasses, finger bowls, individual butters, ice cream plates, ice cream trays, caraffes, pitchers, and flagons. No pains have been spared to make each piece as perfect as possible. The slightest flaw that only a trained eye can see dooms the most valuable piece, so that its only use thereafter is as broken glass to be remelted. Of the 100 men in the shop only twenty of the best ones are employed on this order. The design engraved on each piece consists of the American eagle perched on a shield above the words 'E Pluribus Unum'. It is the design that has always ornamented ware for the White House... The patterns on the glassware consist of sets of parallel lines, crossing at different angles, and forming many-sided diamonds and stars which are changed by additional complex cuts."[18]

A comparison of the article with the actual order illustrates how risky it is for the researcher to rely on newspaper stories for accurate information. The description of the pattern is too general to allow much identification, but the evidence does establish that the glassware was another reorder of the Lincoln pattern set, (Fig. 10-2) not the Hawkes *Russian* pattern which was first supplied to the White House in 1891. The engraved design as described matches that of the Lincoln pattern. The inclusion of both colored glasses and Roman punch glasses points to the earlier pattern because the *Russian* service had neither. That Hawkes was directed to furnish glass identical to examples supplied to him by the White House steward and the odd quantities confirm that this was a reorder and not a new service.

I have gone into this at some length, because most published accounts, beginning with Dorothy Daniel[19] in 1950 and including my own earlier work in 1978, have reported that the 1885 order was the *Russian* service. Daniel received the information from Samuel Hawkes, son of Thomas Hawkes, and most subsequent authors have taken her statement at face value. *Hawkes Cut Glass*, the advertising booklet published by the company for customers around 1898-1900, even gives the date of the first presidential order as "the spring of 1886" when the National Archives papers show that the order was a year earlier.[20] It's not then surprising that the evidence of the set itself proves that Samuel Hawkes's memory was wrong. Hawkes supplied glass for the White House a number of times, but in 1885, the glass was not in the *Russian* pattern which was not to be used for a state service for six more years.

Hawkes was paid in October, and he found that the government bureaucracy was as difficult then as it is now. A letter from Colonel Wilson on October 8th referring to the payment due says, "There are returned herewith the vouchers for the glassware furnished by you to the Executive Mansion, which appear to have been signed for you by 'Mr. Sinclaire.' This signature will not be accepted by the accounting officers of the Treasury who require the signature of the principal... I have therefore prepared a new set of vouchers..."[21]

Benjamin Harrison took office in March, 1889, and two months later Colonel Wilson, who was still in charge of public buildings, received a letter from T. G.

18. *Crockery & Glass Journal*, 22, No. 10 (September. 3, 1885), p.28.
19. Dorothy Daniel, *Cut and Engraved Glass, 1771–1905*. (New York: M. Barrows & Company, 1950), 184.
20. *Hawkes Cut Glass*, n.a., n.d., p.27.
21. Col. John Wilson, Washington, to T. G. Hawkes, October 8, 1885.

Hawkes soliciting another order for glassware. He replied: "I regret to say that it is not the custom to refurnish the Executive mansion once in four years. Unfortunately Congress makes no appropriation for such elaborate expenditures, and for the coming year the funds available will hardly be sufficient to keep the Mansion in good order."[22] However, by 1891, the need for new glass was such that an order for an entirely new set was placed with Beveridge and was delivered in November of that year. The letter from the commissioner of public buildings said: "The samples of table glass which were submitted by you have been examined, and the one selected for acceptance has the straight shape and the *Russian* cut, with the coat of arms of the United States engraved in medallion, like the finished goblet."[23] Beveridge placed this order with C. Dorflinger & Sons of White Mills, rather than with Hawkes and five dozen place settings were supplied, along with eight water bottles and eight decanters.

The Dorflinger firm may have been responsible for the design of the engraved insignia, but because Hawkes had more copper-wheel engravers on staff than Dorflinger, many of the glasses were engraved in Corning. Joseph Haselbauer, Hawkes' senior engraver, worked on the set according to later newspaper stories,[24] but the work was being done by the Hawkes firm at Dorflinger's request, as correspondence between the two companies makes clear. On October 17, Dorflinger wrote to Hawkes: "We are very anxious to get the full line of samples of the White House order about which Factory wrote you some time ago. Can't you express samples of the pieces not yet in?"[25] Another letter on the same day says, "Please advise us how you are getting along with the Russian ware that you are engraving and when you will have it all completed, and oblige…"[26] On October 27, Louis Dorflinger wrote: "Will you kindly let us know when we may expect all the rest of the 'Russian' ware that you are engraving for us, We are anxious to get the shipment off. The time is about up. We are only waiting for the pieces to come in from you."[27] The complete order was delivered to the White House in November of 1891. Unfortunately, there is no way to tell which pieces, or how many of them, the Hawkes firm engraved.

In 1896, and again in 1898, the White House needed replacements for the State Service and ordered them from M. W. Beveridge, who placed the order with Hawkes.[28] The 1896 order was for eight dozen pieces of *Russian* cut stemware, finger bowls and tumblers plus two dozen handled punch cups cut in *Strawberry Diamond and Fan* pattern.[29] The 1898 order, reported in the local paper,[30] was for 11 ½ dozen pieces of *Russian* cut stemware, finger bowls and ice cream plates, cut salt cellars, water bottles, punch glasses and a dozen green white wines cut "to sample" which must have been replacements for the 1860s service, since no colored "Russian" pattern glassware was ever used in the White House. In 1900 and 1901, further replacements were supplied to the White House through Dulin & Martin, Beveridge's successor. The 1900 order was varied,[31] but that of 1901 was for only a dozen ice cream plates.[32] This service continued to be used until Prohibition was enacted in 1919.

22. Col. John Wilson, Washington, to T. G. Hawkes, May 6, 1889.
23. National Archives, Office of Public Buildings and Grounds, Record Group 42, Letters Sent, Col. Oswald Ernst to M. W. Beveridge, June 17, 1891.
24. Estelle Sinclaire Farrar and Jane Shadel Spillman, *The Complete Cut & Engraved Glass of Corning* (New York: Crown Publishers, Inc. and The Corning Museum of Glass, 1979), 141.
25. C. Dorflinger & Sons to T. G. Hawkes, October 17, 1891.
26. C. Dorflinger & Sons to T. G. Hawkes, October 17, 1891.
27. Louis Dorflinger for C. Dorflinger & Sons to T. G. Hawkes, October 27, 1891.
28. *Hawkes Cut Glass*, 26.
29. National Archives, Miscellaneous Treasury Accounts for the President's House, Record Group 217, Accounts Received, Voucher 10, June 26, 1896.
30. *Corning Daily Journal*, August 4, 1898.
31. National Archives, Office of Public Buildings and Grounds, Record Group 42, Letters Sent, Theodore A. Bingham to Dulin & Martin, April 18, 1900.
32. National Archives, General Accounting Office, 22485, Voucher 36, June 24, 1901.

When Prohibition was repealed in 1933, Franklin and Eleanor Roosevelt began to serve wine at state dinners, using the remains of the two 19th century services supplied by Hawkes and Dorflinger. It quickly became apparent that a new service would have to be ordered. In 1937, the order was placed with Martin's China and Glassware, successor to Dulin and Martin, and it was manufactured by T. G. Hawkes & Company.[33] (Fig. 10–1) The Roosevelts chose a pattern that Hawkes had marketed as "Venetian" but which the company renamed "White House." The coat of arms was added to the pattern for the Roosevelts. By this time, the Hawkes company had trouble finding enough skilled engravers to do the work. The Depression, and Prohibition, had both hit the fine glass trade severely and new engravers were not being trained. However, Edward Palme and Joseph Sidot, two of the older engravers, did most of the work on the White House order. The first samples had the eagle's head facing the wrong way for the drinker so Roosevelt, a former assistant secretary of the navy and avid sailor who was interested in military symbols sent them back. The insignia as it was finally engraved was a simplified version of the one used in 1861 for the Lincoln service.

Hawkes ordered the blanks from the Tiffin Glass Company, of Tiffin, Ohio, where he had been getting blanks for some time. The closing of Sinclaire's glasshouse in Bath in 1928, and the change in direction at Steuben in 1933, meant that Hawkes no longer had a local supplier and all blanks had to come in by rail, which added to the expense of doing business. Hawkes supplied Tiffin with a special high lead formula which Tiffin used for all Hawkes blanks. Ten dozen goblets, finger bowls and wine glasses were ordered in 1937 and 1938 and in April of 1939 Hawkes provided drawings and estimates for hollow-stem champagne glasses in a trumpet shape at $160 a dozen or saucer-shaped glasses at $140.[34] Eventually the Roosevelts opted for solid-stem champagnes at a cheaper price and added cordial glasses, sherry glasses and small wine glasses in 1939, 1940, and 1941. In 1946, 1947, and 1950 the Trumans reordered the service from Hawkes, but without the engraved insignia in order to save money. The last White House order filled by Hawkes was in 1955 and this time they were unable to supply an engraver to do the insignia. One of Corning's proudest traditions had come to an end.

Although John Hoare exhibited at the Chicago World's Fair of 1893, Hawkes chose not to go to the expense of doing so. However, according to the Special Trade Edition of the *Daily Journal*, published in 1895, he did display wares there: "The firm made no special exhibit at the world's fair at Chicago, but their goods were exhibited by some of the largest concerns in the country. One very prominent jewelry house in St. Louis, viz. The Mermod & Jaccard Co. made a large display of the goods and received there fore special award. Another notable exhibit was that of Lazell, Dally and Co the celebrated perfumers, for whom this firm manufactured special lines of immense bewildering cut glass bottles. These were filled with perfumes and lit by electricity, and those who saw this display will never forget the wonderful prismatic effects of the same."[35]

33. Jane Shadel Spillman, *White House Glassware*, (Washington: The White House Historical Association, 1989) 121.
34. Office of the Curator of the White House, correspondence from T. G. Hawkes and Company, April 3, 1939.
35. *Corning Daily Journal*, September 4, 1895.

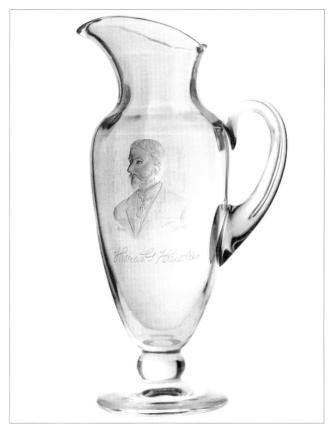

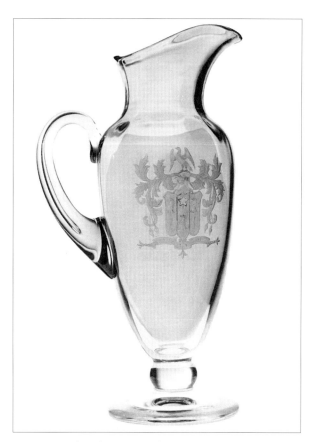

10-8. *Pitcher with a portrait of Thomas G. Hawkes, probably done after his death in 1913. The pitcher belonged to the company until it was sold after 1962. This photograph is an original one from the Hawkes archives.*

10-9. *Reverse of Hawkes portrait pitcher.*

One of Hawkes' more notable "special orders" was the bed created for the 1901 Exposition in Buffalo. This was not actually designed or exhibited by Hawkes. It was the brainchild of the Oliver Brothers Company of Lockport, a furniture company. (Fig. 10–4) According to a story in the Corning paper, this was: "a cut glass bedstead valued at $3,000. The glass for this bedstead was made and cut by T. G. Hawkes & Co. of Corning for the exhibition, for Oliver Bros. Co… Critics who have seen this novel piece of furniture pronounce it to be magnificent and by far the finest work of its kind ever produced and put on exhibit in this or any other country."[36]

The only picture of this piece is on a tradecard printed by Oliver Brothers where it is referred to as a "CRYSTAL BED MADE OF CUT GLASS & SILVER" and which does not mention Hawkes. However, Hawkes's turn-of-the-century cash books record three payments from Oliver Brothers in 1901: an initial payment of $492.70 on April 16, and bills for $50.35 and $17.26 on April 22 and April 23. The last two are probably for replacements for broken parts. Judging from the picture, the cut glass parts are relatively small and probably just slipped on to the metal framework and it is doubtful if Hawkes had the framework in Corning. They probably made the parts and shipped them to Lockport or to Buffalo to be assembled on site. Unfortunately, there is no record of what happened to the bed after the Fair. It may have remained with the Oliver firm, or possibly it was bought by a wealthy customer.

36. *Corning Daily Journal*, June 12, 1901.

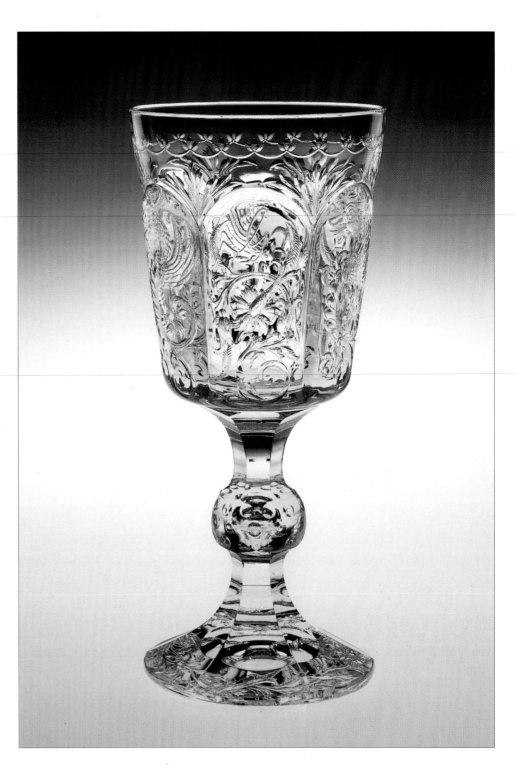

10-10. Sample goblet from the E. H. Gary service, T. G. Hawkes & Company, about 1900–1910. H: 19.3cm, trade-marked. Hawkes Collection.

With the White House orders or the Paris Exposition pieces, it is possible to know what they looked like on the basis of publicity at the time, or surviving recorded examples. In the case of orders for private citizens, the actual pieces are harder to trace. Hawkes apparently made a specialty of pieces engraved with running horses in the 1880s. Three letters in the archives from C. F. Houghton, brother of Amory Houghton, Jr., president of Corning Glass Works, seem to indicate that Houghton ordered gifts for his best customers from Hawkes, or offered to place orders for them with Hawkes. On February 4, 1883, he wrote

10-11. Sample tumbler from the service made for Sir Thomas Lipton, about 1900–1910. H: 13.8cm, trade-marked. Hawkes collection.

from New York: "Dear Tom, Please have monogram R. W. H. put on pair colognes eng'd with horses. Will give you shipping directions when I return. Yours truly, C. F. Houghton. shall want case also."[37]

Two weeks later, he ordered another pair, with different initials. "Dear Tom, Send to J. L. Yale, Kinnard House, Cleveland O., 1 pair 'Horse' colognes & case, monogram J. L. Y. / Have them nice. He will send you a $200. order soon & will show these pieces to some of the wealthiest people in Clev'd which is a wealthy town. Yours Chas. F. H."[38]

37. C. F. Houghton to Thomas G. Hawkes, February 4, 1883.
38. C. F. Houghton to Thomas G. Hawkes, February 17, 1883.

A subsequent letter from J. L. Yale to C. F. Houghton which was forwarded to Hawkes says: "Mr. Hawkes sent me 'blanks' showing shapes of glasses. And in reply I would say they are all satisfactory barring the cutting on the bottom of stem goods. My friends want the cutting to extend clear to edge of the base thus Do you follow? And the water tumblers they wish hobnailed on the bottom as well as sides. Champagnes they are looking for of the old – very old style – something thusly. Do you – can you make such a thing and if you do – can you send a sample hobnail cut? Ice cream tray all right except handles which they want plain & not scolloped thus. The photo Mr. Hawkes sent has them thus. Can these things be done. Sorry to trouble you but I'm in for it and must do all I can for my friends."[39]

The letter is nicely illustrated with pen and ink drawings of a heavily cut foot, a champagne flute glass, and rectangular ice cream trays with plain and scalloped handles and an indication that an order for stemware, tumblers and nappies would follow soon. One can only hope that the size of the order eventually justified the effort that C. F. Houghton and Tom Hawkes put into soliciting it.

In 1889, C. F. Houghton received a large order for glass from Enoch Lewis of Philadelphia after he had sent Mr. Lewis a box of Hawkes's photographs. Houghton sent the order to Hawkes with the note: "Dear Tom, Please fill & chge C. G. W."[40] A letter from L. C. Higgins, the purchasing agent for the Lake Shore and Michigan Southern Railway Company, to Houghton gave at least one reason why he ordered from Hawkes through Houghton, "Will you kindly let me avail myself of your offer and ask you to have the above sent to my house... with bill for same? I only venture to trouble you because... it will save me the difference between the wholesale and retail prices."[41] And finally, a letter from a St. Louis dealer in railway supplies, to Corning Glass Works, gives another motive: "Our mutual friend, Mr. H. H. Williams, a firm friend of the great Corning Globe, wants a glass Celery Dish for his wife's birthday... to match the square piece you sent him some time ago."[42] In fact, most of Houghton's gifts and special orders are connected with railroad executives, probably because it was Amory Houghton Jr.'s red railroad globe which was responsible for much of the company's prosperity at this time.

We know what the "horse" colognes looked like, because at least one pair has survived which we can match with the order. (Fig. 10–3) The archives include a letter from S. B. Wellington, brother of Corning banker Quincy Wellington, to C. F. Houghton ordering a similar pair of colognes. S. B. Wellington was a New York stockbroker. "My Dear Charly. I enclose herewith a paper which Mr. Bowden left with me on which is his letter R. and if it can be done will you please tell Mr. Hawkes to put it on or rather have R cut on the Toilet Bottles." Houghton forwarded this to "Tom" a couple of days after he had sent a note saying, "Sam Wellington gave me inclosed order for toilet bottles. He wants something nice and will take your judgment on them."[43] The Corning Museum collection includes a pair of toilet bottles which were published by George S. McKearin in

39. J. L. Yale, Cleveland, to C. F. Houghton, Corning, March 16, 1883.
40. Enoch Lewis, Philadelphia to C. F. Houghton, Corning, February 27, 1889; T. G. Hawkes to C. F. Houghton, March 8, 1889.
41. L. C. Higgins, Cleveland, to C. F. Houghton, Corning, April 22, 1887.
42. M. Buck & Company, St. Louis to Corning Glass Works, October 1, 1887.
43. S. B. Wellington, New York to C. F. Houghton, Corning, December 1, 1883; C. F. Houghton to Thomas G., November 30, 1883. The actual order which Houghton sent on November 30, is missing; only the letter about the engraving survives.

1941 as having been a gift to Miss Ellen Rogers from her uncle, a New York banker named Bowden, who acquired them from Corning Glass Works through Quincy Wellington.[44] These, undoubtedly, are the toilet bottles referred to in the 1883 letters. A third letter from C. F. Houghton says: "Tom, Pls. send the pair decanters ordered by Joe Bole to this address. Bill to him at Cleveland. He is worth 250 thousand so don't ever hesitate to fill orders. Yours C. F. H."[45] This and similar correspondence indicate that there was a fairly close relationship between the Houghtons and Tom Hawkes, a little surprising in view of the fact that John Hoare's company occupied the upper floor of Corning Glass Works and was considered the "Glass Works cutting shop" by most people. It may have existed simply because C. F. Houghton and T. G. Hawkes were friends.

Many of the special orders were considerably more elaborate than the horse colognes. Design drawings exist for services ordered by Henry C. Frick, the Pittsburgh industrialist (Fig. 10–6) and E. H. Gary, the first president of U. S. Steel. (Fig. 10–5) However, the pieces of the Gary set which have survived are signed with the names of English engravers – "Fritsche", "Hall", and "W. Kny" – and were made at Thomas Webb & Company, or possibly at Stevens & Williams. The pattern is a Stevens & Williams one,[46] but Fritsche worked only for Webb, as far as is known. William Kny worked for Webb Corbett after 1900, although he probably worked with his father at Webb earlier and with his brother at Kny Brothers. The glass set was originally ordered between about 1900 and 1910 by the Garys from Tiffany & Company when they commissioned Tiffany to supply them with an elaborate service of gold flatware and serving pieces with a script initial "G" which is very similar to the "G" on the glassware.[47] The gold service includes some matching glass pieces with Gorham gold tops, perhaps an indication that the English silver tops which had come with the glass were replaced by the American gold ones when the gold service was acquired. Mr. Gary died in 1927 and his wife died a few years later, and 311 pieces of the glass service were sold in 1934. The service is described in the sale catalog as "A SUPERB CARVED CRYSTAL DINNER SERVICE/FROM TIFFANY & CO. NEW YORK" and the individual lots are described as "Stourbridge" crystal.[48] A letter from Otto Bernet, in Sotheby's files, written the following year, mentions that some of the pieces were signed by Fritsche.[49] However, in addition to the design drawing, one goblet from this service is in the National Museum of American History's Department of Ceramics and Glass, a gift from Sarah Hawkes Thornton, who inherited it from her father, Samuel Hawkes. Another remains in the family collection.(Fig. 10–10) The blank shown in the design drawing and the blank at the N.M.A.H. are not exactly the same, and neither is exactly like the existing signed goblets, none of which have turned up with a Hawkes trademark. It's possible that Tiffany & Company placed the original order with Hawkes, who ordered the set from England and added the engraved initial before sending the set to Tiffany. However, a more likely hypothesis is that the Hawkes firm was asked to make some replacement pieces for the set. In that case, the sample pieces,

44. George S. and Helen McKearin, *American Glass*, (New York: Crown Publishers Inc., 1941), Plate 57A, 161.
45. Charles F. Houghton, Corning, to Thomas G. Hawkes, n.d.
46. Stevens & Williams pattern no. 8675, first made in 1884, according to a letter in CMG files from Royal Brierley Crystal.
47. "The Gary Gold Dinner Service by Tiffany & Company" Sotheby's, New York, Wednesday, October 19, 1994.
48. "IMPORTANT RUGS, PAINTINGS, GEORGIAN SILVER AND ENGLISH FURNITURE FROM THE ESTATE OF THE LATE ELBERT H. GARY AND FROM THE ESTATE OF THE LATE EMMA T. GARY" American Art Association/Anderson Galleries, Inc., December 7 and 8, 1934.
49. Otto Bernet, American Art Association, New York to Clarence L. Harper, Philadelphia, March 20, 1935. I am indebted to Fred Grabb for a copy of this letter.

10-12. *Tableware from the service made for Mrs. Marjorie Meriwether Post's yacht, the Sea Cloud, in 1935. Hillwood Museum, Washington, D.C.*

which have no engraver's signature, were probably engraved in Corning.

Because several signatures, especially some of Fritsche's and at least one of Kny's, seem to be acid-etched rather than engraved, there has been some speculation that the signatures were added in the last decade or two, when Fritsche glass has become much better known among collectors than it was before 1960. However, in view of the fact that the service was signed when it was auctioned in 1935, this seems impossible.

In 1915, the Hawkes building was extensively remodeled and at that time, diamond-paned windows engraved with the Hawkes insignia were placed in the Market Street facade and in several doors to the offices on the second floor. One of these panes has an engraved list of customers for whom Hawkes had made special orders. Unfortunately, the list has no dates and some of the names were added after 1915, but most of the orders are from before that year. The list of names for whom special orders were made is impressive: "W. H. Vanderbilt, Harold V. Vanderbilt, F. W. Vanderbilt, J. J. Astor, E. H. Gary, F. T. Stotesbury, H. C. Frick, F. O. Armour, H. P. Whitney, W. H. Whitney, Cyrus Curtis, Edith Rockefeller McCormick, Joseph Chamberlain, Chauncy Depew, F. W. Underwood, O. H. P. Belmont, Sir Thomas Lipton, Senator W. A. Clark, President Diaz of Mexico, Palace at Havana, Mrs. Joseph E, Davies, The White House." Most of the men on this list came to national prominence in the 1890s and most of the orders were probably made between 1890 and 1910. Since the list is not alphabetical, it may be chronological; W. H. Vanderbilt received glass in the 1880s, and Sir Thomas Lipton wasn't knighted until 1902, which tends to support that assumption. The order for the Palace at Havana was placed with Tiffany & Company or Tiffany

10-13. *Display photograph used by T. G. Hawkes & Company showing the glass from the Sea Cloud on the yacht.*

Studios in 1918, when Mario Menocal was president and the Tiffany firm was decorating the palace; it seems to have been placed by Tiffany with both Dorflinger and Hawkes. Although no paperwork has been found to indicate the size or exact date of the order, samples of the service have descended in both the Dorflinger and Hawkes families. The Corning Museum of Glass owns a fingerbowl and plate which was a gift from Isobel Dorflinger, and the National Museum of American History owns a wineglass which was a gift from Sarah Hawkes Thornton. In fact, Mrs. Thornton's 1965 gift to the N.M.A.H. included samples from the orders of Gary, Stotesbury, Frick, Mrs. McCormick, Lipton, the presidents of Mexico and Cuba, and the White House Russian pattern service and Roosevelt service, as well as glass used by Teddy Roosevelt's family. Examples of some of these services are also still in the Hawkes family.

The service for Mrs. Joseph Davies was first ordered by her for her yacht, the *Hussar*, in 1930 when she was Mrs. E. F. Hutton. She reordered it in 1935 and renamed her yacht the *Sea Cloud*. (Fig. 10-13) The bill shows that this engraving was polished and redone to change the ship's name. Pieces of this service are in the N.M.A.H. collection and at Hillwood, her Washington home, (Fig. 10-12) but the remainder is still in use at her daughter's home. (Mrs. Davis was none other than Marjorie Meriwether Post, the cereal heiress.)

Isabella Stewart Gardner, the legendary Boston art collector, owned a set of Hawkes stemware which she used in her Brookline House, not in the house where her museum is now. The fact she specifically mentioned her "Hawkes stemware" in her will proves that it was more prestigious than glass from other companies.[50]

50. Records Boston Court Probate Division. I'm indebted to John Keefe, New Orleans Museum of Art, for this reference.

"Special order" generally implies a one-of-a-kind piece or set to most of us, but in the 1880s and 1890s the term was used more generally. Hawkes's biggest customers, Davis Collamore, Richard Briggs, and J. E. Caldwell & Company kept large inventories of Hawkes cut glass and ordered more on a weekly basis. Anything monogrammed or engraved with an inscription was a special order; thus, Briggs' orders of his *Louis XIV* pattern were all special orders because almost all were monogrammed. The letters from these and other customers frequently specified special combinations of cutting, or cutting and engraving, and much of the correspondence in the archives is devoted to these "special orders" which were distinct from the glass that the stores already had in stock.

One letter from Hawkes to Caldwell says: "Replying… to the prompt delivery of Special Orders, would say that we always do the best we can for you. But, as we have previously explained, it is not possible, in the great majority of cases to send these orders on time, especially if the time is nearly always so very short—on the average nine days and for a great many of these orders we do not have the blanks on hand, and have to make them which takes generally from two weeks to a month, a number of these Specials require moulds, the getting out of which adds to the delay. We sincerely wish there was some way in which we could deliver all Special Orders promptly but you cannot ask us to do Impossibilities."[51]

A similar letter to Davis Collamore explains why it is hard to fill these orders: "Now we wish to impress upon you the importance in giving us the longest time on glass where it is ordered specially for a certain day. A few hours in many cases makes a great difference to us in the case of some on order. So as not to disappoint you on the Russian glass ordered for Dec. 3, we had to put a dozen of our best hands on it; it cost us in actual cash $25.00 more than we get for the goods, and from your letter of this morning, you evidently had several days to spare, as you say you must complete this set this week; besides it is almost impossible for us to give you as good goods as we like when you hurry us so much."[52]

As example of these "Specials," a letter from Briggs says: "Also can you make me a dish the same as your Ice cream tray without handles but an inch and a half shorter cut Russian."[53] Another example from Briggs later that year says: "I also want you to cut for me at once, as samples some pieces, say a 9in. nappy cut in Russian in the most magnificent manner, say two or three times as deep as usual. I want this to be a most superb specimen as I think I can sell a lot of this very rich glass. I have had similar pieces from T. Webb & Sons Stourbridge which have always sold."[54] An order from Davis Collamore marked "(special)" included eighteen each of a variety of stemware including ruby hocks and green hocks, finger bowls and ice plates, handled punch glasses "shape of our straw diamond sample, handles cut on sides, to hold same quantity when finished", and two pairs of handled decanters flat "all of the above to be thin & clear at top, no stones or bubbles. Full pattern on all pieces as on the goblet."[55] Collamore had sent samples for this and he gave Hawkes the entire summer to supply the order.

In 1889, J. E. Caldwell sent a sample pitcher and ordered celery trays cut in the

51. Thomas G. Hawkes to J. E. Caldwell & Company, Philadelphia, October 14, 1888.
52. T. G. Hawkes to Davis Collamore, New York, December 5, 1888.
53 Richard Briggs, Boston, to T. G. Hawkes, May 31, 1882.
54. Richard Briggs, Boston to T. G. Hawkes, December 26, 1882.
55. C A C for Davis Collamore & Company to T. G. Hawkes, June 13, 1882.

same pattern, which he called "Passion." He concluded, "Also please take a design of cutting as we will want more goods of this cutting. Return pitcher as soon as possible."[56] More typical was an inquiry in 1891 from Irwin R. Brayton, a jeweler in Buffalo who handled Hawkes glass there. Mr. Brayton telegraphed, "Have you eight inch Comports the foot Separate. What pattern and price" and Hawkes replied, "No, but could make to special order."[57] Brayton then explained: "Six or seven years ago I bought a set of 5 pcs. at Baccarat that the dish was separate from the foot. A customer now wants 4 of them. Can you give me an idea of the shape of foot and the cost – in a rich cut pattern say the Chrys – or Grecian – and how soon you could make it after accepting the order."[58] A couple of weeks later, a further letter from Brayton says that he is returning the wooden model Hawkes sent to show the shape and "my customer wants it one inch higher and a 9 inch diameter of top made in straw diamond and fan. I want the fan around the bottom of stand. Of course you understand it is to be in two pieces – the top sitting into the foot, Send as early as possible."[59] The profit margin on an order like this, for which Hawkes had to have a special model made and then perhaps a mould to shape the blank, could not have been large. Nonetheless, the letters are full of similar inquiries.

Sometimes the requested special pieces were nearly impossible to make. One letter from Hawkes to a New York retailer explains: "To make a globe of best metal in one piece with opening at one end 21 inches in diameter cut deep hobnail would cost $300. We would not take an order for four of these at this price until we had cut one to see what we could do, as we do not know whether we could make it satisfactory or not in heavy glass. This is a very large piece, as you will see from enclosed paper pattern, and made heavy enough to stand deep cutting – it would weigh 88 pounds, as near as we can estimate, and you can imagine the difficulty of handling a piece of this size. We would have to get up special slings, etc. We could make it in a much lighter weight and shallow cutting for a much less price. We could also make this globe in two pieces in heavy cutting of best metal for $200, We think it would be equally as well if were put together in the center and a silver plated band put around it to secure it."[60] Unfortunately, the orders do not indicate whether the order was ever made. The standard day-to-day correspondence from Richard Briggs, J. E. Caldwell and Company, and Davis Collamore indicates that at least a quarter of their orders, and perhaps more than that, were special orders, a way of doing business that is unheard of today.

56. J. E. Caldwell, Philadelphia to T. G. Hawkes, November 12, 1889.
57. Irwin Brayton, Buffalo to T. G. Hawkes, October 13, 1891, with penciled reply from Hawkes.
58. Irwin Brayton, Buffalo to T. G. Hawkes, October 14, 1891.
59. Irwin Brayton, Buffalo to T. G. Hawkes, October 28, 1891.
60. T. G. Hawkes to Gilman Collamore & Company, New York, September 20, 1892.

CHAPTER ELEVEN

Hoare and Hawkes and Their Relationships with Gorham and Tiffany

From the beginning of the glass industry in Corning, John Hoare's firm supplied glass to Gorham and other companies to be silver mounted. His advertisement in a New York City directory of the 1870s emphasizes "ALL GLASS PERTAINING TO THE SILVER AND PLATED WARE TRADES ON HAND OR MADE TO ORDER."[1] The Gorham Manufacturing Company appears as a Hoare customer in 1879, buying inkstands, bottles, and castor bottles to be silver mounted. Simpson, Hall, Miller & Company in Wallingford, the Derby Silver Company in Birmingham, the Wilcox Silver Plate Company in Meriden, all in Connecticut, the Racine Silver Plate Company in Wisconsin, and the Aurora Silver Plate Manufacturing Company of Aurora, Illinois were also buying glass from Hoare for mounting in silver in 1879–1880.[2] From 1880 to 1883, Thomas Hawkes bought silver fitters from Gorham in small quantities, mostly for "flask tops", but

1. Undated photocopy in Museum files.
2. The customer names are taken from a set of postcards which were on loan to The Corning Museum of Glass briefly in 1972. The postcards had been found in a Corning attic, and were all addressed to John Hoare from various customers and dated 1879 or 1880. The present whereabouts of the cards is unknown, but some notes on their contents remain in Museum files.

Figs. 11-1 through 11-22 are taken from scrapbooks in the Gorham archives in the John Hay Library of Brown University. The Gorham company cut up pages from its catalogs and reassembled them in sections by shape, which accounts for the look of the pages here and for the fact that they are not in strict numerical order. These designs date from between 1898 and 1909.

11-1. Bowls. The glass for nos. 206, 207, 209 and 210 was provided by Hoare.

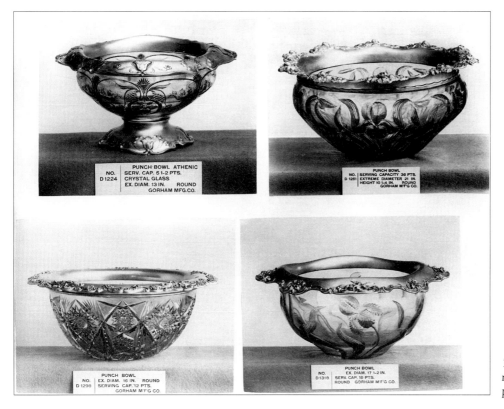

PUNCH BOWL ATHENIC
NO. D 1224 | SERV. CAP. 5 1-2 PTS. | CRYSTAL GLASS
EX. DIAM. 13 IN. ROUND
GORHAM MFG. CO.

PUNCH BOWL.
NO. D 1251 | SERVING CAPACITY 38 PTS. | EXTREME DIAMETER 21 IN. | HEIGHT 10 1-4 IN. ROUND
GORHAM M'F'G CO.

PUNCH BOWL
NO. D 1298 | EX. DIAM. 16 IN. ROUND | SERVING CAP. 12 PTS.
GORHAM M'F'G CO.

PUNCH BOWL
NO. D 1318 | EX. DIAM. 17 1-2 IN. | SERV. CAP. 18 PTS.
ROUND GORHAM M'F'G CO.

11-2. Punch bowls. The glass for nos. 1224, 1251 and 1318 was provided by Hawkes.

NO. D 1305 | BOWL | DIAM. 12 1-4 IN. ROUND
GORHAM M'F'G CO.

NO. D 1306 | BOWL ATHENIC | EX. DIAM. 12 1-8 IN. ROUND
GORHAM M'F'G CO.

NO. D 1307 | BOWL | EX. DIAM. 11 IN. ROUND
GORHAM M'F'G CO.

11-3. Bowls. All three of these designs were purchased from Hawkes, Dec. 9, 1903.

NO. D 1433 | BOWL | DIAM. 12 IN. ROUND
GORHAM MFG. CO.

11-4. Bowl, engraved Wild Rose, Hawkes.

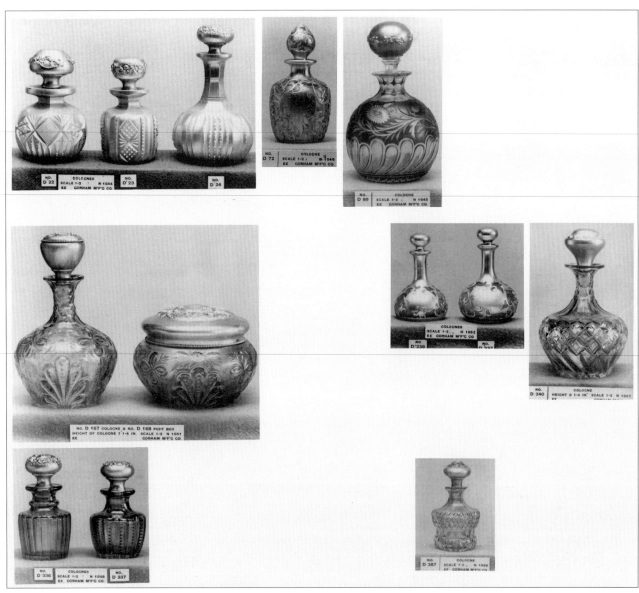

11-5. Colognes. 22, 23, 24 are Hoare; 99 is from *Stevens & Williams*; 167, 168 and 240 are from *Hawkes and the remainder are unidentified.*

no correspondence indicates that Gorham was buying glass from Hawkes before 1884, except for one set of monogrammed tableware.

Gorham's name is first found as a Hawkes customer beginning with an order for $1300 worth of colognes in June, 1884[3] and the association continued into the early 1890s and in the ledgers of the first decade of the 20th century. This order from Gorham to Hawkes in 1889 is typical: "Please send us 175 Glass Flasks to sample sent you this day... These Flasks want to be made as uniform as possible for them to be. Any variation in the size obliges us to change the Silver... We think you made a few of these Flasks for us a while ago. If we have sent you this order by mistake, you will please transfer the whole matter to Mr. Hoare. We are unable to trace from whom we had the others. Please bill these to us as S602 Flasks."[4]

By 1913, Hawkes had started its own department for silver mounting and,

3. Gorham Mnfg. Company, Providence to T. G. Hawkes, June 13, 1884.
4. Gorham Mnfg. Company, Providence to T. G. Hawkes, August 9, 1889.

11-6. Colognes. 594, 595, 603, 604, 605 and 606 are from Hawkes. The remainder are unidentified.

although Gorham continued to buy glass from both Corning firms, Hawkes no longer purchased silver mountings. The Hawkes "Price Book," from the teens (which succeeded an earlier one) has a 13-page section titled "Gorham Mnfg. Co." which makes them the second largest customer (fewer pages than Collamore but more than Briggs, Burley and Caldwell who had the other multi-page sections in the book). A variety of shapes and patterns are listed, including nappies and plates in *DuBarry* (an engraved pattern), *Raleigh, Kensington, Sonora, Queen's, Princess* (probably the 1910 version rather than the earlier one), and *Panel*. There is also a list of "Exhibition Vases", six numbered shapes ranging in price from $12 to $16 with a note that the minimum purchase for each shape is six pieces, and another note that prices for everything have been raised 20% as of May 15, 1916.

The last section included three lamps in Shape 1932, at 13½in., 15in. and 17in. in Sapphire, Diamond and Ruby, but no indication is given whether these are pattern names or colors. However, it is clear that Gorham was still using Hawkes blanks as late as 1916.[5]

Fortunately, the Gorham archives at the John Hay Library of Brown University are extensive, and it is possible to check some silver-mounted designs and find out from where Gorham purchased the glass. In the 1880s and 1890s, the Gorham code for silver-mounted ware was S, but the "S" ledger books were temporarily unavailable in 1994 so only a few of these designs could be identified. However, the Gorham scrapbook from the Rakow Library's Hoare archives contains material cut from Gorham catalogs for which the glass was probably supplied by Hoare. These S designs probably date from the mid-1880s to 1898. Their inclusion in the Hoare scrapbook means that at one time Gorham ordered these cut pieces from Hoare, but it does not mean that the pieces could not have been ordered from another source at a different time.

S624–626: Colognes, Russian & Pillar.
S629: Cologne.
S698: Bottle.
S702, 709: Colognes.
S757: Decanter, Crystal City pattern.
S830: Whiskey decanter.
S834: Pitcher.
S837: Cologne.
S1002: Decanter.
S1067: Decanter.
S1322: Pitcher.
S1361: Tantalus stand – 3 decanters.
S1411: Cologne.
S1465: Bitters bottle.
S1744: Whiskey jug.
S1746–1748: Tumble-ups.
S1781: Butter plate.
S1910: Vase, "like Hawkes".
S1933: Decanter.
S1996–1998: Colognes.
S2120: Puff box.
S2166: Bottle – "6/27/96".
S2170: Engraved Cologne – design drawing.
S2171–2172: Engraved Claret pitchers.
S2184: Butter dish.
S2311: Water color design drawing for an engraved decanter with gilded base and collar dated March 16, '95.
S2318: Berry bowl.
S2402: Silver handled claret decanter.
S2416: Puff box.

S2439: Finger bowl.
S2466, 2467: Cracker jars.
S2472: Cologne.
S2507: Tabasco bottle.
S2510: Puff box.
S2549: Butter dish.
S2550–2553: Bon bon dishes.
S2559: Cologne, Sept. 10, 1898.
S2565: Pitcher.
S2606: Pitcher.
S2629, 2630: Syrup jugs.
S2631, 2632: Pitcher.
S2635: Decanter, Tantalus set.
S2660: Salad bowl.
S2742, 2743: Cologne.
S2746: Cologne.
S2784: Whiskey jug.
S2801: Ice bowl.
S2803: Pitcher.
S2805–S2807: Salad bowls.
S2808–S2809: Claret jugs.
S2820: Cologne, "like Hawkes, 2/14/13".
S2873: Cracker jar.
S2897: Loving cup.
S2900, 2902: Claret decanters.
S2991, 2992: Claret decanters.
S3020: Cologne.
S3049–3051: Salad bowls.
S3116: Pitcher, April 7, 1898.
S3119, 3120: Loving cups.
S3158–3160: Ice cream sets.

In 1898, Gorham changed the designation for silver-mounted wares to D. The D designs are recorded in a ledger book which lists the shape, the price and (about half of the time), the source of the glassware. The existing ledger book covers the period from February 1898 until December 1909. The companies

5. "Price Book", T. G. Hawkes & Company, ca.1913–1918, Hawkes Archives (R804d).

11-7. *Colognes. 634 through 641 are from Hawkes, ordered between 1901 and 1915; 706 is unidentified and 782 is from Hoare although it appears in the ledger as a decanter.*

most frequently listed as suppliers of glassware are the Hope Glass Works in Providence, T. G. Hawkes and Company, J. Hoare and Company, and McCue & Earl in New York. A confusing aspect of this to a glass collector is that the Gorham design numbers were, of course, for the silver parts and they had no relation to the cut or engraved design on the glass. Therefore, two Gorham design numbers could be listed for the same glass blank with the same glass cutting or engraving, but with only slightly different silver parts. In most cases, the D number is on the silver mount, near the Gorham mark.

Blanks were obtained from Stevens & Williams in England and some very simple blanks were ordered from Baccarat. D68, in April 1898, was listed as a green cameo cut claret jug from Stevens & Williams and the following month, one entire page in the ledger is filled with a Gorham order to Stevens & Williams for overlay blanks of various shapes and colors, all cut in a pattern usually attributed

11-8. Claret jugs. 194 and 235 are Hoare, decanter 218 is Hoare; the remainder are unidentified.

6. Ledger VI. 4. Gorham Archives, p.4; see Herbert Wiener and Freda Lipkowitz, Rarities in American Cut Glass, (Houston, 1975) pp.163–164 for illustrations of this pattern.

to Dorflinger.[6] (Fig. 11-5, D99; 11-9, D170) Gorham also bought glass for silver mounting from Dorflinger and the Quezal company, and pottery from Rookwood, although these names occur infrequently in this particular ledger.

As an example of how much the silver cost added to the cost of the glassware, one Hoare entry, D192, is a salad bowl, 10 inches in diameter for which the glass to be mounted cost $14 and the price of the metal and labor was $32. Gorham's internal cost for the bowl was $46, but neither the wholesale or retail prices are

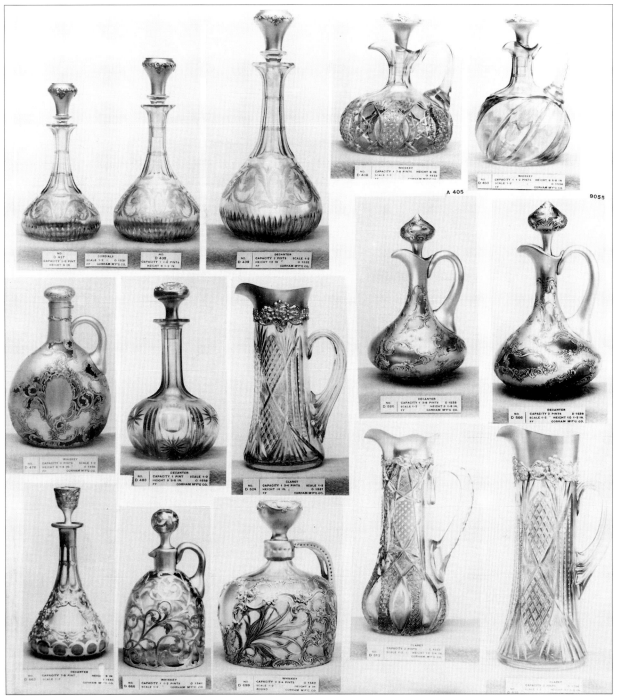

11-9. Claret jugs. 170 is from Stevens & Williams; 194, 208 and 234 are Hoare; 200 is Hawkes, the remainder are unidentified.

given. Fortunately, by cross-checking the Gorham illustrated catalogs, where the pieces are listed by shape and design number, it is often possible to find an illustration of a given piece.

The numbers in the chart below show which Corning pieces were supplied for which design numbers. The entries are given as written, including dates when they occur. Since only about half of the entries have a glass supplier listed, there are more designs which were made in Corning but cannot be identified today.

(Some Hoare designs which are not identified in the "D" ledger turn up in the Hoare archives in Corning and some of these were published by the A.C.G.A. in 1993.) Several designs were listed for each date and the dates seem to represent completed orders since occasionally a given design will have a second, later, date after the first one, sometimes with a different price. The earlier designs do not have a Hawkes or Hoare trademark on the glass, but some of the later ones do.[7] Gorham may have asked its glass suppliers not to mark the ware to be mounted, but Hawkes "Gravic" signatures are sometimes found. Most of the designs on the list are illustrated here in photographs taken from Gorham catalogs in the John Hay Library.

D2–3: Flasks, Horseshoe, Hoare, February 12, 1898.

D4–6: Salve Boxes, sml., med. and large, 1550, Hoare February 15, 1898.

D9: Whiskey jug, Hoare Prism jug with plug February 17, 1898.

D22–24: Colognes, Hoare 9230, March 31, 1898.

D31: Ink, Hoare.

D108: Cruet, Hoare (Hoare archives).

D133–134: Atomizers, Hawkes, not used, changed to D151, 150.

D135–137: Loving cups, 3 pts. Hoare.

D147–148: Paprica Bottles, Hoare May 20, 1898.

D162: Bowl (Hoare archives).

D167–168: Cologne and puff box, Hawkes, Shell pattern, June 14 (in production until 11/25/16).

D192–D198: Set of salad bowls, claret pitcher, ice bowl, cracker jar, cigar jar and sherry decanter, all J. Hoare & Company, August 15, 1898.

D199: Salad bowl, Hoare.

D200: Claret jug, 2 1/2 pints, Hawkes.

D201, 203: Ice Cream set, Hoare (Hoare archives).

D206: Salad bowl, 9in., Hoare, August 18, 1898.

D207: Salad bowl, 10in., Hoare.

D208: Claret jug, Hoare.

D209: Salad bowl, 9in., Hoare, August 30, 1898.

D210–212: Salad bowls, 10in., Hoare.

D218, D219: Pint and quart decanters in same pattern, Hoare.

D234, 235: Claret jugs, Hoare, August 19, 1898.

D240: Cologne, Hawkes.

D336: Cologne, (Hoare archives).

D396–D398: Claret cup pitchers, Hoare, February 6, 1899.

D399: Bitters bottle, Hoare.

D400: Whiskey Jug, Hoare 9403, February 20 1899.

D401: Butter dish, 5in., Hoare 9406.

D402: Butter dish, 5in., Hoare 9404.

D435: Ink, Hoare 9392, March 7, 1899.

D436: Whiskey jug, Hoare 9341.

D437–439: 1/2 Pt, Pt. and Qt. decanters, Hoare 9388, March 7, 1899 (price raised 2/19/17).

D528–531: Vases, engraved, Hawkes, June 14, 1899.

D594–595: Hawkes.

D603–606: Colognes, Hawkes, "intaglio" engraved, September 18, 1899.

D634–D641: Colognes, Hawkes, flutes, September 17, 1901 (last order 2/8/15).

D643: Whiskey jug, Hoare, 3/22/1900.

D646–647: Old Stone jugs, Hoare.

D676–689: Inks, Hawkes.

D699: Whiskey jug (blank same as D643).

D700: Ink, Hoare.

D701–705: Inks, Hawkes.

D714: Engraved bowl, Hoare, December 13, 1900.

D723: Ink (maker not named, but the costing slip gives the maker as Hoare on an order of November 28,1908.)

D764–767: "Chain" clarets, engraved in a shell pattern, Hawkes, November 27, 1901, last order 2/12/06.

D778–782: Whiskey decanters, Hoare.

D802–804: Whiskey decanters, all cut "snail", Hoare.

D805–806: Whiskey decanter and tumbler, Hoare.

D809–810: Decanters, Hoare, February 27, 1901.

D820–823: Whiskey decanters, Hoare.

D824–825: Whiskey set, Hoare.

D838, 848: Athenic design jug and vase (Hoare archives).

7. The following list was compiled from the book designated Gorham VI. 4 by the John Hay Library and titled "Gorham Silver-glass." Production D1-D2425, February 11, 1898–December 22, 1909 with additions from the costing slips and some other archival material.

11-10. Claret jugs. 235, 396, 397, 398 are Hoare, 490 and 512 are unidentified.

D850: Bowl (Hoare archives).

D852: Butter dish, Athenic design (Hoare archives).

D854, 860: Ice cream trays (Hoare archives).

D855: Fruit plate (Hoare archives).

D892: Decanter with cut decoration, Hoare.

D909–910: Marmalade jars, Hawkes.

D911, D914: Whiskey jugs, Hawkes.

D916–917: Decanters, Hawkes.

D998: Vase, Rock Crystal engraved, 17in. high, Hawkes, February 19, 1902 (price raised 2/12/06).

D1051: Horseradish bottle, Hoare.

D1064: Salad bowl, Hoare (Maker not named in ledger, but in Hoare archives).

D1179–1192: Stemware, Hawkes, September 5, 1902.

D1208–1226: Pieces in Gorham's "Athenic" pattern, various shapes, Hawkes, January 29, 1903.

D1251: Punch bowl, Hawkes engraved Iris.

D1293–1295: Colognes, Hoare.

D1305: Bowl, 9in., engraved Tulips, Hawkes, December 9, 1903.

D1306: Bowl, 9in., engraved Carnations, Hawkes, December 9, 1903.

D1307: Bowl, 9in., engraved Narcissus, Hawkes, December 9, 1903.

D1318: Punch bowl, Hawkes.

D1319: Bowl, Hawkes.

11-11. *Decanters. 400, 436, 437, 438, 439 and 699 are Hoare; the remainder are unidentified.*

D1433: Bowl, 9in., engraved Wild Rose, Hawkes, (reordered August 6, 1913).
D1699: Tooth Brush Tubes, Hawkes.
D1757: Bowl, 9in., Hobnail, Hoare, March 22, 1905.
D1771: Vase, "Lorraine", Hawkes.
D1772: Vase, R. C. Hawkes.
D1773: Jug. R. C. Hawkes.
D2142: Cologne (this design ordered from Hawkes 1898–1904; from Pairpoint after 1904).

D2266–68: Bowl, Hoare 870 (Hoare archives).
D2269: Whisky jug, Hoare (Hoare archives photograph marked "our 9658, cut 1112").
D2273: Bowl, Hoare, (Hoare archives photograph marked "our 8049, cut 1284").
D2282,2283, 2285, 2287: Decanters, Hoare, (from Hoare archives).
D2340–2342: Decanters, Hoare, March 22, 1909.
D2776: Decanter, Hoare (Hoare archives).

11-12. Both designs are whisky decanters from Hoare; 646 is listed as an "Old Stone Jug".

11-13. Decanters. 764–767 are listed as "Chain" decanters from Hawkes; 778, 779 and 881 are from Hoare. Decanter 783 is unidentified.

11-14. *All of the decanters and tumblers on this page are from Hoare.*

11-15. *Whiskey set from Hoare.*

11-16. Decanter 892 is from Hoare, Whiskey jug 911 is from Hawkes, 913 is unidentified.

11-17. Decanters 914, 916 and 917 are Hawkes, 922 may be Hoare although it is not identified in the ledger; 919 is not identified.

271

11-19. Engraved vases from Hawkes,
ordered June 14, 1899.

11-18. Pitcher from Hawkes.

11-20. Rock crystal engraved vase.
The 17in. piece was received from
Hawkes, Feb. 19, 1902, and again
on Feb. 2, 1906.

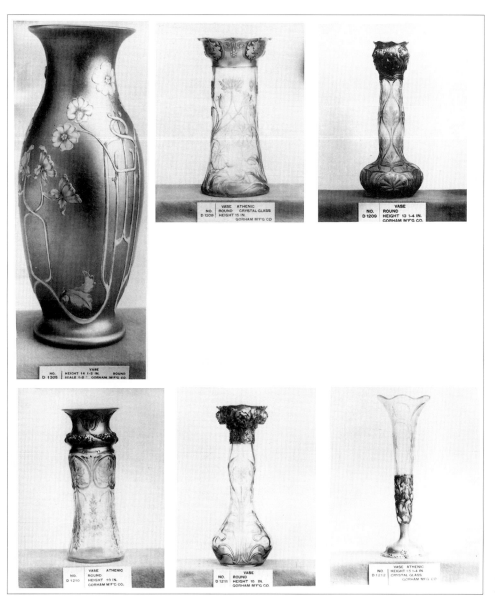

VASE
NO. | VASE ATHENIC CRYSTAL GLASS
D 1208 | ROUND
HEIGHT 15 IN.
GORHAM M'F'G CO.

VASE
NO. | ROUND
D 1209 | HEIGHT 13 1-4 IN.
GORHAM M'F'G CO.

VASE
NO. | HEIGHT 14 1-2 IN. ROUND
D 1205 | SCALE 1-2 " GORHAM M'F'G CO.

VASE ATHENIC
NO. | ROUND
D 1210 | HEIGHT 10 IN.
GORHAM M'F'G CO.

VASE
NO. | ROUND
D 1211 | HEIGHT 15 IN.
GORHAM M'F'G CO.

VASE ATHENIC
NO. | HEIGHT 15 1-4 IN.
D 1212 | CRYSTAL GLASS
GORHAM MFG CO.

11-21. *Vases in Gorham's "Athenic" patterns, 1208–1212 ordered from Hawkes. 1205 is from an unknown supplier.*

NO. | VASES
D 1771 | HEIGHT 19 IN.
D 1772 | " 20 "
CRYSTAL GLASS
GORHAM MFG CO.

11-22. *Vase in Lorraine pattern, and rock crystal engraved vase, both from Hawkes.*

The other silver firm most closely associated with Corning's cut glass is the silver department of Tiffany & Company of New York. Fortunately the archives of the Tiffany silver department are in good order and it is possible to check their ledgers and design files. It emerges that although Tiffany sold English cut glass tableware in the 1880s and 1890s, (purchased through a different department) they bought cut glass for silver mounting exclusively from J. Hoare & Company of Corning from 1888 to 1898. The cash books of the silver department for the early 1880s show only scattered payments to glass companies, generally to the Walker Glass Mnfg. Company and Holbrook Bros. Glass Company. Sometimes these payments are marked "for plateaux" and since the companies listed are not known as tableware producers, it seems likely that Tiffany's silver mounting department did not start to work on cut glass until March 12, 1888, when they paid .55 to receive an express box from Corning. For the rest of that year, Tiffany's monthly payments to Hoare totaled over $6000, which probably made Tiffany a major customer for Hoare, although no Hoare financial records survive to confirm this. The following year, payments recorded in the ledger total nearly

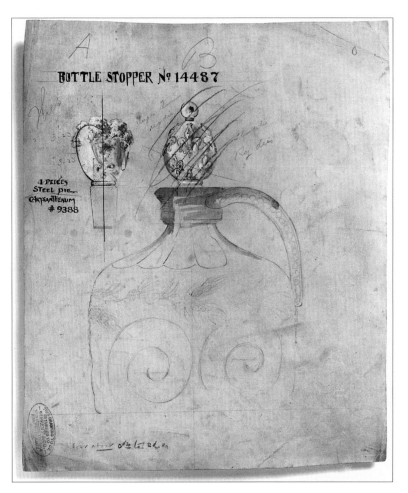

11-23. Design drawing for a whisky jug with silver stopper, engraved in Hoare's Wheat pattern.

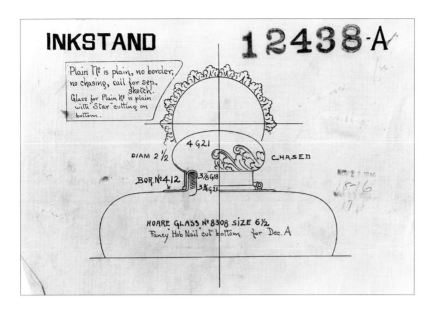

11-24. Design drawing for an inkstand with glass from Hoare, dated Nov. 23, 1910.

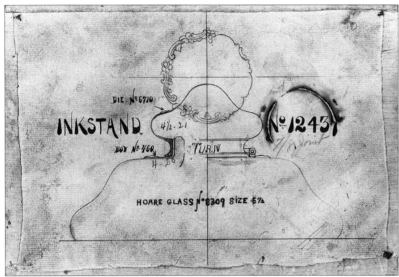

11-25. Design drawing for an inkstand with glass from Hoare.

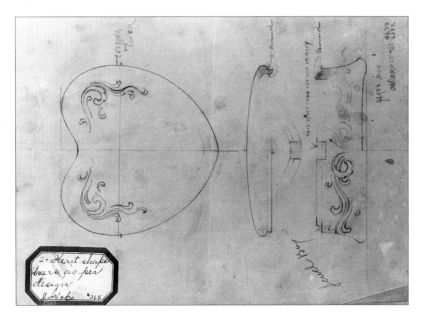

11-26. Design drawings for a heart-shaped cut glass jewel box and matching lid from J. Hoare & Company for Tiffany.

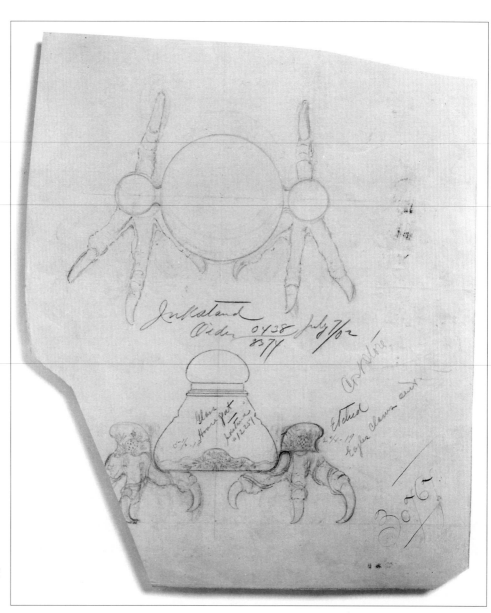

11-27. *Design drawing for an inkstand to be mounted on eagle claws provided by the customer; glass provided by Hoare, dated July 7, 1902.*

$10,000 and in 1890, the total was about $9000. According to Hawkes, Tiffany exhibited silver-mounted cut glass made by Hoare at the 1889 Paris World's Fair (See Chap. 9) but none of the available records list or describe these pieces. However, the popularity of this glassware probably contributed greatly to the fact that Tiffany continued to buy glass from Hoare. Tiffany paid Hoare at the end of each month, but apparently the glass came up several times a month because express payments from Corning occur more often than glass payments. The ledger for 1891 shows around $10,000 but the total went up to $12,000 in 1892, which was the peak year in this collaboration. Payment in 1893 fell to under $5000 and in 1894, 1895, and 1896, they were about $3000. Finally, in 1897 and 1898 payments to Hoare were under $1000 a year. However, all of the payments of the silver department gradually diminished from 1895, so this business was apparently being reduced. This is not to imply that Tiffany produced no silver-mounted cut glass before 1888 or after 1898, but it was a big business only during this decade, according to the records of the silver department. In

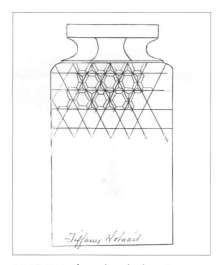

11-28. Design for a cologne bottle cut in Tiffany Hobnail pattern.

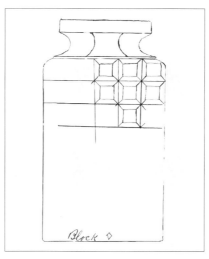

11-29. Design for a cologne bottle cut in Block Diamond pattern.

Figs. 11-28 through 11-35. Group of design drawings for cologne bottles provided by J. Hoare & Company to Tiffany and Company, probably in the early 1890s. The drawings are on the back of J. Hoare & Company stationery dated "189-". Probably these were prospective designs for bottles to which Tiffany would add silver stoppers and there is no indication of whether or not they were actually produced.

11-30. Design for a cologne bottle cut in Richelieu pattern.

11-31. Design for a cologne bottle cut in pattern no. 5480.

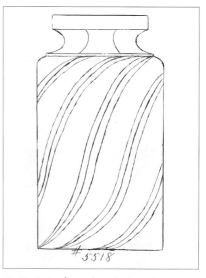

11-32. Design for a cologne bottle cut in pattern no. 5518.

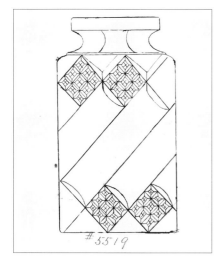

11-33. Design for a cologne bottle cut in pattern no. 5519.

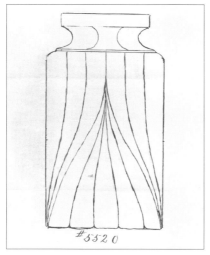

11-34. Design for a cologne bottle cut in pattern no. 5520.

11-35. Design for a cologne bottle cut in pattern no. 5521.

Figs. 11-36 through 11-41. Group of design drawings for cologne bottles provided by J. Hoare & Company to Tiffany and Company, around 1890. The group includes the Mikado pattern patented in 1887. Probably these were prospective designs for bottles to which Tiffany would add silver stoppers and there is no indication of whether or not they were actually produced.

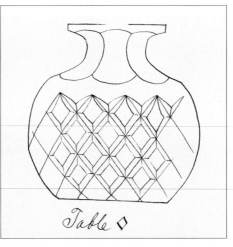

11-36. Design for a cologne bottle cut in Table Diamond pattern.

11-37. Design for a cologne bottle cut in Twist Pillar pattern.

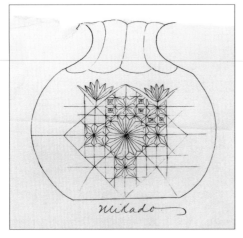

11-38. Design for a cologne bottle cut in Mikado pattern.

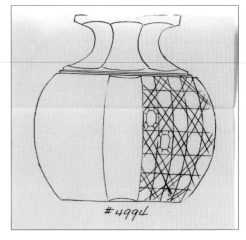

11-39. Design for a cologne bottle cut in pattern no. 4994, Octagonal Hobnail.

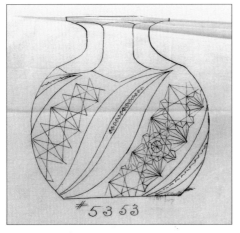

11-40. Design for a cologne bottle cut in pattern no. 5353.

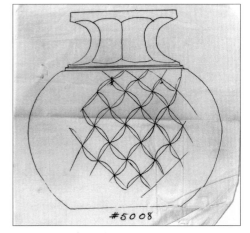

11-41. Design for a cologne bottle cut in pattern no. 5008.

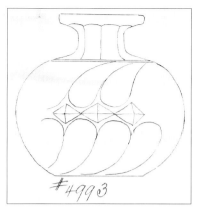

11-42. Design for a cologne bottle cut in pattern no. 4993.

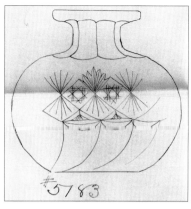

11-43. Design for a cologne bottle cut in pattern no. 5183, Croesus.

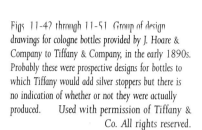

Figs. 11-42 through 11-51. Group of design drawings for cologne bottles provided by J. Hoare & Company to Tiffany & Company, in the early 1890s. Probably these were prospective designs for bottles to which Tiffany would add silver stoppers but there is no indication of whether or not they were actually produced.   Used with permission of Tiffany & Co. All rights reserved.

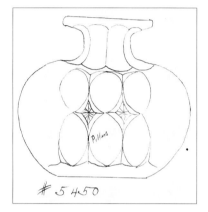

11-44. Design for a cologne bottle cut in pattern no. 5450.

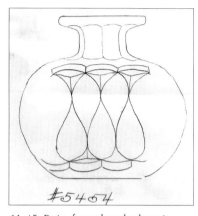

11-45. Design for a cologne bottle cut in pattern no. 5454.

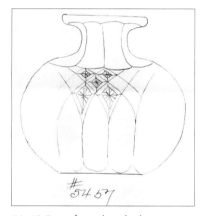

11-46. Design for a cologne bottle cut in pattern no. 5457.

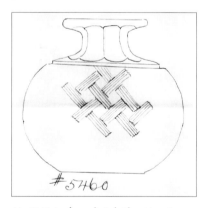

11-47. Design for a cologne bottle cut in pattern no. 5460, Basket.

11-48. Design for a cologne bottle cut in pattern no. 5479.

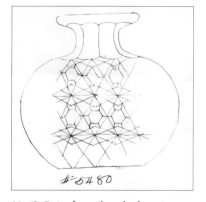

11-49. Design for a cologne bottle cut in pattern no. 5480.

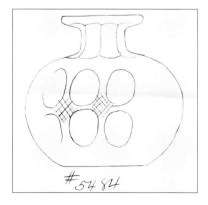

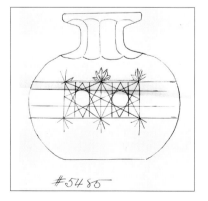

11-50. Design for a cologne bottle cut in pattern no. 5484.

11-51. Design for a cologne bottle cut in pattern no. 5485.

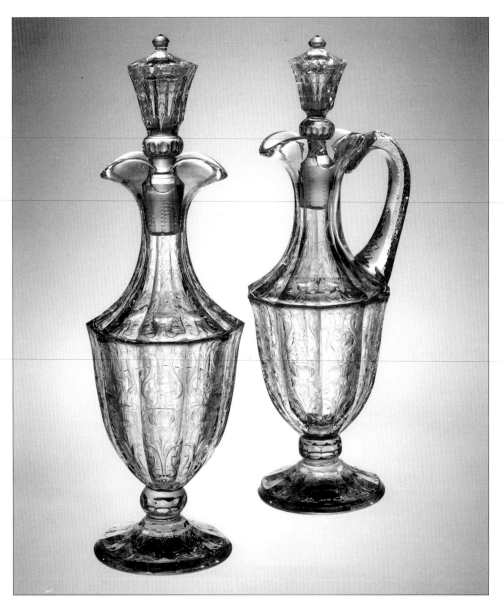

11-52. *Decanters from the set made for "Diamond Jim" Brady by J. Hoare & Company about 1900. Designed by Paulding Farnham of Tiffany & Company H: (taller) 38.4cm. Gift of M. H. Riviere (CMG 88.4.15, 16).*

other time periods, the cut and/or engraved blanks may have been purchased through another department.

The Hoare template book in the Rakow library shows a number of shapes supplied to the Tiffany and Gorham firms between 1900 and 1920, but there's no indication of the cut or engraved pattern or of what Tiffany or Gorham intended to do with the pieces. One silhouette shows a cylindrical cologne bottle with the notation "Gorham's 8136D with lip/Tiffany's 3409 without lip/Iron mould 1622 9/18/09". The Hawkes firm was supplying Tiffany as well as Gorham in these decades, since a Hawkes Gravic fruit set engraved with fruit which was found in a Tiffany presentation case was illustrated in a company history.[8]

Tiffany's blue books in the 1880s and 1890s have no illustrations, but they do list "English table glass" and no American cut glass is specifically mentioned. In

8. John Loring. *150 Years of Tiffany*, New York, 1987, p.143.

11-53. *Place setting from the set made for "Diamond Jim" Brady by J. Hoare & Company about 1900. H: (goblet) 18cm. Gift of M. H. Riviere.(CMG 88.4.17A–J).*

1893, a radical change was announced. The company decided to sell less tableware, and more artwares, and it announced that it would sell antique glass and china, reproductions, and wares from the 1889 exposition in Paris, including glass by Gallé and others. This is probably why pieces engraved with "Tiffany & Co. /1889/Paris Exhibition/ Thomas Webb" turn up from time to time.

Unfortunately, the Tiffany design records fail to record all of their glassware patterns, nor do they show much of the glass bought for resale. The "blue books" are not illustrated, and so it is impossible to identify most of the glass which Tiffany offered in its china and glass department. Some of that must have been from Hoare as well but there is no way to tell, if the glass is not marked. Fortunately, the Tiffany design archives do have some drawings of glassware made by Hoare, and although most of these are not dated, they probably are from the

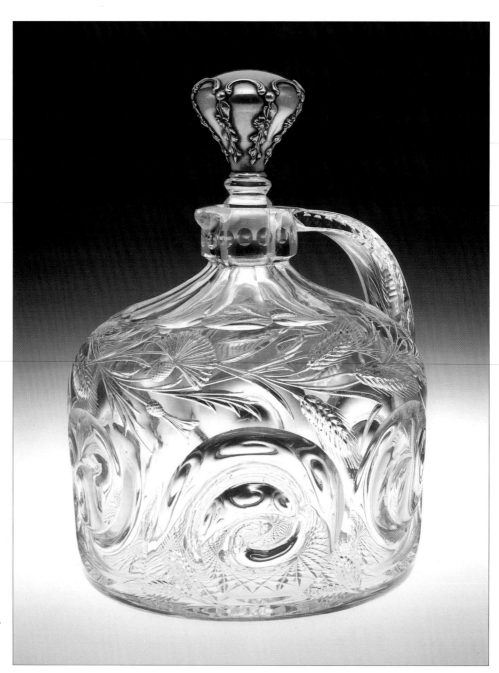

11-54. Whiskey jug, "cut snail", according to ledger description and engraved in Hoare's Wheat pattern. Gorham D643, about 1900–1910, H. 22.7cm. (94.4.165). This design was also used by Tiffany, see Fig. 11-23.

1888-1898 period. Most of these are illustrated in this chapter. One set of glassware cut and engraved by J. Hoare & Company, and probably retailed by Tiffany & Company, is the set of tableware made for James Buchanan Brady, better known as "Diamond Jim" Brady. Brady was a colorful character, a salesman of railroad equipment who controlled the United States supply of an essential piece of machinery for the railroads, part of a rail car's undercarriage. He made his fortune in the 1880s and 1890s and was one of Tiffany's best customers. When he died in 1917, this set of glassware was sold at auction as having been made by "James Hoare of the Corning Glass Company" (James Hoare had testified in a suit in 1902 that his company was often confused with Corning Glass Works because of its location in the Corning plant). None of the surviving pieces is marked, but the auction attribution is firm, coming as it does directly from the estate. The lack

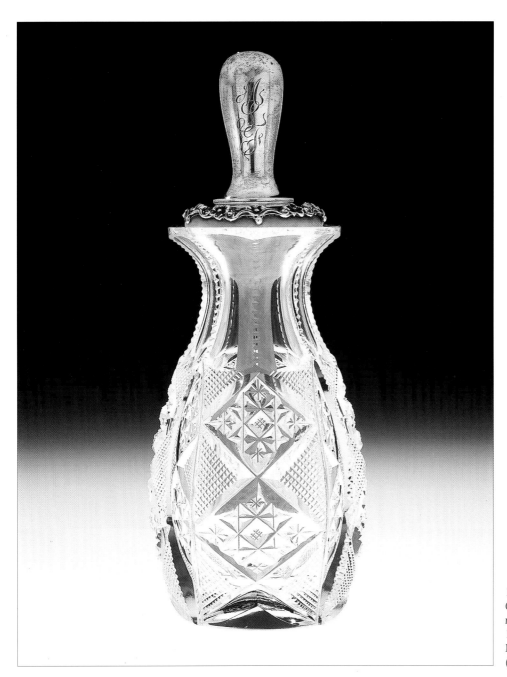

11-55. Horseradish jar, J. Hoare & Company, Gorham's D1051 with monogrammed stopper, about 1902–1910, H. 15.7cm. Gift of Mr. and Mrs. Clifford G. Maynard (CMG 84.4.24).

of a trademark might mean that it was made in the 1890s, and it may be a set which Hoare exhibited at the Chicago World's Fair in 1893 where one of their prize citations was for "rock crystal glassware." However, the identical engraved pattern on very similar blanks is shown on silver-mounted glass[9] designed by Paulding Farnham of Tiffany & Company and retailed by that firm in 1905. If the engraved design was created by Farnham, it was done after 1900, when many of his designs were inspired by Renaissance rock crystal pieces. Therefore, this set may have been made between 1900 and 1908 when Farnham resigned from Tiffany. The omission of the trademark was in that case probably a request from Tiffany since James Hoare testified in the suit mentioned above that the Hoare firm trademarked its wares unless it was requested not to do so by a customer like Gorham.[10]

9. Zapata, Janet. "The Rediscovery of Paulding Farnham, Tiffany's Designer Extraordinaire", The Magazine Antiques, Vol. 139 (April, 1991), p.729.
10. Papers on Appeal, p.304. Record, Corning Glass Works v. Corning Cut Glass Company et al., 126 A.D. 919, 75 A.D. 629 (Fourth Dept., 1902), p.140.

Egginton, Sinclaire, Steuben
and other firms

The Rakow Library has no archival material from O. F. Egginton & Company and little information about its daily operations is available. Oliver Egginton (1822-1900), the founder, was an English-trained cutter who came to the United States around 1863, and worked until 1867 in Portland, Maine where his brother, Enoch, was superintendent of the Portland Glass Company and another brother, Joseph, was head of the cutting shop. Oliver and a fourth brother, Thomas, accompanied Enoch to Montreal in 1867 when he went there to run a newly built factory, and when Enoch died in 1869, Oliver succeeded him as superintendent. When that factory closed in 1873, he brought his family to Corning and went to work for John Hoare. Egginton went from Hoare's company to the Hawkes firm shortly after it opened in 1880, and was first foreman and then general superintendent until he left Hawkes to start his own company in October, 1896.

His small cutting shop was located on Fifth Street in Corning, in a frame building erected for that purpose only a few blocks from his home. Initially, it was quite successful and he was able to repay the local investors within a couple of years and to enlarge the building and expand to about eighty employees. During the peak fall cutting season, he often had as many as 120 people working. He was assisted by his younger son, Walter, who had been trained as a cutter at Hoare and Hawkes. After Oliver's death in 1900, Walter ran the company until it closed in 1918. Walter was relatively conservative, preferring heavily cut patterns to the lighter cuttings popular after 1900, and producing very few engraved patterns. Because it was always a small firm, and was in business for a comparatively short period, Egginton produced much less glass than Hawkes or Hoare. During the twenty-two years it was in operation, however, O. F. Egginton & Company made a great deal of high quality glass and since the firm used an acid-stamped trademark at least from 1900, its products are easy to identify.

Unfortunately, all of the correspondence and ledgers of O. F. Egginton & Company were apparently discarded when the company closed in 1918, and only

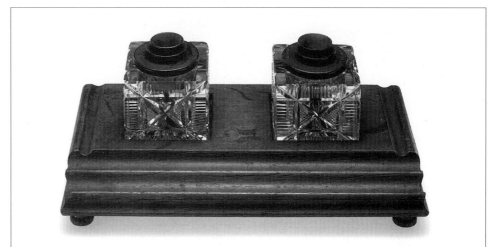

12-1. Inkstand made by the Bronson Inkstand Company of Painted Post, 1896–1900. L. 28.8cm. (CMG 94.4.35). The inkstand was invented by the Rev. Mr. Smith of Painted Post, and manufactured for only a few years.

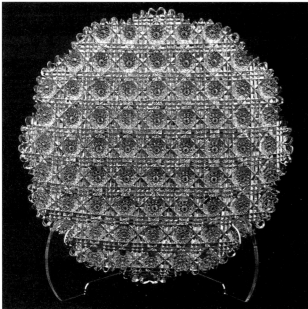

12-2. Decanter cut in Creswick pattern, O. F. Egginton & Company about 1900–1910. H. 30.5cm. trade-marked. Gift of Mrs. Richard O'Brien in memory of Mr. and Mrs. John Ryan (CMG 86.4.5ab).

12-3. Vase, engraved on a figured blank. O. F. Egginton & Company, 1916. H. 31cm., trade-marked. Gift of Mrs. Edith Weaver (CMG 86.4.88).

12-4. Tray cut in Calvé or Trellis variant pattern, O. F. Egginton & Company, about 1900–1910. D. 36cm, trade-marked. Courtesy Tom and Marsha de Graffenreid. Crofford photo

12-5. *Five-part epergne cut in Strathmore pattern, O. F. Egginton & Company, about 1900–1915. H. 76.2cm, trademarked.*

Courtesy Martin Folb. Folb photo

1. Farrar and Spillman, p.136.
2. Ibid, p. 134, Fig. 472.

one catalog has been found. That one is in a private collection, but was reprinted by the A.C.G.A. in 1982 and it is the best guide to Egginton patterns. Several of the pattern names provided by Miss Lucille Egginton (Walter's youngest daughter) in 1978[1] have never been found illustrated, and others were mis-identified by her at that time (understandable, given that she was trying to remember pattern names fifty-seven years after the company closed). Regrettably, the undated Egginton catalog does not include the *Trellis* pattern patented by Walter Egginton in 1908 or the variation (named *Trellis variant* by collectors) which is more common and is often found with the Egginton trademark. (Fig. 12-4) The *Trellis* variant was identified as *Calvé* pattern by Miss Egginton in 1977,[2] but no corroborating information has been located. As the looseleaf catalog does not include the *Magnolia* pattern patented in 1903 or *Trellis*, we can assume that neither pattern was very successful.

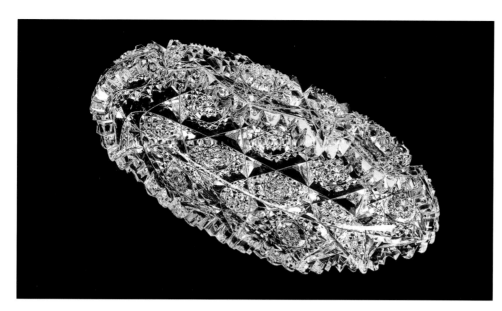

12-6. *Spoon tray, cut in Creswick pattern, O.F. Egginton & Company, 1896-1910, L. 20.2cm. trademarked. Gift of Ruth L. Gay, granddaughter of Walter Egginton (CMG 95.4.276).*

12-7. *Plate, cut in Arabian pattern. O.F. Egginton & Company, 1896-1910. D. 18cm. Gift of Ruth L. Gay, granddaughter of Walter Egginton (CMG 95.4.274).*

The Egginton company used a variety of blanks suppliers, but very few from Corning Glass Works. The Libbey Glass Company, the Union Glass Company, and later the Jeannette Glass Company were its American suppliers and some may have come from Dorflinger, although there is no record of that. The Eggintons also bought foreign blanks, principally from Baccarat in France and Val St. Lambert in Belgium. Oliver Egginton had plenty of connections in England had he wished to order blanks from his homeland, but there is no indication that he did so.

The Bronson Inkstand Company was founded in 1896 in Painted Post, a village about three miles west of Corning, to make an inkstand designed by the Reverend Mr. Smith of the village. The business was soon sold to Clute & Drake, a stationery company, although the Bronson name was retained. Corning Glass Works made the blanks for the inkstands and they were cut by George W. Drake & Company, a

3. "Engraved and Etched Glassware", *Pottery And Glass*, August, 1909, pp.73–74.

12-8. *Puff box engraved in Athens pattern. John N. Illig, about 1915–1925. D. 11.2cm., trademarked. Gift of Mr. and Mrs. Richard H. Parsons (CMG 82.2.44).*

small cutting shop owned by one of the Clute & Drake partners. By 1900, Clute and Drake had parted company and the inkstand was no longer in production. The inkstand in Fig. 12-1 is marked "Bronson Inkstand Company" and is one of the few surviving remainders of this small business.

John N. Illig was an engraver from Alsace who had worked first for Hawkes and then for the Sinclaire firm while operating his own home business. An article on Illig's company can be found as early as 1909,[3] and he advertised in the trade papers without listing a factory address from 1910 until 1915, when 136 Tioga Avenue appears for the first time. In 1921, Illig moved to the vacant Egginton factory, perhaps with a view towards expansion, but in 1924, he was forced to close at that location and work at home. Given the small size of Illig's business, it is surprising that he produced a catalog, but one Illig catalog, dating from 1917, is in the Corning Museum's Rakow Library and was published in 1979.[4]

As might be expected from the company name, John N. Illig Artistically Engraved Glassware, Illig products are engraved, although a few do have a combination of cutting and engraving. The blanks shown in the catalog are relatively lightweight. Some of them seem to have come from Steuben, but the source of the others is unknown. The most impressive piece in the catalog is a table center, done in the style of the 1870s, with three trumpet vases surrounding a fourth larger one, each trumpet engraved with a different flower. This was featured in *The Pottery, Glass & Brass Salesman* in 1913,[5] and is done on Steuben blank 1386.

It is unlikely that the firm had more than fifteen or twenty employees at best, so the total output must have been small. The puff box illustrated in Fig. 12-8, bears the company trademark, the words "ILLIG/CORNING" across a leaflike design. Only a few pieces bearing the trademark have been found, so it may not have been in use during the company's entire life.

4. Ibid., pp.266–275.
5. *Pottery, Brass & Glass Salesman*, May 15, 1913, p.17.

12-9. *Punch bowl cut in Coromandel pattern, H. P. Sinclaire & Company, about 1904–1920. H. 42cm,*
trade-marked.   *Courtesy Martin Folb. Folb photo*

Henry P. Sinclaire Jr. was the son of the Corning Glass Works corporate secretary. He moved to Corning at the age of four and joined T. G. Hawkes as bookkeeper at the age of nineteen, when he had finished a course at business school. He soon became a salesman as well and the Hawkes Archives document his increasing responsibilities during the two decades he worked for the company. In 1904, he left Hawkes to start his own cutting and engraving firm which was so successful that he was able to expand into glass manufacture in the 1920s. Sinclaire used mostly Dorflinger blanks, but some came from Corning Glass Works, Pairpoint,

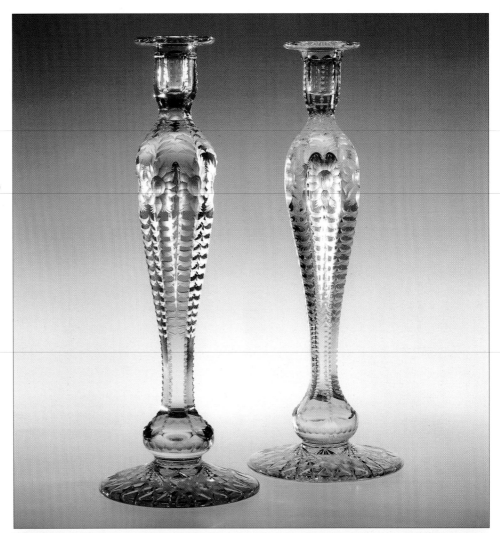

12-10. Pair of candlesticks, H. P. Sinclaire & Company, about 1910–1928. H. 35.8cm, trademarked. Courtesy George and Billie Harrington.   T. A. & M. photo

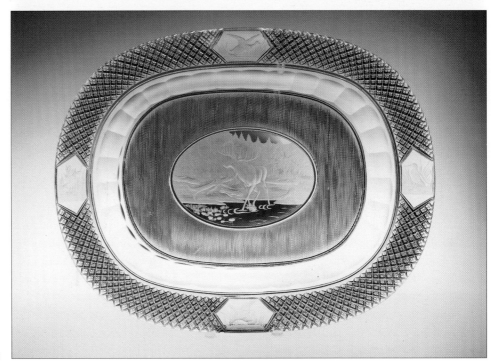

12-11. Tray cut in Silver Diamonds and Silver Threads and engraved with a moose, H. P. Sinclaire & Company, about 1904–1920. L. 36.9cm, trademarked. Courtesy Del and Elone Tipps.   T. A. & M. photo

12-12. *Punch bowl, H. P. Sinclaire & Company probably 1914. D. 41cm, trade-marked. Gift of Mr. and Mrs. William H. Morris, Richard H. Eisenhart, and Edward C. Eisenhart in memory of Mr. and Mrs. M. Herbert Eisenhart (CMG 86.4.194.).*

Steuben, and Libbey as well. Sinclaire also bought a few shapes from Baccarat and from Webb. The colored and cased glass made in the 1920s is very similar to that made by Steuben during the same period, although many of the Sinclaire colors were the same as Dorflinger's as the White Mills factory had gone out of business and former Dorflinger workmen were staffing the Sinclaire glasshouse in Bath, New York.[6]

H. P. Sinclaire & Company was the largest firm specializing in engraving, and the Rakow Library has received its extensive design archives, several hundred drawings in separate folders. Although H. P. Sinclaire created almost all of the designs for his company, the drawings are probably the work of a draftsman employed to make drawings for the workman to use as guides. A different drawing was needed for each shape, and sometimes the patterns had to be somewhat altered to make them fit on a particularly small or exceptionally large

6. Estelle Sinclaire, "C. Dorflinger & Sons from a Corning Viewpoint", *The Glass Club Bulletin*, No. 156. Fall, 1988, pp.9–13.

12-13. Goblet, cut in Sinclaire's Adam pattern on shape #1530 marked "STEUBEN", Steuben Glass Works, probably in the 1910s. H. 18.6cm. Gift of Corning Glass Works (CMG 75.4.592).

piece. Most of the patterns in the Sinclaire design archive are shown in the two volume set, written by his granddaughter[7] or in the Sinclaire chapter in *The Complete Cut & Engraved Glass of Corning*. A selection of previously unpublished designs is illustrated in Figs. 12-40 to 12-52.

Sinclaire's glass was all trademarked and can be dated to 1904-1928, the years of the firm's existence. However, a close study of the books mentioned above can sometimes enable a collector to narrow the time frame somewhat. As with most of the larger Corning firms, sets are frequently found with both Sinclaire and Hawkes, or Sinclaire and Hoare trademarks. The place setting in Fig. 1-25 is an example of this practice, since some pieces in it have Sinclaire trademarks and some Hoare trademarks while the pattern is found in the catalogs of both companies. The set is supposed to have been a gift in 1912, but there is no way to know which firm received the order from J. E. Caldwell & Company.

Steuben Glass Works, under the artistic direction of Frederick Carder, made an extensive line of blanks for cutting for T. G. Hawkes & Company, but also sold blanks to other Corning cutting firms and probably to companies outside of Corning. The company was a project of Thomas Hawkes, and not a branch of his cutting firm, and there was no reason it should not enter the profitable blank manufacturing business and market them aggressively. However, it did make some blanks for Hawkes exclusively; these are illustrated in *The Glass of Frederick Carder*.[8] The same book has a few illustrations of Carder's cut designs sold by Steuben from 1903 until 1918. These are conventional "rich-cut" designs in the

7. Estelle Sinclaire Farrar, *H. P. Sinclaire Jr. Glassmaker*, Vols. I, II. Farrar Books, Garden City, New York, 1974, 1975.
8. Paul V. Gardner, *The Glass of Frederick Carder*, Crown Books, New York, 1970, pp.323–342.

12-14. Champagne, goblet and wine glass in Queen Anne pattern on shape #6268, Steuben Division, Corning Glass Works, 1925–1935. H. of goblet: 13.8cm. Gift of Corning Glass Works (CMG 75.4.320, 75.4.765, 75.4.764).

12-15. Champagne glass, shape #7270 and finger bowl, cut in a variant of Queen Anne pattern on shape #7301, Steuben Division, Corning Glass Works, 1925–1935. H. of glass: 10.3cm. Gift of Corning Glass Works (CMG 75.4.583, 75.4.538).

12-16. Goblets cut on #6192, possibly in designs 10035, 10036 and 10037. Steuben Division, Corning Glass Works, 1920–1930. H. 14.6cm. Gift of Corning Glass Works (CMG 75.4.601, 75.4.586, 75.4.589).

12-17. Goblet, cut in Thistle pattern on #6183, and another cut in a simple pattern on a Hawkes shape, but marked "STEUBEN". Steuben Division, Corning Glass Works,1925–1935. H. of taller, 19.6cm. Gift of Corning Glass Works (CMG 75.4.566).

12-18. Goblet and champagne glass engraved in Lambeau pattern on shape #7390. Steuben Division, Corning Glass Works, late 1920s. H. 15.5cm. Gift of Corning Glass Works (CMG 75.4.604. 75.4.603).

12-19. *Wineglasses engraved in Coat-of-Arms and an unidentified pattern on shape #7081. Steuben Division, Corning Glass Works, late 1920s. H. 15cm. Gift of Corning Glass Works (CMG 75.4.788, 75.4.560).*

12-20. *Goblet engraved in Marina pattern on shape #6869, Steuben Division, Corning Glass Works, 1925–1935. H. 16.6cm. Gift of Corning Glass Works (CMG 75.4.613). This is in the 1932 Steuben catalog.*

12-21. *Goblet engraved in Mariette pattern on shape #7353, Steuben Division, Corning Glass Works, 1920s. H. 15.3cm. Gift of Corning Glass Works (CMG 75.4.618).*

12-22. *Goblet engraved in Freyburg pattern on shape #6959, Steuben Division, Corning Glass Works, 1920s. H. 15.3cm. Gift of Corning Glass Works (CMG 75.4.563).*

12-23. *Two goblets engraved on shape 3551 and one on an unknown blank. The pattern at left is Van Dyke, at center Verdun. Steuben Division, Corning Glass Works, 1915–1925. H. 20.2cm. Gift of Corning Glass Works (CMG 75.4.692, 75.4.786, 59.4.113).*

12 24. *Goblet cut in Old English*, No.3, *Steuben Division, Corning Glass Works, 1920–1930. H.14.1cm. Gift of Corning Glass Works (CMG 59.4.240).*

American style with a liberal use of hobstars and are not distinguishable from the cut glass patterns produced elsewhere in Corning. They were apparently not marked, since no marked Steuben cut glass in this style has been found. It is possible that a paper label was used, however, as Steuben decorated in other ways was always marked.

This could not have been a very large proportion of Steuben's business though, as so little evidence of it remains compared to the thousands of pieces of Carder-designed colored wares which are in museums and private collections. Frederick Carder stated in the 1960s, that he often used blanks returned from Hawkes as unsuitable, to make his own cut wares, thus cutting the factory losses.[9] The photographs in the Carder Archives in the Rakow Library include one electric lamp priced at $64.00 in a pattern called *Majestic*, and a three trumpet centerpiece

9. A. C. Revi, *American Cut and Engraved Glass*, New York, 1965, p.75.

12-25. *Goblet with an amethyst bowl, shape 3586, engraved. Steuben Division, Corning Glass Works, 1915-1925. H. 18.6cm. Gift of Corning Glass Works (CMG 59.4.246).*

12-26. *Two engraved goblets, shape 8351, in an unknown pattern, and 6861 engraved Roslyn. Steuben Division, Corning Glass Works, 1925-1932. H.(left) 25.1cm. Gift of Corning Glass Works (CMG 59.4.127, 75.4.578).*

12-27. *Goblet and wineglass, shapes 6928 and 6714. Steuben Division, Corning Glass Works, about 1925-1932. H.(right) 20.4cm. Gift of Corning Glass Works (CMG 75.4.577, 75.4.573).*

12-28. *Two goblets, shapes 7341 and 6505. Steuben Division, Corning Glass Works, about 1925-1932. Hts. 19.9cm. 20.9cm. Gift of Corning Glass Works (CMG 75.4.611, 59.4,300).*

12-29. *Three goblets, shapes 6947, 6728 and an unidentified shape, all cut in variations of the same pattern. Steuben Division, Corning Glass Works, about 1925-1932. H.(tallest) 24.2cm. Gift of Corning Glass Works (CMG 75.4.569, 75.4.148, 70.4.120).*

12-30. *Goblet engraved in Torino pattern on shape 6765; iced tea glass engraved in an unidentified pattern. Steuben Division, Corning Glass Works, 1925-1933. H.(left) 23.1cm. Gift of Corning Glass Works (CMG 75.4.678, 53.4.55). The Torino pattern is in the 1932 Steuben catalog.*

on the same blank as the one mentioned above by Illig, which was cut with a diamond and fan pattern and priced at $28.00. Steuben made other less glamorous products as well, listing itself as a manufacturer of jelly jars, electrical goods, opal ware, tubing, blanks for cutting and cut glass in the 1912 *American Glass Factory Directory*.

After 1918, when Steuben was sold by the Hawkes family to Corning Glass Works, Frederick Carder continued as its chief designer as well as manager and his cut and engraved designs for Steuben were much more modern, influenced by the prevailing angular style now called "Art Deco". Several patterns are reminiscent of the 19th-century Anglo-Irish cut designs with which Carder must have been familiar in England. Many of the engraved designs also hark back to 19th century designs. According to Corning Glass Works records for the period, cut and engraved glass comprised less than 15% of Steuben's output from 1918 until 1933 and this was probably a larger percentage than in the years when Hawkes owned the factory. The Steuben stemware shown in this chapter is from this period and dates mostly from the 1920s, although a few of the designs were continued into the early 1930s, including *Marina* and *Queen Anne*, both of which are in the 1932 Steuben catalog. These all bear the Steuben banner and fleur-de-lis trademark, and were originally design samples which were kept for many years by Steuben and its parent, Corning Glass Works, before they were given to The Corning Museum of Glass in 1975. It is likely that earlier design samples were discarded in the 1920s after styles changed.

12-31. Three goblets with cut decoration in the color Carder called *Wisteria*. This dichroic glass is bluish in daylight and pinkish in incandescent light and is usually called *alexandrite* (after the mineral) by European factories. The left and center ones are shape 7382 and the right one 7383. Steuben Division, Corning Glass Works, about 1920-1930. H.(left) 19.9cm. Gift of Corning Glass Works (CMG 69.4.239B, 75.4.802, 69.4.239C).

12-32. *Three goblets with applied color and engraved decoration, shapes 7336, 7283 and 7353. Steuben Division, Corning Glass Works, about 1925-1933. H.(left) 20.2cm. Gift of Corning Glass Works (CMG 70.4.117, 70.4.116, 59.4.452).*

12-33. Champagne glass engraved in Fountain pattern on shape 6395 or 6445; goblet and champagne glasses engraved in Cordova pattern on 6728. Steuben Division, Corning Glass Works, about 1920-1930. H.(left) 19.8cm. Gift of Corning Glass Works (CMG 75.4.838, 75.4.790, 70.4.123).

12-34. Three goblets, shape 6727 engraved in the Virginia pattern, 6728, and an unrecorded shape; Steuben Division, Corning Glass Works, about 1925-1933. H.(left) 25.5cm. Gift of Corning Glass Works (CMG 75.4.644, 59.4.290, 59.4.249).

12-35. Three engraved goblets, shape 6505. Steuben Division, Corning Glass Works, about 1925-1933. H.(left) 21cm. Gift of Corning Glass Works (CMG 75.4.698, 75.4.704, 75.4.810).

12-36. *Wineglass and goblets shapes 6735, 6563 and 6735. Steuben Division, Corning Glass Works, about 1925-1932. H.(center) 23cm. Gift of Corning Glass Works (CMG 75.4.635, 75.4.679, 75.4.626).*

12-37. Pitcher cut in Bengal pattern, H. P. Sinclaire & Company, about 1904–1920. H. 29.2cm. trade-marked. Courtesy of Tom and Marsha de Graffenreid. Crofford photo

12-38. Plaster cast of a tray like the one in Fig. 12-11.(CMG 90.7.2). This is one of a number of plaster casts of engraved objects from H. P. Sinclaire which were part of the Hawkes purchase in 1990. It was common practice for engravers to make a cast of the first piece engraved in a pattern so that the succeeding orders would be exactly the same.

12-39. Cordial and sherry glasses, H.P. Sinclaire & Company, 1924. H. (taller) 12.1cm, trade-marked. Gift of Mrs. Edwin S. Underhill, Sr. (CMG 85.4.7AB).

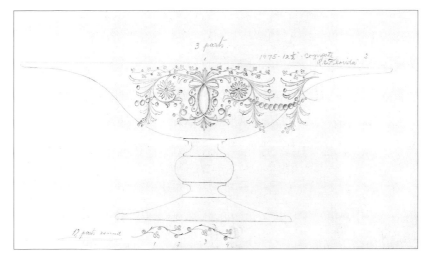

12-40. Drawing of a compote in R. C. Florida design. Sinclaire Design Archives.

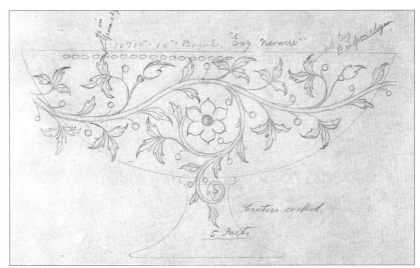

12-41. Drawing of a compote engraved Navarre design. Sinclaire Design Archives.

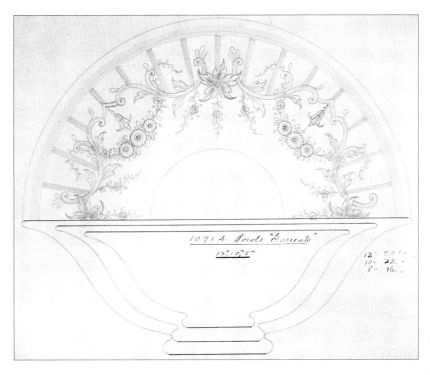

12-42. Drawing of a bowl in Sorrento design. Sinclaire Design Archives.

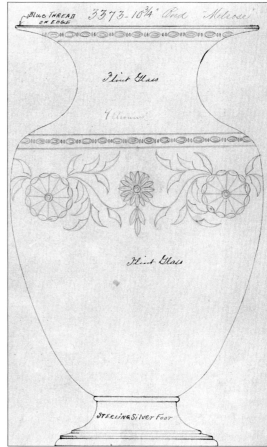

12-43. Drawing of a vase engraved in Melrose design. Sinclaire Design Archives.

12-44. Drawing of a goblet in R. C. Savoy design, 1918. Sinclaire Design Archives.

12-45. Drawing of a champagne glass in Fontaine design. Sinclaire Design Archives.

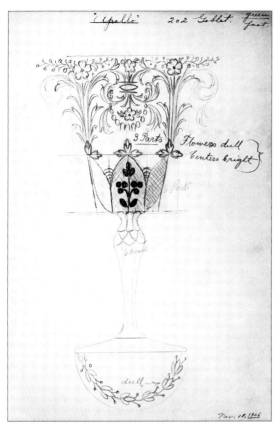

12-46. Drawing of a goblet in Apollo design, 1926. Sinclaire Design Archives.

12-47. Drawing of a cocktail glass in Essex design. Sinclaire Design Archives.

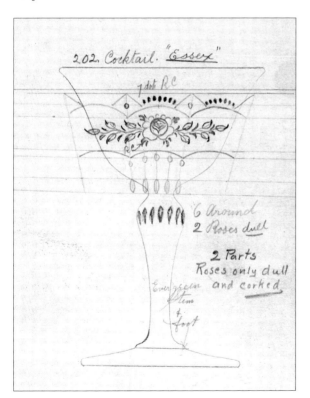

12-48. Drawing of a champagne glass in Regal design. Sinclaire Design Archives.

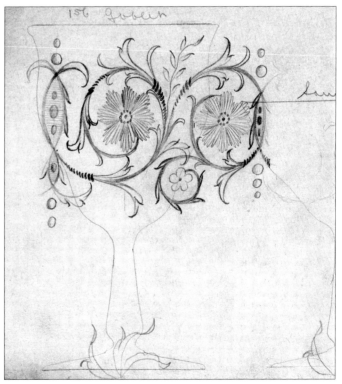

12-49. Drawing of a goblet in R. C. Princeton design. Sinclaire Design Archives.

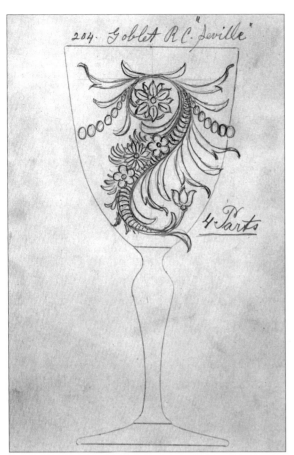

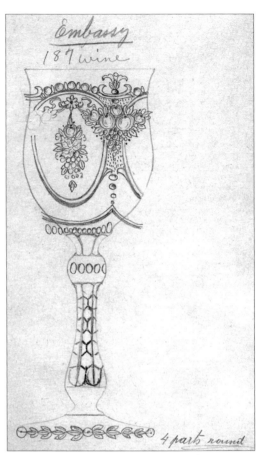

12-50. Drawing of a wine in Embassy design. Sinclaire Design Archives.

12-51. Drawing of a goblet in R. C. Seville design. Sinclaire Design Archives.

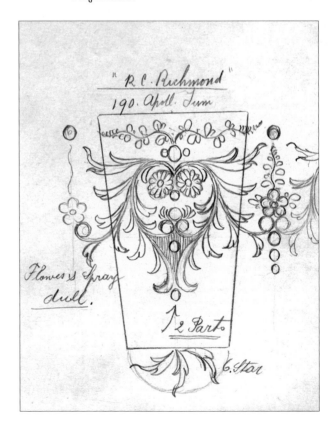

12-52. Drawing of an apollinaris tumbler in R .C. Richmond design. Sinclaire Design Archives.

12-53. Goblet cut in an unknown pattern on shape #6505, Steuben Division, Corning Glass Works, 1920s. H. 20.8cm. Gift of Corning Glass Works (CMG59.4.243).

12-54. Wineglass and goblet cut in a honeycomb pattern and engraved with crests on a Hawkes shape, but marked "STEUBEN". Steuben Division, Corning Glass Works, 1925–1935. H. 19.9cm, 15.5cm. Gift of Corning Glass Works (CMG 75.4.493, 75.4.492). These two pieces and the goblet in 12-17, may have been ordered from Steuben by Hawkes for replacements to sets.

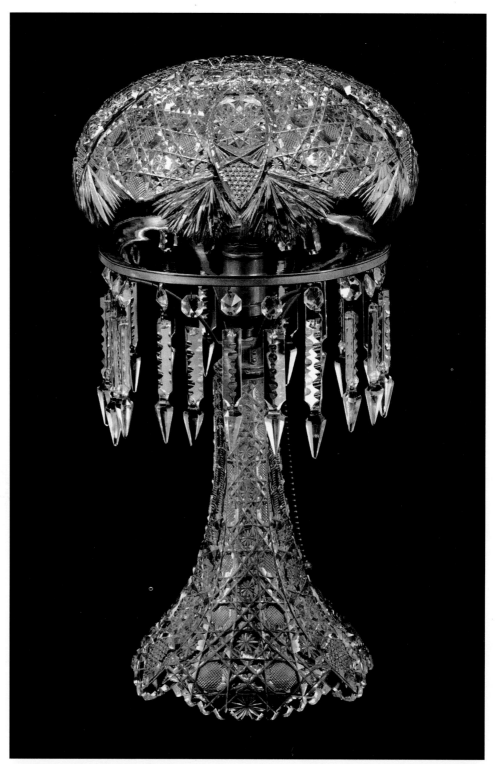

12-55. *Electric lamp cut at Giometti Brothers, Corning, 1903-1910. H. 45.8cm. Gift in memory of Atty Claude V. Stowell from his family (CMG 95.4.256).*

Giometti Brothers was another small cutting firm which opened in Corning in 1902, the venture of Clarence Giometti, a cutter trained at Hawkes in the 1890s, and his brother C. J. Giometti, who was an experienced salesman. The company stayed in business until the beginning of the Depression, but remained very small.

12-56. *Electric lamp, Corning, New York, possibly Hunt Glass Works, about 1910. H. 44.5cm. Gift of Mrs. Florence Emilson Vang in memory of William Vang and his parents, Eugene and Agda Vang (CMG 92.4.131). Photograph by Frank J. Borkowski.*

Since their wares were never marked, few can be identified. However, the lamp in Fig. 12-55 was a gift to their company treasurere (and financial backer), Corning attorney Claude V. Stowell.

Bibliography

Unpublished material in the Rakow Library of The Corning Museum of Glass includes: *Carder Archives*. Documents relating to Frederick Carder and Steuben Glass Works, mostly gifts from Carder and his family.

Hawkes Archives. This includes several thousand letters, catalog pages, drawings, photographs, advertisements, brochures, financial ledgers and memoranda, gathered from several sources.

Hoare Archives. This includes mostly catalog pages and photographic material gathered from several sources.

Sinclaire Design Archives. This consists of hundreds of design drawings, in pen or pencil, identified by pattern name, some dated, all acquired in 1990.

Farrar, Estelle Sinclaire and Spillman, J. S. *The Complete Cut and Engraved Glass of Corning*. New York: Crown Publishers, Inc., 1979. (Reprint available from The Corning Museum of Glass and Syracuse University Press in 1997.)

Farrar, Estelle Sinclaire. *H. P. Sinclaire, Jr., Glassmaker*, vol.1.; *H. P. Sinclaire, Jr., The Manufacturing Years*, vol.2. Garden City, New York: Farrar Books, 1974, 1975.

Revi, Albert C. *American Cut and Engraved Glass*. New York: Thomas Nelson & Sons, 1965.

Spillman, Jane Shadel. *White House Glassware, Two Centuries of Presidental Entertaining*. Washington, DC: The White House Historical Association in cooperation with the National Geographic Society and The Corning Museum of Glass, 1989.

Spillman, Jane Shadel and Farrar, Estelle Sinclaire. *The Cut and Engraved Glass of Corning, 1868-1940*. Corning: The Corning Museum of Glass, 1977.

Catalog reprints available from the American Cut Glass Association (P.O. Box 482, Ramona, CA 92065-0482) include:
Egginton's Celebrated Cut Glass, 80 pages, 50 patterns
T. G. Hawkes & Co. 1900-1905. 228 pages, 124 patterns
J. Hoare & Co. — 1882-1915. 144 pages, numerous patterns (Another Hoare catalog will be reprinted in 1997)

Index